The Noise of Change:

Russian Literature
and the Critics
(1891-1917)

Edited and Translated by
Stanley Rabinowitz

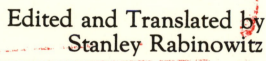

Ardis, Ann Arbor

Grateful acknowledgment is made to Yale University Press for permission to reprint a translation of Fet from *The Imagination of Spring: The Poetry of Afanasy Fet,* by Richard F. Gustafson, page 20. Copyright © 1966.

Ardis Publishers
2901 Heatherway
Ann Arbor, Michigan 48104

Library of Congress Cataloging in Publication Data
Main entry under title:

The Noise of change.

Translated from Russian.
1. Russian literature—19th century—History and criticism—Addresses, essays, lectures. 2. Russian literature—20th century—History and criticism—Addresses, essays, lectures. I. Rabinowitz, Stanley J.
PG3017.N65 1986   891.7'09'003   85-15056
ISBN 0-88233-525-1 (alk. paper)

To My Parents

Contents

Preface   9

Introduction   13

1   Literature and Writers   29
    M. Menshikov

2   Without Wings: Chekhov and His Work   37
    M. Nevedomsky

3   A Survey of Some Themes in Gorky's Work   67
    A. Volzhsky

4   Ivan Bunin   85
    A. Derman

5   Summing Up Russian Symbolist Poetry   101
    P. Gurev

6   Estranged: Toward a Psychology of Sologub's Work   123
    A. Dolinin

7   Between "Holy Russia" and "a Monkey":
    The Work of Alexei Remizov   149
    R. Ivanov-Razumnik

8   The Farsighted Ones: Bryusov's *Fiery Angel*
    and Kuzmin's *First Book of Stories*   169
    L. Gurevich

9   Russia's Temptation: On Bely's *Silver Dove*   183
    N. Berdyaev

10   An Astral Novel: Some Thoughts on
     Andrei Bely's *Petersburg*   197
     N. Berdyaev

11   The Inspiration of Horror: On Andrei Bely's *Petersburg*   205
     V. Ivanov

12   Symbolism's Successors   217
     V. Zhirmunsky

Preface

Several goals underlie this book, but it is based on only one assumption, namely that pre-Revolutionary Russian literature, especially its prose, has not achieved the broad familiarity it deserves, given its rich and serious quality. Roughly between 1890 and 1917 Russia experienced one of the greatest cultural revivals in its history, the impact of which still resonates in the West. In the area of painting, music, dance, theater, and, not least of all, belles-lettres, the Russian landscape underwent significant, often revolutionary change. Yet while the names and accomplishments of Stanislavsky and Meyerhold, Chagall and Kandinsky, Diaghilev and Nijinsky, Scriabin and Stravinsky enjoy at least some familiarity among growing segments of today's public, the same cannot necessarily be said, with few exceptions, of writers such as Remizov, Bely, Bryusov, Sologub, Bunin, Kuzmin, and others.

What might explain the sad fact that, until fairly recently, the remarkable variety and sophistication of Russian verbal art has been grossly overlooked—even by specialists in the field? Surely the problem has something to do with translation, although the continuing appearance of more and better English renderings of the works of this period is a hopeful sign. It goes without saying that the profound and subtle richness of poetry and prose (and particularly the former) stands to suffer enormously when this writing is not conveyed in its language of origin. But this hardly accounts for the frequent gaps in knowledge among those who have a command of Russian. Here something else is at work, especially regarding narrative prose. Sandwiched between the monumental achievements of Russia's classical age of fiction (Pushkin, Gogol, Turgenev, Tolstoy, Dostoevsky) and the compelling contemporary productions of the twenties and beyond (Babel, Bulgakov, Zamyatin, Olesha, Pasternak), the work of the late nineteenth and early twentieth centuries has remained virtually hidden from view. Many readers have tended to pass all too easily from Dostoevsky to Bulgakov, from Tolstoy to Babel without an awareness of, or perhaps even an interest in, what occurred in between.

The present volume at least partially seeks to redress this wrong. The twelve essays offered here touch upon virtually all of the major prose writers and literary currents (futurism excepted) of pre-Revolutionary Russia. And while the book is in no way offered as an all-inclusive history of the period, it does seek to begin that full-scale discussion which has been so sorely lacking. Gathered between the covers of a single book, these extended analyses of individual writers, specific works of literature, and important aesthetic trends should provide the reader with a deeper understanding of this remarkably productive era than such general surveys as Mirsky and Slonim currently offer. No consistent point of view, no fixed interpretation of the period in general or of any writer in particular is advanced; the essays are as varied, hopefully as provocative, as the works they treat. Poetry and drama are discussed, as are contemporary aesthetic values and cultural expectations. But the selections clearly emphasize works of narrative fiction—both long and short. Part of the reasoning behind this strategy is that the volume will address a larger audience, since the vast majority of the writing it discusses exists in English translation.

Such a strategy, however, combined with considerations of space and available material, has forced me to exclude from the collection a few important figures. I regret the absence of Zinaida Gippius and Dmitry Merezhkovsky, and my only consolation is that neither's reputation was based on imaginative prose: Gippius was a far more original poet; Merezhkovsky—a much more compelling critic. The stress upon prose has by definition required me to eliminate sustained evaluations of such notables as Balmont, Blok, and Vyacheslav Ivanov. However, references to the writing of all three do occasionally appear in the text.

A glance at the table of contents will immediately inform the reader of some of the book's other goals. All of the articles are concurrent with the literature under review, written by eyewitnesses who were attempting to understand and evaluate what they saw and read, as it was being produced.

In the West we know precious little about pre-Revolutionary Russian critics and literary criticism, and this volume seeks to fill an unfortunate gap by offering a compendium of the different critical methodologies which existed in Russia before the Bolshevik seizure of power. I have tried to make the selection as representative as possible, including approaches which range from the biographical (Nevedomsky), psychological (Dolinin), and religio-philosophical (Berdyaev; Ivanov) to the Marxist (Gurev), and the formalist (Zhirmunsky). Some of the critics represented here are better known than others, and certainly all deserve greater attention than has heretofore been afforded them. In criticism, too, interesting figures and noteworthy writing lie buried between the representatives of Russia's classical age (Belinsky, Chernyshevsky, Dobrolyubov, Strakhov, Grigorev) and the major talents of the twenties and beyond (Tynyanov, Eikhenbaum, Shklovsky, Jakobson).

A strategy which presents contemporary responses to cultural phenomena is not devoid of some genuine problems—and this is all the more true for the period under consideration. Such "on the spot" writing obviously has none of the benefits of hindsight and tradition, and years later we are always in a better position to modify certain claims. Yet, overall, there is little of what I would call major lapses of critical judgment in these articles, and any lack of profound insight tends to find compensation in the forthright and open airing of concerns which were of primary importance at the time. All the pieces are written with serious intent, and although none of them is likely to produce unanimous agreement, each should provoke in the reader further thought about the issues in question. The most persistent difficulty with these essays reflects a more general problem. With few exceptions, Russian literary criticism never became, or aspired to be, the sophisticated art that we find, say, in the British tradition. Particularly in the pre-Revolutionary period, the writing of the best critics often lacks stylistic grace and proportion: repetitiveness and long-windedness are not uncommon. Due to these characterisitics, some abridging was done in articles by Menshikov, Nevedomsky, Volzhsky, Derman, Gurev, and Ivanov-Razumnik.

Many people helped me during the various stages of this project, and it is my great pleasure to be able to thank them in print. June Pachuta of the Slavic division of the University of Illinois library was extremely helpful in locating many documents which were useful to me in putting together this volume. Kevin Moss and John Weeks prepared original drafts of the Gurevich and Gurev translations respectively. Kay Halpern researched many of the critics' biographies. My colleagues, Dale Peterson and Frederick Griffiths, read over several sections of the book and offered valuable advice. Thanks also go to Deans Mary Catherine Bateson and Richard Fink who made available much appreciated funds to see this project through. My major debt of gratitude is to Angelia Graf. A skilled translator and perceptive reader of literary and critical texts, Ms. Graf scrupulously edited over two-thirds of the essays in this collection, constantly providing useful tips.

Amherst, Mass.
July 1985

Introduction

"Disappointment, apathy, frayed nerves, and weariness are the inevitable consequences of excitability, and this excitability is to a great degree characteristic of our young people."[1] So generalized Dr. Anton Chekhov in a letter of 1888, after carefully explaining the symptoms of his suffering protagonist—the recently created Ivanov in the play of the same name. Chekhov's confused and directionless hero was an apt emblem for the generation that came of age in the 1880s and whose spiritual emptiness signalled the much larger socio-cultural vacuum Russia was experiencing at that time. Never before had Russians been so cognizant of a national malaise or so preoccupied with their collective sense of impotence and general stagnation. In his gloomy and naively sentimental poetry Semyon Nadson (1862-1887) had already fashionably reproduced the psychic state of the "diseased" intelligentsia, and despite his limited experience and lack of depth, he had touched the very nerve fiber of those with crushed hopes and lost ideals. "Do not laugh at Nadsonism," wisely cautioned the poet Osip Mandelstam. "It is the enigma of Russian culture and the essentially uncomprehended sound of it, for we do not understand and hear as they understood and heard."[2] Despite a tendency to ignore the period as one of political reaction and pitifully low aesthetic achievement, the 1880s constitute an extremely important chapter in Russian cultural history whose significance Mandelstam well understood, although it has yet to be properly investigated. Little did Russians know that precisely in those years were planted the seeds of a major artistic revival, known as "modernism," which would only fully blossom during the two decades preceding the Revolution of 1917.

With so much talk of sickness and its various causes, Russia was especially fortunate to have a writer-physician enter the scene, and this Chekhov did with an unrivaled talent for careful, sober diagnosis. "When people have a fever," he told his publisher Suvorin in another of his famous letters, "they do not want to eat, but they do want something, and express that undefinable desire by asking for 'something slightly sour'. Well, I too want something slightly sour. Nor am I alone in this sensation; I notice the very same mood all around me. It's as though everyone had been in love and gotten over it, and was looking around for new interests."[3]

If we apply the last sentence of Chekhov's statement to the situation prevailing in literature just prior to the upheavals it would experience in the 1890s, we observe the following dilemma. By 1883 the three bulwarks of

Russian realist prose had either died (Dostoevsky in 1881; Turgenev in 1883) or had largely retired from the realm of imaginative literature (Tolstoy), thus terminating Russia's love affair with fiction which had run continuously for almost fifty years and had included such prominent figures as Pushkin, Lermontov, Gogol, and Goncharov. Nor was lyric poetry ready to fill the void. The great Pushkin had been placed in virtual oblivion after a vehement drubbing by the popular utilitarian critic Dmitry Pisarev in 1865; the profound mystical-romantic verse of Tyutchev had never had a wide audience; and the talented civic poet Nikolai Nekrasov was already in eclipse, having bequeathed to the 1880s a string of second- and third-rate imitators. The seemingly unshakeable foundation of a long tradition of solid literary accomplishment began to crumble, as did the belief in those religious and social programs which were supposed to have brought comforting enlightenment, if not salvation, to Russians. Tolstoy's description of his spiritual state during these years, so vividly conveyed in his *Confession* (1882) captures the impasse which existed in literary matters as well. "I felt," he writes, "that what I had been standing on had collapsed and that I had nothing left under my feet. What I had lived no longer existed, and there was nothing left."[4]

The respected Soviet critic G. Byaly has recently noted the prevalence of words signalling doom in the writing of the period, particularly the phrase "the world is crumbling" ("mir rushitsya").[5] This ominous forecast of the loosening of ideas, values, and systems appears in Chekhov, Saltykov-Shchedrin, and Turgenev; the latter's piece "The Destruction of the World" ("Konets sveta," published in his *Poems in Prose*) characterizes with particular effectiveness the oppressive mood of chaos and disintegration. Not only in diction and vocabulary, but in form as well the disturbing end of an entire tradition became visible. Wasn't, for example, the very genre of Tolstoy's singularly important *Confession* a statement about the exhaustion of previous literary models and their failure to deal adequately with man's current spiritual and emotional crisis? Particularly at a time when the position of literature was so weakened and demoralized, how could one not interpret the *Confession* as both a literal and symbolic refutation of fiction's (and particularly the novel's) ability to retain its formerly sacred place as the primary medium of profound soul-searching?

Combined with, and related to, imaginative literature's decline was the Russian public's low level of aesthetic sensitivity. Indeed, the master diagnostician insisted to Suvorin in a letter of December 17, 1892 that "no matter how low literature has fallen, the public is still lower than it." Jeffrey Brooks has carefully studied the critical question of readership and literary manners in late nineteenth- and early twentieth-century Russia, and his analysis is mandatory for a full understanding of the period's complicated socio-cultural dynamics.[6] Suffice it to say for now that the beginning of mass literacy in Russia in the 1880s and the appearance in unprecedented numbers of new magazines ("thick journals," as they were called) to meet the more literate public's growing needs did not, ironically, constitute a hopeful sign for the overall health of literature. To the contrary, it exacerbated the problem, for we see at this time a growing gap between the readers of serious or "high" literature—the kind we associate with the national classics mentioned above—and the more numerous consumers of popular, or mass, culture whose tastes the "new journalism" was increasingly feeding. Where was the readership for the kind of great literature which Russia had so recently experienced, and where could such work appear? Had Russia's unprecedented fifty-year literary flowering come to an irrevocable end?

Mikhail Menshikov's (here considerably abridged) essay "On Literature and Writers" (No. 1) captures some of the frustrations mentioned above and expresses hope for a complete turn-around in Russia's literary situation; as such it serves as a fitting prologue to the exciting events which would shortly follow. Whatever the peculiarities of Menshikov's taste or personal vision of literature's role in society, his remarks bespeak a protest against outmoded themes and forms and a widespread dissatisfaction with the low level of Russian critical awareness, a complaint commonly heard in commentaries on the Russian literary scene of the 1890s. The most famous, comprehensive, and profound of these was, of course, Dmitry Merezhkovsky's manifesto "On the Causes for the Decline and the New Currents of Contemporary Russian Literature" (1893),[7] which might in some respects be seen as a companion piece to Menshikov's work. Each critic acknowledges realism's (and particularly the realist novel's) outdatedness; each derides the currently fashionable naturalism for its incapacity to satisfy man's deepest needs for faith. And there is a mutual commitment to Russia's renewed ability to seek, as it had in the past, the universal ideals which characterized its greatest works, although each critic would define and reach those ideals quite differently. In the tradition of Russia's most famous nineteenth-century literary critic, Vissarion Belinsky (1811-1848), Menshikov stresses the social and ethical significance of literature—its need ultimately to improve man's material conditions and morally regenerate his spirit. Although no champion of the populist literature of the 1870s and 1880s (he deprecatingly refers to its representatives as "tendentious writers"), Menshikov's sense of an author was nevertheless that of a prophet whose duty it was to promote the nation's welfare. For him, perfect form resulted from a vague blend of the writer-seer's spiritual depth and civic consciousness. Menshikov's assumptions about literature inevitably led him, as they did most critics of his day, to reject the aesthetic emphasis on stylistic perfection and experimentation, advocated by the early Merezhkovsky and the modernists who followed shortly after. Menshikov prefers looking back to the "good old days," to older forms, which he believes need only to be "transfigured," whereas the modernists largely preferred to reject tradition and create a literature which was more ground breaking. Menshikov's essay is perhaps most notable in that it reflects the breakdown of previously accepted literary guidelines while also suggesting the simultaneous sense of opportunity and confusion that existed during this transitional literary era.

The greatest writer of this interim period, and one of the genuine Russian national classics, is Anton Chekhov (1860-1904), to whom the longest essay in this collection, "Without Wings: Chekhov and His Work" (No. 2), is appropriately devoted. Chekhov's writing displays many characteristic features of Russian realism (e.g., a lucid, unadorned style in the tradition of Pushkin and Tolstoy) while simultaneously revealing some traits frequently associated with the post-realist or modernist period of literature (e.g., the emphasis on mood and atmosphere, as seen in his plays and in such late stories as "The Bishop"). Nevedomsky rightly attempts to explain Chekhov's unique style and world view at least partly in terms of the period which shaped him, and he makes the interesting claim that the lack of absolutely firm foundations—philosophical, socio-political, literary—during the 1880s complements, and perhaps directly causes, the characteristic elusiveness of Chekhov's work. The decade which was known as a time of "reevaluation of values" finds a literary echo in Chekhov's work. His characters are often presented at a moment when their firmest preconceptions crumble before them, and his compositional strategy is such that diverse, often contradictory issues are presented "democratically" and totally objectively, thus causing his writing to resist ideological straight-jacketing. Unlike his contemporaries, Nevedomsky accepts and praises this latter feature of Chekhov's work. Two years after the writer's death, Nevedomsky almost alone appreciated what some of today's best Chekhov critics have only recently affirmed: of all writers, the supremely adogmatic Chekhov defies easy categorization and must be judged on the basis of his *entire* corpus.

How wise—and brave—Nevedomsky is in taking to task such distinguished figures as Merezhkovsky, Shestov, and Mikhailovsky for squeezing Chekhov into their own biased critical framework and thus seriously underestimating his complexity. Unfortunately Nevedomsky cannot possibly manage to unpeel all of the labels which were affixed to Chekhov: he was deemed a decadent and a symbolist as well. Nevedomsky does seem to get carried away, however, when he erroneously claims that Chekhov was no thinker; "ideologue" would have been the better word to use here. Chekhov's writings show considerable philosophical depth, but his is not a philosophy with a capital "P," such as one finds in Dostoevsky or Tolstoy.

On balance, Nevedomsky's analysis is remarkable for its many original insights, some of which beg for further expansion, such as the role that medicine played in Chekhov's world view. (One of Nevedomsky's findings is that the only theories Chekhov preached were medical ones). The critic's approach to the writer—his underscoring of Chekhov's early comic sketches and his insistence that they anticipate the essentially anecdotal basis of his writing—would later be assumed and expanded by one of the greatest Chekhov scholars, P. Bitsilli.[8] One of the latter's basic tenets—that the pathos of distance makes Chekhov simultaneously compassionate and dispassionate—also owes something to Nevedomsky. And last, but not least, later criticism is anticipated by Nevedomsky's astute attempt to distinguish Chekhov as a writer who, unlike most of his predecessors, treated art as an absolute value in itself, devoid of any "great idea" other than the idea of its own autonomy. Chekhov was, as Nevedomsky instructs us, the freest of Russian artists and has thus been among the hardest for his countrymen to decipher.

If there is one writer who has managed to enjoy extreme, almost unheard-of popularity among his own countrymen, then as well as now, it is Maxim Gorky (1865-1936). Although he had been known since 1892, Gorky's fame peaked around 1898-1899, when a two-volume edition of his best stories was published and his novel *Foma Gordeyev* appeared. He would continue (although less frequently) to create works of quality until the first world war, most notably his play *The Lower Depths* (1903) and the first volume of his fictionalized autobiography, *My Childhood* (1913). Only after the Russian Revolution did Gorky's presence become again as formidable as it was in the late nineties, and he currently enjoys almost mythical status in the Soviet Union. Prolific and at times immature in his literary craft, Gorky produced large amounts of hastily written stories and sketches during the first decade of his career. But his best works created a literary sensation quite unlike anything Russia had ever experienced, and his writing plays an important role in the history and development of Russian literature. A major virtue of Volzhsky's article, "On Several Themes in Gorky's Work" (No. 3), is its emphasis on the writer's finest works, the fiction and drama written before 1904 which established Gorky as a bold, innovative talent.

Not that everyone agrees with this last statement. Gorky's writing has occasioned some of the most malign attacks in the history of criticism— Russian and Western—ranging from Merezhkovsky's claim in 1909 that his poetry of the tramp "deserves nothing but condescending oblivion"[9] to Nabokov's recently published and dismissively reductive remarks about "the poverty of his art."[10] Both as a social phenomenon and as a literary event, Gorky's significance is almost universally conceded. But if one discounts the frequent and often useless panegyrics of kindred Marxist spirits, there have been precious few scholarly evaluations of Gorky's writing as art. Perhaps the essential peculiarity of this art is that its strength often constitutes its greatest weakness. The boldness of its imagery, the startling and occasionally even refreshing crudity of its dialogue and characterizations, the pulsating, at times uncontrollable rhythm of its diction can, if one is so inclined, be seen as vices instead of virtues. Let it be noted, however, that an author as discerning as the symbolist Bryusov, who was known for the insightfulness of his critical judgments, could write the following in 1900: "To Maxim Gorky—strong and free, from someone who passionately loves his work."[11]

The aspect of Gorky's work on which Volzhsky focuses is its Nietzscheanism or, strange as it may seem, its "decadence." Although Gorky was an implacable foe of literary modernism and had gone on record in 1896 as saying, "Decadence is a dangerous, anti-social phenomenon which must be combatted,"[12] some contemporaries observed a strongly decadent strain in his own early writing. Indeed, when the history of Russian modernism is finally written, Gorky's most noteworthy contribution may be precisely that of an early and minor decadent. Nietzsche played a crucial and still not fully documented role in the early twentieth-century Russian literary revival, and Volzhsky provocatively, if somewhat long-windedly, establishes some of the major points of contact between the German philosopher and the Russian author. An aesthetic based on the rights of the strong; an artistic/philosophical system which calls for beauty as art's final goal—a beauty which is synonymous with the fully autonomous, self-fashioning individual; an attraction to, and inspiration by, nothingness itself, the relativism of truth and the potency of "the lie"—all of these are common thematic features of Gorky's and Nietzsche's writing.

That Gorky was attracted to one of the gods in the modernist pantheon should really not surprise us; in fact, the Gorkian hero-individualist derives his very essence from this attraction. Both Gorky and the decadents-symbolists (as Merezhkovsky observed quite early) grew from the same anti-naturalist soil which strongly resisted biological determinism and the laws of necessity. Nietzsche's superman and Gorky's tramp gratified a sorely felt need to "épater le bourgeois" and to counter the impotence of an enfeebled generation of Ivanovs with brazen strength and the power of action. Menshikov, we remember, had called for a "great deed," although the kind Gorky's rebels accomplish mortified him (and Volzhsky as well) by its irreverence and anti-Christian glorification of the man-God. The Russian press was filled with requests for a rejection of apathy, and along these lines Gorky himself provided the best description of his writing to Chekhov in 1899: "The time has come when we need the heroic; everyone craves something exciting and bright, something which will not be life-like, but higher, better and more beautiful than it."[13] Whatever one's ultimate evaluation of Gorky is, his early work surely met a fundamental need of the growing Russian audience of literate consumers, and Volzhsky, in part through his extensive use of citations, provides some of the reasons for the writer's seductiveness. But while Volzhsky illustrates, he also, like many, bemoans Gorky's lack of realism. Gorky's characterization of his tramps as self-analytic philosophers betrays a sentimental and naive romanticism, not to mention a distasteful amoralism. Yet in documenting these features Volzhsky always proceeds with sobriety and a due respect for Gorky's position as a writer of talent and substance, giving us a view of the writer which strikes us as unusual, even startling, but ultimately sound.

Frequent disagreement combined with overall fairness also characterizes Abram Derman's judgment of Ivan Bunin (1870-1953) in article No. 4, which rightly notes from the beginning some of the similarities and differences between Bunin as poet and prosaist.

Bunin's highly competent verse is of a traditional sort, breaking no new formal ground at a time when the experimentation of the decadents and symbolists was permanently affecting the course of Russian poetry. But his narrative fiction—beginning with the impressionistic "Antonov Apples" in 1900 and even before—betrays a unique and unmistakably innovative stamp, precisely because of its lyrical features. Colorful diction, the importance of the acoustical quality of words, and a compact, often turbid style (which the otherwise well-disposed Chekhov once called a "thick soup") constitute some of the major formal aspects of the writer's prose. Bunin's writing occasionally seems self-conscious—Derman might add self-indulgent—in the way it allows the dazzling array of its linguistic detail to predominate over the psychological and social presentation of character. This is a crucial feature of Bunin's work which the prominent literary historian D. S. Mirsky would later define, although without Derman's largely negative assessment, as "the enchantment of things" in Bunin. Although these latter features liken him to the modernists, as do several similar thematic concerns (e.g., the prevalence of death and decay), Bunin continually expressed hostility toward decadence and symbolism. This was surely so because he saw himself dealing largely with "the nobleman's nest," with life in the countryside (as it had been immortalized by such classical realists as Turgenev, Aksakov, Tolstoy, and Goncharov), as opposed to writing about the urban landscape, which was being exploited by the representatives of the "new art" (most notably in Bryusov, Bely, and Blok) and their "fantastic" predecessors, Gogol and Dostoevsky. Yet even as the content of Bunin's work occupied canonical turf, for example *The Village,* whose depiction of provincial life is as brutally realistic or naturalistic as anything in the Russian tradition, its form frequently betrayed non-realist features. *The Village* (like the equally long *Sukhodol*) does not quite belong to any established genre, and its subtitle, "a poem," signals just the kind of break with literary norms that we find in such hybrid narratives as Gogol's *Dead Souls* and Dostoevsky's *The Double* (also called "poems"), and in more contemporary pieces such as Bely's *Symphonies.*

The issue of literary modernism in Russia, its sources, goals, and techniques, is handled squarely and most interestingly in Gurev's "Summing up Russian Symbolism" (No. 5). Contemporary criticism often viewed early modernism's alleged negation of civic-mindedness and desire to emancipate personality from social responsibility at worst as an aberration in Russian culture and at best as an imitation of French "décadence." The entire complex of psychological attitudes—the promulgation of self-worship to the point where "all is permitted," the often perverse attraction to erotic or sensual love and its destructive power, the escape into a world of fantasy and dream closed to ouside reality, the predominance of usually gloomy and melancholic moods—all of this was believed to have sprung from Baudelaire and his European descendants. By looking, as it were, in his own backyard at such renowned figures as Tyutchev, Dostoevsky, Fet, and Vladimir Solovyov, Gurev makes two important contributions to our understanding of the period. First, he challenges common assumptions by showing us the organic nature of Russian decadence and symbolism and by implying that Russia was particularly ripe for the reception of these trends in the late 1880s and 1890s. Second, he demonstrates the difficulty we face in understanding modernism if we rely on judgments made by people who often misread the very classics which they were defending against modernist "aberrations." Although ultimately hostile to modernism, the Marxist Gurev (like the sympathetic and virulently anti-Marxist Merezhkovsky) is able to read the Russian classical writers from a broad perspective and thereby rightly see many of them as harbingers of the new art. He quite perceptively analyzes a phenomenon which almost every article that follows (and some that precede) his affirms: the absolutely inescapable presence of a rediscovered Dostoevsky in pre-Revolutionary Russian literature.

When he chooses to exercise them, Gurev's literary judgments can be rather sound, yet his Marxist approach to literature demands that he focus on the sociological basis of artistic creation. This slant at times provides a refreshingly different, if hostile approach to the phenomenon of Russian symbolism. At the time, though, the majority of Russian critics were anti-modernist, for a variety of reasons. Trouble ensues, however, when Gurev claims that the new art is intimately tied to capitalism and the bankruptcy of middle class values. The fact is that the modernists, and the decadents in particular, were often anti-bourgeois and quite defiant of middle class conventionality. Another weakness in Gurev's analysis is the critic's failure to distinguish some crucial differences between the early decadence and the later symbolism; by 1907-1908 more optimistic and spiritual themes appear in the literature which Gurev discusses. Allowing for these problems, Gurev's indictment of decadent/symbolist art for its limited range of human concerns and emotions still represents a literary judgment which many intelligent readers share. Even the respected formalist critic Victor

Zhirmunsky, whose article on symbolism's successors concludes this anthology, charges symbolism with having a narrow circle of interests although, like Gurev, he appreciates some of its daring and lasting innovations.

An interest in a writer's limited thematic scope and the emotional reasons thereof motivates Dolinin's psychological approach to one of literary modernism's most original practitioners in the article entitled "Estranged: Toward a Psychology of Sologub's Work" (No. 6). Poet, novelist, short story writer, playwright, and essayist, Fyodor Sologub (1863-1927) began to publish in 1894. On everything he wrote Sologub left an unmistakable imprint, and Dolinin detects it with rare objectivity and sympathy. Perhaps no other modernist writer experienced more sustained, more hostile and, frequently, more irrelevant criticism than did the controversial Sologub. Considered—and not without foundation—an arch decadent, Sologub became for many an emblem of the period's unhealthiest excesses. His early writing, particularly before 1907, reads like a compendium of fin-de-siècle themes: a gloomy despair over imperfect reality; an escape into the solitary confines of the absolute ego; an obsession with, and deep attraction to, evil; a pathological interest in the erotic and the morbid, and a curious preoccupation with sex and death; and, finally, a realization of the ultimate impermanence of the ideal, resulting in a fierce struggle to capture and linger over the "moment."

But Sologub's writing never suffers from the cheapness or sensationalism characteristic of many of the period's lesser figures, such as Mikhail Artsybashev, the author of the notorious *Sanin* (1907). Dolinin's great contribution lies in his ability to convey the genuineness and seriousness of Sologub's decadence, to recognize how accurately (and, usually, how successfully) Sologub translates his private mythology into art, producing a body of work which is as absorbing as it is idiosyncratic. At its best Sologub's writing is the meeting point between personal experience and literary fact, the place where the individual psyche, with all its doubts, insecurities, and ambivalences, merges with, indeed *is* the social reality which produced it. By locating the peculiarity of Sologub's writing not in the works themselves, but rather in Sologub's complicated personality, Dolinin does face some serious problems. For instance, Dolinin limits the range of inquiry into Sologub's masterpiece of narrative art, *The Petty Demon,* by regarding it exclusively as an objectification of its author's troubled emotional state. And he comes squarely up against one of Sologub's own objections. "No, my dear contemporaries," Sologub had instructed some misguided readers in the preface to the novel's second edition, "it is you that my novel of the Petty Demon is about . . . (the novel is) about you."

Even more than in the case of Sologub (with whom he has much in common), the interweaving of elements from folklore, myth, and dream

into conventional literary structures pervades the extremely unusual work
of Alexei Remizov (1877-1957).[14] One of the most understudied of all
Russian writers, modernist or otherwise, Remizov, like Bunin, produced
works of high quality both inside and outside of Russia, from which he
emigrated in 1921. And although in many readers' eyes he shares with
Bunin the distinction of having achieved even greater mastery abroad, one
difference is undeniable: unlike Bunin, Remizov abandoned most of the
literary forms (but not the techniques) he had employed in Russia and
moved into other largely uncharted areas during emigration. The epitome
of his "second life" remains the autobiographical *With Clipped Eyes*
(*Podstrizhennymi glazami,* 1953)—a remarkably complex and surrealistic
tapestry which treats his "salad days" in his native Moscow. Together with
Bunin's *Life of Arsenyev,* Nabokov's *Speak, Memory,* and Sinyavsky's
Good Night, Remizov's *With Clipped Eyes* belongs to a distinguished
company of fictive memoirs written in emigration in which the writer's life
is seen as a literary phenomenon.

Ivanov-Razumnik's "Between 'Holy Russia' and a Monkey" (No. 7)
deals, of course, with Remizov's pre-Revolutionary phase, but because it
includes examples from his diverse repertoire, the piece conveys the tension
and sense of instability characteristic of the writer's world view. The short
prose narrative *Sisters of the Cross* is obviously more conventional in form
than the collection of anecdotes about the child's world of imagination and
play, *Sunways.* However, the novel is not without its complexities, as
Ivanov-Razumnik's extensive plot summary helps to illustrate. *Sisters of
the Cross* does, indeed, have Dostoevskian overtones: the very setting of a
Petersburg boarding house and the narration of the fates of its unfortunate
inhabitants, bring us back to Dostoevsky's first published work *Poor Folk*
(1845). Nor is there any doubt that *Sisters of the Cross* rehearses many of
Ivan Karamazov's "eternal questions" about the tragedy of human
suffering. The protagonists of both writers are visionary-idealists who are
confronted with the problem of accepting life in its most complex
manifestations. In both cases reason interferes and yields devastating
consequences. For each writer the attractiveness of children provides a way
of negating the faults of our ugly reality and of finally acknowledging its
beauty. The sequence in which Ivanov-Razumnik presents Remizov's
works allows us to pass from a case of seeing—and rejecting—the world
through the prism of the adult mind (Marakulin in *Sisters of the Cross*) to
an example of viewing—and celebrating—life through the eyes of the child
(Sunways). A similar sequence exists in the work of Sologub, whose
charming *Fairy Tales (Skazochki)* also allow the writer to escape his
tortured bouts with reason and doubt and, like Remizov, transcend the
mundane through the sheer magic of verbal art.

Ivanov-Razumnik cannot be faulted for stressing as he does the
fundamental dichotomy in Remizov's writing, and we must mention his

encouraging and deeply approving voice in a chorus of criticism which frequently disapproved of the author's alleged "exoticism" and "formless chaos." But one wonders whether the boundaries between Remizov's two styles, the borders between his "realistic" *Sisters of the Cross* and his "fantastic" *Sunways,* are as firmly fixed as the critic suggests. The similarities between these two pieces may indeed be as great as the differences; surely a confusion of clear-cut divisions constitutes a major hallmark of Remizov's writing. In both works, for example, the question of survival is essential: each poses the problem of how we may view reality and what we must do in order to endure it. Structural ties exist as well, for *Sisters of the Cross* shares the anecdotal quality of *Sunways.* Embedded in the prose narrative are scores of little tales, each one having its own peculiar resonance or "voice." At least Ivanov-Razumnik had made a beginning in the study of this accomplished stylist's prose, and it is unfortunate that so few have followed his lead.

Another beginning in the study of some now neglected modernist fiction is Lyubov Gurevich's "The Farsighted Ones" (No. 8), which conveniently brings together two major writers who are chiefly read as poets—Valery Bryusov (1873-1924) and Mikhail Kuzmin (1875-1936). Quite different in their poetic sensibilities, both authors share more than a passing interest in decadent/erotic themes, and their prose in particular betrays the presence of Pushkin. Perhaps this link to the "father of Russian literature" explains the interesting phenomenon which Gurevich notes but does not fully investigate: an inclination in some of the best Russian modernist writing toward the past, especially toward classical or neo-classical culture. (Zhirmunsky more broadly treats this phenomenon in his article on acmeism which concludes this volume.) Such fascination for the old is unquestionably stylistically motivated, and from this perspective one can argue that the writers whom Gurevich discusses do not escape to the past as much as they use it to inform the present. In contrast to the often ornamental, turbid and weighty prose of many symbolist writers, the work of Bryusov and Kuzmin employs a style which is lucid, simple, unpre-tentious—in a word, Pushkinian. At least on one level, examples of narrative fiction such as Gurevich analyzes seem to suggest not a rejection of contemporaneity, but rather a return to a more simple and accessible, a more personal and intimate means of expression.

To many, Gurevich's remarks, particularly about Kuzmin, will reflect some serious lapses of critical judgment. But on the whole, her evaluation touches upon some valid points. Bryusov's best narrative fiction—*The Fiery Angel* and the collection of stories entitled *The Earth's Axis* (*Zemnaya os',* 1907)—provides the reader with unforgettable characters and situations; in the case of the former, Bryusov's captivating plot compares favorably with the best adventure novels in world literature. But presentation is another matter, and a reader-critic as astute as the poet

Marina Tsvetaeva once expressed a commonly-held opinion about Bryusov, one which Gurevich shares. "I admired *Fiery Angel* then in both
conception and execution, now only in conception...in its non-reali-
zation," Tsvetaeva wrote. "A master—and such a total miss! Yes, because
craftsmanship is not everything. One needs an ear. And Bryusov was tone
deaf."[15] What Gurevich describes as the plodding and academic quality,
the scientific exactitude of Bryusov's prose, which resembles more the
rational, anatomical style of the historian than of the truly inspired artist,
Tsvetaeva described thusly: "Bryusov's anti-musicality...reflected the
anti-musicality of his essence, of his being: dry land, the absence of a
river...Bryusov was comprised totally of shores—granite ones."[16] Of
course, there are other readers who view the deliberateness and lack of
spontaneity of Bryusov's prose style as a mark of considerable literary
achievement.

In terms of literary achievement, Gurevich underestimates Kuzmin,
although one should note that her review was published before many of the
writer's best works were written. And considering the general outrage at
Kuzmin's professed homosexuality and his open treatment of that theme in
his work, Gurevich's evaluation is a model of fairness and restraint. But
while the critic acknowledges Kuzmin's accomplishments as a stylist, she
requires something more—precisely what, we are not sure. These vague
demands prevent Gurevich from appreciating Kuzmin's miniature art for
what it ultimately is: light, elegant, delicately expressed "chamber music,"
as it were. Her quick dismissal of Kuzmin's stories, for example, misses
their significance; much like Pushkin's *Tales of Belkin* (1831), these are
stylizations, often parodies of traditional literary forms. Kuzmin's claim
that "the best test of talent is to write about nothing"[17] (but to write about it
beautifully!) expresses the writer's intentions in much of his prose, and this
obviously excludes him from occupying a place of greatness in Gurevich's
pantheon of Russian giants.

A writer who does currently enjoy major status in Russian literature
and who recently has been undergoing a significant revival, particularly in
the West, is Andrei Bely (1880-1934). Poet, novelist, critic, and literary
theoretician, Bely can claim unquestionable fame for his three most
important prose narratives: *The Silver Dove* (1910), *Petersburg* (1913), and
Kotik Letaev (1917).* In the year that *The Silver Dove* was published
Kuzmin had noted—with obvious reference to Bely's work—that "as of
late we observe a renewed interest among readers and writers...in the
revival of the genre of the novel...We are on the threshold of a new form of
novel which is both symbolic and realistic."[18] The two novels treated in this
anthology certainly fall under Kuzmin's rubric, and Bely's advances in the

---

* These books, incidentally, closely fit the term "transfigured novel," which Menshikov had
coined at the end of his essay.

mode of narrative fiction make him one of the most important writers of the period. With its provincial setting, *The Silver Dove* recalls Gogol and his novel *Dead Souls* (even Bely's fictitious town, Gugelovo, is a play on the earlier writer's name); the urban setting of *Petersburg* (not to mention its theme of revolution and parricide) echoes Dostoevsky's novel-tragedies and, for Berdyaev's taste, occasionally to a fault.

In his admittedly non-literary approach to *The Silver Dove* in "Russia's Temptation" (No. 9), Berdyaev uncovers some aspects of Bely's writing which resonate on the aesthetic level as well. By evaluating the book from a religio-philosophical point of view, and by seeing it as a kind of allegory of the Russian intelligentsia's doomed attempts to merge with "the people," Berdyaev penetrates to the core of Bely's artistic world. It is a world which, as the critic notes, contains an apocalyptic vision of history (inherited from Vladimir Solovyov) and which demonstrates an omnipresent, occasionally maddening dualism: East vs. West, mysticism vs. rationalism, primitivism vs. culture, peasant vs. intellectual, anti-Christ vs. Christ. Perhaps the most striking paired opposition is poet vs. philosopher, for Bely's temperament courts and includes both categories. As a friend and intellectual equal, Berdyaev recognizes the fierce struggle which raged within Bely between the scientific, ordered mind of the thinker and the intuitive, creative will of the artist. That Berdyaev senses so early in Bely's career his kindredness to Gogol and his fear of sharing Gogol's sad fate represents a high degree of sensitivity. Gogol constituted for Bely a lifelong interest, almost an obsession, culminating in his last published work, the monumental scholarly tract *The Mastery of Gogol* (*Masterstvo Gogolya,* 1933).

As early as 1910, Berdyaev virtually predicts the theme and flavor of Bely's next work of prose fiction. Both his essay "An Astral Novel" (No. 10) and Ivanov's piece "The Inspiration of Horror" (No. 11) acknowledge Bely's ingeniousness in focusing all the ambivalences and tensions of his binary oppositions onto the imperial capital of Petersburg—the traditional literary setting of Russian madness, dualism, and intellectual extremes. Each critic is evaluating not the 1913 serialized version, but rather the separate edition of the novel which appeared in 1916, and none of the pathos or immediacy of this moment in time is lost on either writer. Here history and literature meet: by the time Bely's novel achieved autonomous status, Petersburg was no more, its Germanic sounding name having been replaced by the Russian equivalent (Petrograd) during World War I. The novel's apocalyptic mood of doom and destruction and the final conflagration signified by the explosion of the bomb appear to have come true not only in the loss of a city's name, but in the end of an entire period of Russian history.

According to Berdyaev, Bely's depiction of this end involves a curious interplay of two levels: cosmic occurrences are continually being reenacted on the earthly plane. And such an "astral" view of reality distinguishes *Petersburg* from its Dostoevskian predecessors, for Bely's twentieth-century characters lack the passionate, "flesh and blood" humanity of Dostoevsky's protagonists. Both the times and Bely's own artistic temperament yield a method of characterization which is more Gogolian in its emphasis on the grotesque and the surreal. Even more provocative are Berdyaev's musings about the relationship between the lack of three-dimensional qualities in Bely's characters and cubist art, reminding us of the connection of modernist literature to painting. Spatial form plays a central role in *Petersburg,* and we must *see* this fiction in ways which may be unfamiliar to us. As in cubist art, relationships are presented in an abstract, geometrical fashion; the novel is truly a product of its century in the way that it so persistently calls attention to "how it is made."[19]

The construction of *Petersburg* depends as much on tone and mood to create its effect as it does on purely visual images or spatial relationships. Bely's fellow-symbolist, Vyacheslav Ivanov, appreciates the novel for its unique evocation of atmosphere, which he sees as one of unrelenting chaos, hallucination, and horror. His sincere admission of the difficulty he has in approaching this complex work totally rationally or analytically serves as both a compliment on the novel's effectiveness and a key to the author's intent. "The goal of symbolism," Bryusov reminded the public as early as 1894, "is, via a series of juxtaposed images, somehow to hypnotize the reader, to elicit in him a certain mood."[20] This Bely accomplishes quite admirably. Ivanov does well to advise us to hear the special music of *Petersburg* and to enjoy the book for the sounds which resonate within us after we have completed it. Already in 1916 both he and Berdyaev were noting that in order to appreciate modernist fiction fully we must learn to read in new and potentially exciting ways.

Even before *Petersburg* appeared as a separate edition the practitioners and supporters of symbolism sensed the end of this important phase in the history of modernist art. Gurev already observed in 1914 that writers such as Balmont, Bryusov, and Sologub had reached the pinnacle of their careers years before the outbreak of the first world war and that their talent was at best beginning to become repetitive. Symptomatic of a change in the air was Sologub's 1913-1914 tour of the provinces, during which he lectured on "The Art of Our Day" ("Iskusstvo nashikh dnei," published in *Russkaya mysl',* Dec., 1915), staunchly defending the symbolist *Weltanschauung* while simultaneously singing its swan song.

The philosophical, often mystical orientation of symbolist writing, the vagueness of its moods and the density and weightiness of its style, had run their course. The old gods—Dostoevsky, Nietzsche, Baudelaire, the German Romantics—were regarded as philosophically and literarily cumbersome, contradicting the new simplicity in self-expression which was beginning to be avowed. Symbolist art was hardly one of restraint, and by the mid-teens we note a renewed interest in the Chekhovian ideal of artistic measure, control, and modesty. According to a later critic, the new phase of modernism, usually called "acmeism," came into being primarily because of differences in opinion over the use of language. In his 1923 study of the acmeist poet Akhmatova, Boris Eikhenbaum isolates what he believes to be the major factor in symbolism's demise: "It became necessary to change the attitude toward poetic speech, which had turned into a lifeless idiom, incapable of further growth or free play. It became necessary ... to emancipate the tradition of poetic diction from the shackles of symbolism, and thus to restore the equilibrium between verse and language."[21]

What Gurevich had failed to see especially in Kuzmin's writing, Victor Zhirmunsky in "Symbolism's Successors" (No. 12) is quick to note as the hallmark of the new generation: the presence of "Apollonian" clarity and neo-classical grace and the emergence of Pushkin as the reigning deity. With the exception of Kuzmin, whom Zhirmunsky places in a kind of hybrid category, the acmeists made their greatest contributions in the area of poetry, and a special article about them in a volume devoted largely to modernist prose might be construed as being somewhat out of place. But Zhirmunsky's essay contains many riches.

Firstly, "Symbolism's Successors" (written when the critic was only twenty-five!) is almost as important for its perceptive evaluation of symbolist literary practices (both in poetry and prose) as it is for its sophisticated insights into acmeist technique. Zhirmunsky's brief, scholarly analyses of Akhmatova, Mandelstam, and Gumilyov remain, almost seventy years later, models of sober critical judgment. Yet the critic's compare-and-contrast approach also provides us with a greater awareness of certain crucial features characteristic of the writing discussed in the second half of this anthology—of Sologub, Bely, Bryusov, and, of course, Kuzmin. Secondly, in discussing the new drift of modernist art toward greater aesthetic and emotional balance, Zhirmunsky echoes many of the concerns voiced in the first article of this volume, Menshikov's "On Literature and Writers." Viewing this latest phase of modernism as a reaction against the philosophical and linguistic excesses of symbolism, the critic goes so far as to suggest that we appreciate acmeist writing as a "new realism."

Acmeism never achieved the fusion of realism and religion that Zhirmunsky had envisioned in 1916, nor, in fact, did it reign supreme for very much longer. Already in 1914 the drum beat of a new and stridently anti-traditional artistic movement began to be heard—that of futurism, which outlived acmeism, at least officially, insofar as it briefly enjoyed most favored status after the Bolshevik revolution. But this brings us to a period which extends beyond the confines of this book, and a survey of the prose of Pasternak and Khlebnikov, as well as that of the major figures of the twenties—Pilnyak, Babel, Zamyatin, Olesha, Fedin—clearly deserves a volume of its own.

Notes

1. Anton Chekhov, Letter to A. Suvorin, Dec. 30, 1888. Quoted from *Letters of Anton Chekhov*, translated by Simon Karlinsky and Michael Henry Heim (N.Y., 1973), p. 78.

2. *The Prose of Osip Mandelstam*. Translated with an introduction by Clarence Brown (Princeton, 1965), pp. 83-84.

3. Letter to A. Suvorin, March 27, 1894. Quoted from Karlinsky and Heim, op. cit., p. 262.

4. Leo Tolstoy, *A Confession*. Translated by Aylmer Maude (London, 1961), p. 13.

5. See G. Byalyi, "Sovremenniki," in *Chekhov i ego vremia* (Moscow, 1977), pp. 5-18. For another crucial document which employs a vision of the destruction of the world to signal the termination of all former values, see N. Minsky, *In the Light of Conscience* (*Pri svete sovesti*, 1900).

6. Jeffrey Brooks, "Readers and Reading at the End of the Tsarist Era," in *Literature and Society in Imperial Russia, 1880-1914*, edited by William Mills Todd III (Stanford, 1978), pp. 97-150.

7. For a helpful synopsis and discussion of this document, see Ralph E. Matlaw, "The Manifesto of Russian Symbolism," in *Slavic and East European Journal*, 1957, No. 1 (Vol. 2), pp. 177-191.

8. P. Bitsilli, *Tvorchestvo Chekhova: Opyt stilisticheskogo analiza. Godishnik na universitet sv. Kliment Okhridski*, XXXVIII, 6 (Sofia, 1942); English translation by T. W. Clyman and E. J. Cruise (Ardis: Ann Arbor, 1983).

9. D. Merezhkovskii, "Chekhov i Gorkii," in *Polnoe sobranie sochinenii*, Vol. XIII (Moscow, 1914), p. 62.

10. Vladimir Nabokov, "Maksim Gorky," in *Lectures on Russian Literature* (New York, 1981), p. 305.

11. V. Bryusov, Inscription in his volume of poetry *Tertia Vigilia*, which he presented to Gorky. Quoted in *Russkaia literatura kontsa XIX-nachala XX vekov: Devianostye gody* (Moscow, 1968), p. 471.

12. Quoted in Ibid., p. 346.

13. Ibid., p. 445. This statement is preceded by Gorky's oft-quoted remark to Chekhov that in stories such as "Lady With Lapdog" Chekhov was killing realism by writing in so succinct a style.

14. The most informative general introduction to Remizov I have come across in English is Alex M. Shane, "An Introduction to Alexei Remizov," in *The Bitter Air of Exile: Russian Writers in the West: 1922-1972*, edited by S. Karlinsky and A. Appel, Jr. (Berkeley, 1977), pp. 10-16.

15. Marina Tsvetaeva, "Hero of Labor" (1924). Quoted in *The Diary of Valery Bryusov* (1893-1905), Edited, Translated and with an Introductory Essay by Joan Delaney Grossman (Berkeley, 1980), p. 162.

16. Ibid.

17. Boris Eikhenbaum, "O proze M. Kuzmina," in *Skvoz' literaturu*, No. 4 (Leningrad, 1924). Quoted in Andrew Field, "Mikhail Kuzmin: Notes on a Decadent's Prose," in *The Russian Review*, July, 1963, Vol. 2, No. 3, pp. 289-300.

18. Mikhail Kuzmin, "Zametki o russkoi belletristike," in *Apollon*, No. 7 (April, 1910). Quoted in *Russkaya literatura kontsa XIX-nachala XX vekov* (Moscow, 1972), p. 452.

19. For an informative discussion of some modernist elements in *Petersburg*, see Donald Fanger, "The City of Russian Modernist Fiction," in Bradbury and McFarlane, eds., *Modernism* (Penguin Books, 1976), pp. 467-480.

20. V. Bryusov (under the pseudonym V. A. Maslov), "Foreword" to *Russkie simvolisty* (Moscow, 1894). Quoted in *Russkaia literatura ...* (Moscow, 1968), p. 305.

21. Boris Eikhenbaum, *Anna Akhmatova* (Petrograd, 1923), p. 66. Quoted in Victor Erlich, *Russian Formalism: History and Doctrine* (The Hague, 1955), p. 224.

1

On Literature and Writers

Mikhail Osipovich Menshikov (1859-1918)

After a brief career as a sailor, Mikhail Menshikov went on to become an important journalist in the 1880s and 1890s. He was editor of the popular magazine The Week (Nedelya) *to which Chekhov had contributed because he found it "congenial." In reference to Menshikov's long article on his story "Peasants," Chekhov wrote in 1897: "Your article on 'Peasants' has made me quite excited and has inspired me to do a great deal of thinking." For a while Menshikov was influenced by the religious ideas of Tolstoy, with whom he briefly corresponded, as he had with Chekhov and the writer Nikolai Leskov. Menshikov's article "Critical Decadence" ("Kriticheskii dekadans," 1892), which Leskov deemed "a bitter and intelligent piece," was a vitriolic attack against the newly emerging modernist views of the critic and early theoretician of the "new" art, A. Volynsky. Menshikov's writings tend to reflect the pervasive strain of moral and religious unctuousness which existed in Russian society of that time. By the turn of the century Menshikov's views became increasingly reactionary; in his articles for* New Times (Novoe vremya) *and elsewhere he exhibited an undisguised anti-Semitism and was accused of promoting the pogroms which followed the 1905 revolution. He published three books of collected essays between 1898 and 1900, which included studies of Griboedov, Gogol, Leskov, Tolstoy, Chekhov, Pushkin, Nadson, A. K. Tolstoy, and others. A staunch traditionalist and "aristocrat" in his literary tastes (as the following selection shows) and social views, Menshikov was especially hostile to Gorky's fiction, for which he earned the warm praise of Tolstoy. To Menshikov is attributed the remarks: "Society is the intelligentsia" and "Let the barefoot peasants, workers, and other outcasts of society rot." In 1918 the Soviets shot Menshikov as "an enemy of the people."*

On Literature and Writers*

... With each passing day literature is losing its former significance as a guider of souls; its inner, ennobling power is waning. From the status of master, literature is changing into the servant and even, repulsive as this may sound, the *lackey* of the public... Fiction is becoming a thousand times more accessible than before; it has become an everyday requirement, like tobacco and music. Nowadays we read as mechanically as we smoke or drink tea: the demand is satisfied, the aroma pleasantly excites our nerves, and if a book is bad we throw it away like a bad cigar and take another one. We read in order to be immediately distracted and to forget what we have just finished reading so that in the evening, while lying in bed, we can take yet another dose of reading. What kind of reading? An "interesting" kind, one which tickles our fancy in a special way. One can meet thousands of "intelligent" people who constantly "smoke" books, so to speak, and who are at the same time uneducated and surprisingly callous and narrow...

Perhaps it is here, in literature's democratization, that one should seek the reason for Russia's, as well as the world's, unfortunate impoverishment. Everywhere one hears cries that talented people do not exist. This is patently wrong. Talented people do exist, and now that the masses are being drawn into the sphere of education, there are more talented people than ever before. But this talent is *impotent* and therefore you don't notice it. Talent is paralyzed by the current literary vogue, by a school which is unnatural for genuine art. The naturalism of today requires above all else the *external* portrayal of life, with all its vulgarity and chaos. But the very nature of art will not tolerate this: for true art, the surface constitutes only the outer crust beneath which life's deeper meaning lies hidden. Unless it is truly heroic, today's talent cannot resist the psychic miasma, and overcome the rut, of our time; either it has to abandon literature or adapt itself to the current fashion and mutilate itself. It is for this reason that talent has lost its ancient power and no longer exerts its previous influence. Take, for example, a powerful artist such as Zola: does he influence you in any way? You read him, you marvel at the skill of his writing, you experience a certain satisfaction, but does it leave the same impression on you as Hugo's, Thackeray's, Dostoevsky's, or Tolstoy's writing? Or take the young stars of France—Maupassant, Bourget,[1] Marcel Prévost,[2] or of Russia—Chekhov and Korolenko.[3] Let us be fair: in what way are these writers untalented? An uncommon intelligence, a sensitive heart, an ability to grasp precisely those tones and colors which nature itself provides, shows through each line of their writing. But at the same time you feel that these talented men hardly affect you, hardly enchant or teach you. It is precisely from them, from the talented, that you expect this rare and happy mood, but they just

* "O literature i pisateliakh"—published in *Knizhki nedeli*, 1891, No. 11, pp. 206-223. The current version represents roughly the last third of Menshikov's discussion.

don't provide it. Nor is it their fault—this mood is greater than them and, perhaps, beyond human power. Can a generation of literary giants which is not equal to, but stronger than the Turgenevs, Goncharovs, and Tolstoys really appear? Can such a generation, with a new fire stolen from heaven, with a completely new word which will be not only literary but also *prophetic,* materialize and shake life up by breaking the burdensome chains that are holding down today's literary talent?...

Russian prosaists have not morally influenced society in full proportion to their talent. Ordinarily the great writers were read immediately after each new work appeared, and if the piece was especially strong *(Oblomov, Fathers and Sons, Anna Karenina),* the critics would stir up a commotion for a while and people would discuss and even argue about it. But two or three years would pass and the novel would be put aside: perhaps only a few would reread it, and the handful of real admirers would read it several times, continually enjoying it, like Mozart's or Chopin's music, or Lermontov's poetry. Yet even among these aficionados one could hardly find individuals for whom the great novel represented more than a pleasant diversion. Neither *Dead Souls,* nor *War and Peace,* nor *Oblomov,* nor *Crime and Punishment* was, or could be, by its very nature what the *Iliad* was for the ancient reader, what the *Divine Comedy* was for the medieval reader, what the Bible was for the Reformation reader: they were not "good tidings," they did not constitute a world of lofty models which could powerfully affect the *very lives* of the reader or of nations. There is no heroic element, no romanticism in the contemporary novel: it is imprinted with a dry, positivist method, with the stamp of a scientific, excessively materialistic attitude toward life. The realist novel is essentially a scientific work executed via artistic means; it provides a "multitude of low truths" and very little "lofty deceit." Just as in science nature contains only "active forces" and nothing supernatural, so in the realist novel there are "active characters"—actors, but no *heroes.* One would have to create these heroes, to extract them from the depths of the imagination, to *invent* them, as Raphael *invented* the heavenly beauty of the Madonna or Schiller *invented* the exalted nobility of the Marquis of Posa.[4] But the realist school, like the exact sciences, considers *invention* to be a great sin. In real life one too rarely encounters the heroic, and the contemporary novel actually denies its very existence. In life we always encounter sick, debased, insolent, and stupid people and among them their typical, archetypal models. The realist school chooses these archetypes with scientific scrupulousness and then draws "life as it is,"—variegated, interesting, picturesque, but essentially in a way which can neither inspire us nor affect our world view. Chichikov, Sobakevich, Khlestakov, Nozdryov, Korobochka[5] are living people, but they in no way ennoble me. Famusov, Molchalin, Tit-Titych,[6] the Karamazovs, the Yudushkas[7] are, if you like, *heroes,* but not the kind you want to imitate or for whom you have great respect. Among these "heroes" you feel uneasy and depressed, and protracted intercourse with them oppresses and weakens you. By their triumphant presence and prevalence in literature, these types poison one's view of life: one loses faith in the possibility of better types, of not only ideal, but simply good people; one becomes a kind of Sobakevich himself. True, honest writers know that good and evil are intermingled in life and therefore in addition to scoundrels they create good, albeit inevitably weak and wretched souls. Furthermore, they endow the most ghastly monsters with certain human feelings: Chichikov dreams of little children, Yudushka prays to God—all of this imparting more life-like qualities to these monsters and making them even more authentic. In a scientifically precise way, the great realist writers have filled the imaginations of readers, including often innocent youth, with trivial, gloomy, repulsive beings who resemble evil spirits. But of the world of radiant geniuses there is not a trace. No objects in the realist novel exist by which man can satisfy his ineradicable instinct to worship and venerate. Rather, these objects elicit an antithetical, essentially sick feeling: disgust and negation which, like genuine poison, is healthy only in small doses:

> The heart which is tired of hating
> Cannot be taught to love.

Thus our literature's inability to regenerate society can be explained by the very nature of the realist novel as the predominant literary form. Borrowed from the sciences, this form has been reduced by naturalism to its ultimate expression—self-negation. In both the West and Russia one senses a crisis in fiction which amounts to nothing less than the extinction of the novel, and even Zola himself is beginning to imagine a new, heretofore unmaterialized literary form. In the Russian novel this crisis has long been anticipated. Pushkin—the Peter the Great of literature (to use his own definition of Lomonosov)[8]—sensed the danger of being restricted to solely negative types in the novel and was able to introduce in his fiction several exquisite, even heroic figures: Tatyana, Marya Ivanovna, the old commandant,[9] and so on. Gogol felt a similar danger. At the end of *Dead Souls* he began somehow to feel suffocated among the distorted and vulgar creatures into whom he had breathed life; he dreamed of furnishing positive, heroic types and tortured himself in struggling with the spirit of the form which he had inductively accepted. Contemporary life did not provide the required "nature," and resorting to romanticism—which Pushkin never feared to do—was something Gogol allowed himself only in his stories. Gogol never succeeded in resolving this insoluble problem. All our great realists have felt this narrowness of form and its oppressive, dry materiality. All of them struggled with and expanded it until the breaking point, as we see in several novels of Dostoevsky *(The Possessed, The Brothers Karamazov),* Tolstoy *(War and Peace),* and Goncharov *(The Precipice).* Dostoevsky felt the need to introduce wholly autonomous poems and even treatises into the novel; Tolstoy—entire historical and philosophical digressions. As soon as the writer grasped the surface of life more profoundly, as soon as he conceived a powerful positive figure, his scheme underwent total disorder, his different ends could not be met.

The realist novel has turned out to be an unsuitable form for artistic preaching and prophesying, which is the writer's mission, and it is no accident that Gogol burned his sequel to *Dead Souls* and Tolstoy stopped at *Anna Karenina.* Even Turgenev, the most skillful of the artist-realists, ended with "The Song of Triumphant Love," "Klara Milich" and "Poems in Prose"—pieces which are written in an entirely non-realist style. It was as if by the end of their lives all the great artists recognized the futility of their realist writings—all of those full and beautiful pictures which stood too close to life to be higher than it and thus were unable to move it forward. Seeing that the surface of life remained the way it was—base and full of pain and darkness—the artist involuntarily escaped into his own inner world, into the realm of ideals, and from there, from the beautiful distance, he began to look at life prophetically, with fervent love and fervent hatred for it. Only the writer's flight from the callous exterior surface of realist art into his own self can explain the remarkable emotional upheaval in Gogol, Dostoevsky, and Tolstoy toward the end of their lives. And what a great misfortune that Gogol and Dostoevsky died so early! In Gogol one could have expected another original and no less powerful Dostoevsky, who had gone from laughter to pain. In Dostoevsky there might have developed the current Tolstoy—again, an original and peculiar one, but precisely one who possessed the kind of prophetic inspiration that has given us "The Death of Ivan Ilych" and "The Kreutzer Sonata." And although of the three, Dostoevsky was the closest to the new prophetic literary school, if fate allows Tolstoy to live longer, perhaps we shall finally see this new aesthetic type of writing and new order which will be able to establish the influence of literature. That Tolstoy will abandon art forever is a psychological impossibility, for it would be a betrayal of his personality; but that he will no longer write novels is possible and even probable.[10] The novel is obsolete, and for the new prophetic word the artist will undoubtedly find a new form. Of course the novel will long remain in the theory and practice of art, but for moving society forward, for its rebirth through prophetic supplication, another form must appear—the transfigured novel, the drama, the poem, or whatever.

In essence this will not be a step ahead, but a *return*—specifically from psychically dead forms, which perhaps were freer and more beautiful for their own times, to a structure which is freer and more natural for our own. Not only literature but all art is now more or less feeling the weight of obsolete styles which have lost their roots in peoples' psyches. For example, in architecture, the Greek and Gothic styles are beautiful, but who builds buildings (or temples) now in these styles? If we have reluctant recourse to these structures because of our distressing lack of more native ones, then we still try to change them (although we only end up distorting these dead, yet beautiful systems). Of course, porticos, columns, capitols, battlements, and the like are all very popular, but all of this is not style, but rather the *remains* of a style, just as, for example, currently fashionable stories and novellas are nothing more than the remains of the novel. In painting, sculpture, music—in all spheres of art—one senses exhaustion due to the redundancy of old forms, and one feels the painful and madly pressured search for new ones (recall, for instance, Claude in Zola's *L'Oeuvre*)[11] Just as in the animal world various creatures from time to time shed their old, moulted coat, sensing the growth of a new one which is organically tied to their new body, so the genius of contemporary art—including literature—is attempting to find for itself its own organic form.

Perhaps the conditions for new spiritual forms are taking shape among the popular masses. But a great soul, a powerful, passionate impulse is needed in order for these conditions to come to fruition. Essentially here, as in all spheres, the decisive act for any momentous event is the *deed* of a great person, in this case the deed of a great writer. What the substance of this necessary deed in literature should be, I shall speak about separately.[12]

Notes

1. Bourget, Paul Charles Josef (1852-1935). French poet, essayist, and novelist. Some of his early fiction (e.g., *Mensonges,* 1887 and *Le disciple,* 1889) appeared in Russian translation shortly before Menshikov wrote his essay.

2. Prévost, Eugene Marcel (1862-1941). French novelist who began his career under the influence of Émile Zola. Several of his early works (e.g., *Le skorpion,* 1887 and *Chonchette,* 1888) appeared in Russian translation at the turn of the century.

3. Korolenko, Vladimir Galaktionovich (1853-1921). Realist writer and social thinker whose many short stories are often marked by a sentimental, usually cheerful and optimistic humanitarianism. In addition to several outstanding stories, Korolenko left a superb autobiography of his youth, *The History of My Contemporary (Istoriia moego sovremennika,* 1922).

4. A character in Friedrich Schiller's drama in blank verse *Don Carlos* (1797).

5. Khlestakov is a character in Gogol's comedy *The Inspector General (Revizor,* 1836); the other characters are from the novel *Dead Souls (Mertvye dushi,* 1842).

6. Characters in Alexander Griboedov's comedy in rhymed verse *Woe From Wit (Gore ot uma,* 1824).

7. Yudushka (Judas)—despicable protagonist of Saltykov-Shchedrin's novel *The Golovlyov Family (Gospoda Golovlevy,* 1880).

8. Lomonosov, Mikhail Vasilievich (1711-1765). Writer, philosopher, scientist, and one of the founders of Moscow University, after whom the institution is currently named. To Pushkin is also attributed the line "Lomonosov himself was a university."

9. Tatyana is the heroine of *Eugene Onegin.* Marya Ivanovna and the old commandant are characters in the novel *The Captain's Daughter (Kapitanskaia dochka,* 1836).

10. Menshikov was correct in his assessment that Tolstoy would not and could not abandon fiction, but his prediction that the writer would no longer produce novels did not come true. After Menshikov's article Tolstoy wrote *Resurrection (Voskresenie,* 1899) and Hadji-Murat (published posthumously in 1912).

11. A novel by Émile Zola (1886), the best-known writer in France during the last two decades of the nineteenth century.

12. Menshikov's sequel followed shortly.

2

Without Wings: Chekhov and His Work

M. P. Nevedomsky* (1866-1943)

Trained in Petersburg as a mathematician and physicist, Nevedomsky (pseudonym of Mikhail Petrovich Miklashevsky) began writing literary criticism in 1889 and for over twenty-five years contributed to such popular journals as God's World (Mir bozhii), Education (Obrazovanie), *and* The Contemporary World (Sovremennyi mir). *He is the author of over fifty articles and reviews, covering painting and theater as well as literature, a large book of collected essays on Russian literature from Belinsky through Gorky and Andreyev (entitled* Originators and Continuers [Zachinateli i prodolzhateli], *1919), a history of Russian literature of the 1880s and 1890s, and, toward the end of his life, an impressive monograph on the late nineteenth-century landscapist A. I. Kuindzhi (published in 1937), which is a continuation of a work which he had co-authored with Repin in 1913.*

Politically, Nevedomsky supported the Menshevik faction of the Social Democrats, a fact which endeared him neither to Lenin nor the editors of the Soviet Literary Encyclopedia, who find his work too free of political ideology and too insistent on the concept of the artist's "inner freedom." Nevedomsky's critical methodology is succinctly expressed in his article "The Zig-Zags of Our Criticism" ("Zig-zagi nashei kritiki"). Here he calls for an approach which combines the inner and outer world of artistic creation, one which stresses the connection between the subjective realm of an author and the objective world in which he resides. Nevedomsky argues that the comprehension of the creative personality is a basic element in the critical evaluation of art and that such comprehension must begin on the firm ground of social conditions: "Only an approach which totally and synthetically encompasses both the nature of the author-creator's intuition and objective (i.e., biographical and social) data can yield the best possible understanding of fiction." The article on Chekhov, which was originally intended as the first part of a book, admirably lives up to Nevedomsky's credo. It combines analysis of individual works with biographical data (gleaned from reminiscences and letters) and a socio-historical excursis on the decade of the 1880s (partly abridged here) when Chekhov matured into a major writer.

Occasionally assuming Marxist positions on art, Nevedomsky more often employed exclusively aesthetic criteria in evaluating the merits of fiction. Thus, he appreciated the early writings of Gorky, but found his political novel Mother *(Mat', 1907) highly schematic and "a sign of Gorky's diminishing talent." Essentially Nevedomsky saw the history of Russian literature from the end of the nineteenth through the beginning of the twentieth century as a process departing from the often rigid and constricting moralism of the populists and others (such as Tolstoy, Dostoevsky, and Saltykov-Shchedrin) and moving toward a freer aestheticphilosophical synthesis, which he saw best manifested in the work of Chekhov and Andreyev. In Nevedomsky's eyes the major and determining idea of the evolution of Russian literature was the development of the free personality. However, Nevedomsky drew the line at the decadent and symbolist writers of the early twentieth century and came out strongly against the religious and mystical trends which he found in their writing.*

Without Wings: Chekhov and His Work*

Chekhov and his work...Judging by the "literature on the subject," it is hardly possible to find in our entire fiction a more complex topic for critical analysis than the work of this melancholy artist. He is positively an enigma. Literature on Chekhov is not in short supply; we have a whole series of critical articles and memoirs about him. But in my view the Chekhov question is far from resolved: neither the intimate essence of his work nor his personality emerges with sufficient clarity.

"Chekhov was a democrat, he dreamed of the triumph of democratic ideas," comments Lvov[1] in his article on the writer. But several lines earlier this same critic notes: "Unfortunately, Chekhov did not live to the present day, when even the blind have gained sight,"—using this as an excuse to explain both the absence of "young Russia" in the gallery of Chekhovian types and the appearance of only rare and "symbolic" rays of light in his work. Chekhov did not live to see *the blind* gain sight. But obviously those who *did* have sight saw the light and perceived everything that they should have perceived; they did so earlier on, probably quite some time ago. Then why did not "the subtle, sensitive artist and democrat"—as this critic describes him—see these things? Lvov does not linger on this question, yet it is one of no small importance; it is precisely one of the "riddles" which the late writer has posed us: such a "perceptive" artist as he should have had to live until the blind gained sight in order to see!

"Cold-blooded" is how Mikhailovsky[2] harshly and concisely summarizes his description of Chekhov in his first piece on the writer in connection with the collection *Gloomy People*. However, some Moscow students, in a telegram to the late artist's widow, declared that they particularly valued Chekhov's teaching them "to love and to pity our gloomy people." Another enigma.

Bulgakov[3] sees in Chekhov "an optimistic idealist," on the one hand, and a kind of secret adherent to Christianity, something along the lines of the New Testament Nicodemus,[4] on the other. This view, we may assume, can be attributed to the usual zealousness of the neophyte who aspires to discern in everything and everyone elements of the truth he has discovered. But if this is to be accepted, there should at the very least be no elements in Chekhov's work contradicting it, no indications that ought to prevent the new prophet from reckoning him among "the chosen." However, in his perceptive and interesting article on Chekhov, Shestov[5] considers himself justified in describing the author as follows: "Art, science, love, inspiration, ideals, the future—choose any word with which humanity, past and present, has comforted or diverted itself—Chekhov has only to touch it for

* "Bez kryl'ev: A. P. Chekhov i ego tvorchestvo"—published in *Yubileynyi chekhovskii sbornik* (Moscow, 1910), pp. 55-113. The article first appeared, without the postscript, in *Mir bozhii* in 1906.

it to fade instantly, wither, and die." And a bit further on he continues: "Maupassant often had to strain every nerve to do in his victim. The victim often escaped from him, crushed and broken, yet alive. In Chekhov's hands, nothing escaped death." It is clear that, in Shestov's opinion, Chekhov is not so much a "secret" adherent to Bulgakov's religion as he is a manifest pessimist who destroys all religion with his "gnawing skepticism." I am purposely citing critiques which get at the heart of Chekhov, attempts to define the ideological side of his work; and I believe that these diametrically opposed and mutually exclusive positions are sufficient testimony to the enigmatic character of Chekhov's writing.

Merezhkovsky[6] has gone even further than Shestov. From the heights of his new "religion of the Trinity," he likens Chekhov to a "naked tramp." Of Chekhov's world view he says, as he does of the world view of all the contemporary intelligentsia, "this is genuine death, both corporeal and spiritual, which is forecast in the Apocalypse," and so on. This evaluation has been current for a long time. Protopopov[7] tried to show that Chekhov was lacking a "general idea," while Skabichevsky[8] has called him an "extreme idealist." Volzhsky[9] now sees this same "extreme idealism" in Chekhov, only he describes it as *pessimistic;* whereas Batyushkov,[10] concurring with Bulgakov's view of Chekhov as an "optimist-idealist," resolutely denies the current charges that Chekhov is a pessimist and, contrary to Lvov, who had practically turned Chekhov into a Social-Democrat, assures us that had the writer lived until our day he probably would have been a Cadet.[11]

With his somewhat "Spencerian" cast of mind, Gornfeld[12] finds purely Spencerian comfort in the thought that differences among critics are the best proof of the originality and *significance* of a writer's talent. This may be comforting, but it is not entirely fair; and in any case, it does not get us very far. Only one firm and indubitable fact emerges from all these contradictory analyses, namely, that Chekhov's critics tend to discuss the object of their criticism very much in terms of their own image and likeness. From these descriptions we essentially know that Lvov is an undisputed democrat; Bulgakov is a very zealous and philosophically refined Christian, like any number of Catholic priests or like Chichikov, who even recruits "dead souls"; Shestov is a writer filled with "gnawing skepticism"; Batyushkov is an optimist-idealist with a clear weakness for the Cadet party, and so on. All of this is of course very interesting. However, what is Chekhov himself? This is also an interesting question, which remains wide open...

Let us try to strike up an initial "acquaintance" with Chekhov. The wording I have happened to use makes this sound like a sad paradox; however, in the case of deceased writers, reminiscences facilitate this first acquaintance rather significantly. Afterwards we can more conveniently turn to the conditions of surrounding life, the influence of environment, and the historical situation which nurtured the artist. We shall use both approaches, i.e., we shall look at "reminiscences" of Chekhov and at the environment that cultivated him.

Chekhov's writings have always reminded me of a somewhat clouded mirror, as if someone had "breathed" on the smooth and perfectly polished surface of the glass so that the mirror became covered with a haze or with a certain *frostiness*. Objects are reflected in it accurately and in all of their variations, but the colors are a bit dull, the contours are not completely clear. Something is always left unsaid in Chekhov's images, and they are always a bit gray and sadly lackluster, as if the author is afraid or unable to convey everything that he knows about his characters. Of course, I am speaking about the second, "gloomy" period of Chekhov's work. In the brief first period of Chekhov's career, which lasted only two or three years, the period of "Antosha Chekhonte,"[13] of the *Dragonfly,* and partially of *New Times,* the mirror was completely bright. This was a time of gay laughter and pure comicality. Yet even later—to the very end—at the slightest glimmering of humor, whenever there was the barest reflection of a comic figure, this reflection invariably hit the mirror's bright spot, and the depiction simply stood out against the general background—sharp and distinct. Think of the baliff Epikhodov or the bankrupt landowner Simeon-Pishchik in *The Cherry Orchard.* Is this not the same old Antosha Chekhonte deriding them with his good-natured, radiant laughter? However, Chekhov specializes in semi-clear, muted images. Compare them with the multi-colored "living" people, full of blood and life, who emerge from under Tolstoy's pen—so three-dimensional and full-blooded that it seems as if you could walk around them. Or with the transparent, see-through images of Turgenev. The idea-laden images of our neo-Romantics are also clear and transparent, whether sketched in the strikingly colorful and impatient strokes of the Romantic Gorky or outlined by the delicate symbolic brush of Andreyev. In the long line of our old and new artists the muted and melancholy Chekhov stands completely alone.

It is curious that authors of "reminiscences" note that Chekhov had a *muted* voice—a sad, somewhat muffled, and restrained baritone. But alongside of this all of them also mention *"Chekhov's laughter,"* unusual and radiant, which remained intact to the very end, during all the long years of illness and "gloominess."

Shcheglov[14] mentions that Chekhov always had the intention of writing a good vaudeville. "Yes, vaudeville is really something else, and all the rest is stuff and nonsense," Chekhov is supposed to have said on occasion, quoting Griboedov's Repetilov.[15] "He loved jokes, absurd nicknames, all kinds of foolishness and hoaxes," Bunin recalls. Once, beginning a conversation about literature and exalting Lermontov's "Taman," Chekhov quipped, "I can't understand how he could do this while practically a boy. Oh, if I could write such a thing and a good vaudeville as well—then I could die in peace...."

The combination of "radiant laughter," a love for merriment, and a "muted" voice—in the literal and figurative senses—is extremely characteristic of Chekhov. It even seems to me that it defines the essential features of his image, that it may serve as the "sesame" which opens the secret doors of his creative work...

Chekhov's gift was primarily a gift for the comic. This is borne out not only by *his creation of the genre of comic sketches in Russia,* not only by all of those pearls of humor ("The Malefactor," "Surgery," "Shrove Tuesday," and so on) which are scattered throughout the early "cheerful" period of his work and that relapse of "laughter" which I have already mentioned in his last drama, but also by his eternal predilection for the *contradiction between form and content,* which never left him over the course of his entire career. The radiant laughter disappeared. The sickness which had already begun at the end of the eighties (referring to an 1887 letter of Chekhov to his sister, Bunin concludes that the writer's lungs were already then infected with tuberculosis), and the somber period of social stagnation which nurtured Chekhov, caused the carefree, happy Antosha Chekhonte to turn into the "muted," gloomy writer-"whiner," as he ironically called himself. The long procession of gray, hopeless figures—superfluous, impotent, tormented people—started on its way and struck up the doleful song of its bankruptcy. But *formally,* conceptually, Chekhov remained true to his former *comic* method. The artistic lever with which he approached life's phenomena remained the same: the search for *contradictions.*

What is it, for instance, that elicits our *laughter* in "The Malefactor"? On the one hand we have the idyllic naiveté of the peasant who sees in the nut which he unscrews from the railway tracks only a sinker for his fishing rod, for "if you put a worm or other live bait on the hook, how do you think it will get to the bottom without a sinker? What the devil is it good for if it swims on the surface!" On the other hand we have the examining magistrate, who with great seriousness eradicates "evil intent" according to Article 1081 of the Penal Code, and in whose eyes the same nut is sufficient grounds for judging the fisherman to be a malefactor worthy of imprisonment. It is hard to imagine a more preposterous contradiction in views about the same object—particularly an object of such insignificant size. And from the very beginning the reader automatically forgets about the tragic finale of the incident and the deep social content which Chekhov perhaps accidentally has touched upon in this classic comic sketch. Instead he laughs to tears over both—over the fisherman who for the sake of a gudgeon can cause a railway accident and over the eradicator of "evil intent," who makes a mountain out of a molehill. In both there is a flagrant contradiciton between the essence of the matter and its form. Both have wound up in genuinely comic *situations.* I should emphasize that the contradiction here is conditioned more by the external situation than by the inner nature of the characters. Glance over Chekhov's "merry" sketches and you will satisfy yourself that this is typical of them: almost everywhere the question is one of situations rather than types. One recalls "The Burbot" (with the squire and his entire household naked in the water, levelled by their greed as they try to catch the fish, which in the end makes fools of them all); one recalls "The Screw," where some bureaucrats are playing cards with a deck of photographic likenesses of their superiors and where an initially intrigued superior participates in this "sacrilegious" game; one recalls "Albion's Daughter," "Surgery," and so on and so forth. Everywhere we have situation comedy, but this comedy is never superficial. The contradiction between the characters' situations and the essence of the matter almost always in Chekhov corresponds to the universal contradictions which are found in life itself. These are not merely empty farces, but rather "good vaudevilles," as he put it—in the manner of the two which he actually did write, "The Proposal" and "The Bear." Such purely nonsensical trifles as "Romance with a Double Bass," "The Avenger," "A Naughty Boy," and "A Sinister Night" are very rare in Chekhov.

Chekhov's laughter is intelligent, but it is also youthfully light-hearted. His is not the laughter of a Leikin.[16] The merry humor of Chekhov sometimes turns into caricature, but it almost always reflects the far-from-cheerful contradictions of life. In this early period Chekhov does not avoid so-called "civic," accusatory motifs, and at times his comic sketches become light political satire. "The Death of a Government Clerk," "Anxiety," "Staff Sergeant Prishibeyev," "In the Bathhouse," "The Discontent of Minds," and other pieces come to mind. The fledgling, still unformed writer is obviously completely free in his choice of themes; he possesses in full measure that *inner freedom,* that "feeling of personal liberty" which, as Bunin notes, he subsequently elevated to a theory and identified as the major and necessary characteristic of a genuine artist ... One other comment about Chekhov's *laughter.* Gogol also laughed, as did Saltykov-Shchedrin—one with a healthy, radiant, and profound laughter which embraced all our absurd reality, the other with a painfully bitter and prophetically angry one. But neither began with laughter. Gogol romantically composed idylls of Ukrainian life, only occasionally sprinkling them with sparks of humor. Shchedrin began with a sad, perhaps sentimental tale of poverty and misfortune in life. Both began to laugh only when they matured, when they saw laughter as an instrument for ideological and artistic struggle. This is why their laughter was so conscious and serious, if one can indeed describe laughter in this way. The laughter of Chekhov's youth, however, is a carefree exposure and cheerful ridicule of contradictions—and nothing more. He came upon these contradictions and absurd *situations,* put them on exhibit for everyone to see clearly and vividly, and burst into light-hearted laughter. There is no idea present here, no service to any god (except the god of youth). This is completely free and carefree laughter. But could such laughter become a person's goal in life? Or, to take the opposite approach, could Chekhov sustain this original source of his creativity during his entire lifetime? Could he actually preserve it until the very end under the conditions of our Russian reality? And, finally, what did this richly talented artist bring with him into life, with what baggage did he enter it?

We come now to Chekhov's "muted voice" and "lusterless" images, to his constant restraint and his dislike of saying the final word about things. It would be best to begin with posthumous reminiscences...One can find, especially in Kuprin,[17] several characteristic strokes which individualize Chekhov's image and which other authors of reminiscences repeat. One such feature, besides the above-mentioned "muted" voice and uniquely "Chekhovian" laughter, is Chekhov's peculiar *restraint,* which both Kuprin and Bunin mention. The latter, whose reminiscences are particularly close to a "eulogy," sees in this restraint a singularly "strong" and select nature: "His restraint, it seems to me, springs from the noble nature of his soul and, among other things, from his desire to be exact in his every word...Even the people who were closest to him never knew what was going on in the depths of his soul."

Kuprin analyzes this characteristic in more detail. "It appears that he never completely unlocked his heart or opened up to anyone. But he treated all indifferently, in a benign and friendly manner. In his remarkable objectivity, standing above private sorrows and joys...he could be good and generous without loving, tender and compassionate without being attached...And perhaps these traits, which always remained obscure to those near him, hold the essential key to his personality."

And a bit further, the same author notes: "There are people who organically cannot endure, who are painfully ashamed of, overly expressive poses, gestures, expressions, and words. Chekhov possessed this quality to the highest degree. There existed in him a *fear of pathos* and of strong feelings, and the theatrical effects which are inseparable from them." On the basis of this analysis, Kuprin tries in passing to explain why it was never possible to ascertain whether or not Chekhov sympathized with the "intellectual movement, social protest," and the like.[18]

As one can see, not only Chekhov's work, but his very personality have hidden within them, as the authors of these reminiscences attest, certain riddles; he could not be figured out even by "the people who were closest to him." Characteristically, both writers see the root of Chekhov's singularity as lying in his mysteriousness. It is clear that "restraint" was as much a distinctive feature of his personality as it was of his work. What conditioned it? "Nobility of soul," answers Bunin. This is laudatory, but unspecific. More important is the completely different explanation which he gives in the same place, but only "among other things": the "desire to be *exact* in his every word." One senses here a kind of constant, tireless working on himself, a kind of unremitting tension and self-scrutiny out of fear of sinning against *exactitude*. This is certainly characteristic of Chekhov and surely explains something.

Kuprin comes even closer to the point. True, he approaches the tone of obituary; he is afraid of being insufficiently laudatory, and so at times he is a bit ambiguous. He even finds it necessary to qualify his opinion about Chekhov's "benign indifference" toward people, which he is quick to attribute to the writer's "amazing objectivity": "Here I must approach a ticklish spot, which perhaps not everyone will like." Then, after accurately noting a terribly characteristic trait of Chekhov's—*"his fear of pathos and strong feelings"*—he immediately adds: "The somewhat theatrical effects which are inseparable from them," and thereby nearly annuls the first half of his comment. Indeed, who has proved, and where, that strong feelings are inseparable from theatrical effects? I think quite the opposite is true: where there are theatrical effects, do not look for strong feelings and genuine pathos. What did Chekhov really fear? Theatricality or strong feeings? Both, I think. Kuprin's slippery phrase hits the nail on the head and, although somewhat illogical, it provides a very condensed and accurate description of Chekhov.

Namely this: his fear of pathos, strong feelings, and—at the same time—theatricality, or, as Kuprin says a little earlier, "overly expressive poses, gestures, expressions, and words" is the reason for Chekhov's unremitting and persistent "restraint." He really was somehow frightened of something, as if constantly scared, and therefore he continuously watched himself, weighing his every word sparingly and carefully, since he preferred not to say everything where there was a risk of saying more than "was proper" or where there was just an iota of a chance of sinning against "exactness." This hardly resembles the inner freedom of the artist, the complete liberty of his personality about which Bunin speaks in his reminiscences.

Let us turn from reminiscences to Chekhov's works themselves. Fear of pathos is certainly predominant here! Everywhere—in his stories, sketches, and dramas—Chekhov avoids powerful dramatic scenes. In "The Duel," in the very scene where the confrontation takes place, the psychology of the story's hero, Laevsky, is carefully depicted up to the moment when Von Koren's shot is fired. Von Koren misses his mark. What does the surviving Laevsky experience at this moment? What whirl of feelings and thoughts must be rushing through his agitated and tormented soul? We learn nothing about this from Chekhov, for he places a period precisely at this point, and next shows us a Laevsky who is reborn and "reformed." In the tale "In the Ravine," the savage scene in which Aksinya scalds Lipa's baby with boiling water ends abruptly with the child's inhuman scream. Once again it is as if Chekhov cannot bring himself to peer into the mother's soul at this moment. The culmination of "A Boring

Story," the scene between the professor and Katya in the hotel is handled with the same "restraint." The professor definitively acknowledges his inadequacy, which results from the absence of "what his philosopher friends call a general idea," and he retreats from the straightforward Katya's cross-examination (we shall later return to this scene), completely powerless to tell her how to live or what to do. This tragic collision is described in the following brief strokes:

> "Honestly, Katya, I don't know..."
> I was utterly at a loss, disconcerted and touched by her sobs, and hardly able to stand on my feet.
> "Come, Katya, let's have breakfast," I said with a forced smile. "No more crying!"

Katya leaves, not looking at him and not turning back. The only being in the world to whom he is attached has left him. He remains alone. What is he going through? Chekhov draws the curtain. Unlike the former two cases, I do not judge this one to be artistically faulty. Indeed, from the artistic point of view this particular scene may be Chekhov's best. Here his restraint and economy of means transmit with concentrated force the gloomy and mute despair of the professor who has "seen through life." I need only note that this feature of Chekhov's never changes; he is always restrained to the point of stinginess, always frightened by pathos. In "A Boring Story" this stinginess leads to an artistic gain, but such is not always the case.

In *The Seagull,* when Treplev's much-beloved Nina Zarechnaya leaves him forever before his suicide, he says only: "It will be too bad if someone meets her in the garden and later informs mother. That might distress her." Then he tears up all of his manuscripts and goes out to shoot himself. The author leaves all of his feelings to the spectator's imagination and sensitivity. In *The Three Sisters* Tuzenbach's fiancée, Irina, upon learning of his death, responds with only two words: "I knew, I knew." And of the others, practically no one mentions a word about him. True, in the author's conception of things, Tuzenbach's death is merely one episode in the general meaningless burden of life, under which the heroines of the drama languish. But psychologically such an economy of words on the part of the three sisters is not very convincing.

I do not need to demonstrate that Tolstoy, for example, would have been able to find simple, completely "untheatrical" words to depict Lipa's grief or Treplev's feelings, as he did in the scene of Andrey Bolkonsky's death or Anna Karenina's suicide. Nor will I speak of Dostoevsky who, in these cases, forgetting all sense of measure, would have lacerated himself and the reader, although without any "theatricality." It is clear that it was not merely a question of Chekhov's fear of theatricality. He could not find simple and sufficiently powerful words for the expression of strong feelings—such is the hypothesis which these comparisons inevitably suggest. And I do not think it is a mistake to say that as a writer Chekhov *was lacking in pathos* and that this same absence of pathos explains his "benignly indifferent" attitude toward people...

We can note this absence of pathos, passion, and bias as the distinguishing feature of this exemplary contemplator. It undoubtedly results in a certain coldness, "an amazing objectivity, which stands higher *(why higher?)* than private joys and sorrow," as Kuprin puts it; in a certain viewing of people and of life *from without,* from the side, from an outside observer's—and not a participant's—point of view, from the perspective of a spectator and not of a character who is acting in the drama. Yet along with this coldness there is an unusual "spectator's" *interest* in life, an unappeasable *keenness* of observation, as Kuprin perceptively indicates. What I want to say is that there is a certain *technical,* purely artistic interest in the observation and reproduction of life; there is a development, a conscious elaboration of the devices of observation and reproduction such as one encounters in hardly anyone else. From this point of view, Chekhov's work is of quite exceptional theoretical interest.[19]

It is impossible to calculate how many figures in Chekhov are "without pathos." Almost all of his heroes are characterized precisely by their lack of pathos. This is their curse, the reason for their inadequacy and lack of vitality. Some blame themselves for it—like the hero of the wonderful story "Verochka," who, God knows why, has left the girl who loves him and to whom he is profoundly attracted.

> When he reached the bridge he stopped in thought and sought the cause of his strange coldness. That it lay not outside himself but within, he saw clearly. And he frankly admitted to himself that this was not the rational coldness about which clever men boasted, not the coldness of inflated egotism, but simple *impotence of soul* (my italics—M. N.), an inability to feel beauty deeply, and premature old age, brought about by his education, his grim struggle for a living, his bachelor, hotel life.

Both the bureaucrat and the revolutionary in "The Story of an Unknown Man" suffer from this impotence of soul, as do the educated merchant Laptev in "Three Years," the gentleman-of-the-bedchamber husband in "The Wife," the businesswoman Anna Akimovna in "A Woman's Kingdom," the man of letters Trigorin in *The Seagull,* the brother of the *Three Sisters,* and even the wealthy peasant Lopakhin in *The Cherry Orchard.* This impotence is manifested in different areas, beginning with the simple love between a man and a woman, as in "Verochka," and ending with social calamaties and the ability to react to them, as in "The Wife." But everywhere the basic reason is the same: dull stifled emotions, an incapacity for pathos, for vital impulses, for deep feelings.

The somber, lackluster, impotent soul is Chekhov's constant theme. Of course, daring social commentators such as Lvov explain this by "the era," which, they say, Chekhov merely reproduced. They do not even stop to consider the impotence in the area of love, the string of unloving men and women which extends through all of Chekhov's works. "That is the

way those abominable eighties were," the publicists will tell you. Lvov
actually maintains (true, quoting some author of "reminiscences") that the
eighties "destroyed Chekhov's lungs," so that even the writer's tuberculosis,
in his opinion, is explained by the "era"! I cannot settle for such diagnoses. I
will grant, however, that in Chekhov's penchant for depicting lackluster
souls there is something subjective, something in the nature of self-
reproach or self-duplication on his part. Actually, "self-reproach" is not the
right word. Gogol's confession that he was trying to "escape" from his
"vices," as if, by endowing his types with them, he were handing them over
for punishment, is famous. All of his life Turgenev depicted weak-willed
"Hamlets" and juxtaposed them to strong, active "Don Quixote" figures,
as though confessing his guilt before the latter. True, as Mikhailovsky
perceptively remarked, Turgenev never completely repented and cunningly
provided each Don Quixote with two or three characteristics which
considerably undermined the cause of the "Don Quixote" and tipped the
scales in favor of the Hamlet. But this still was self-punishment to a certain
extent. From this point of view, too, Chekhov only depicted, only
reproduced, only reembodied himself in his heroes. With few exceptions,
such as the above-cited sentencing of the hero of "Verochka," he never
judged; he preferred, instead, to allow the reader to pronounce the verdict.
But if he was not "cunning" like Turgenev, one must nevertheless admit
that for all his "supreme objectivity," he could, when he wanted to, put in a
word for the "impotent souls" and make them likeable—although perhaps
this was unconscious...

Without question the central point in Chekhov's work is not a
"glorification" of impotence, but rather an obvious and intense interest in
it, as well as some elements of defense of and sympathy for it. It should be
said right here that Chekhov is a great psychologist of the "impotent soul,"
and that the characters he depicts as being struck by an absence of "pathos"
will always remain models of such types.

The *artist of the soul's impotence,* the painter of life *without pathos*—
such is the first definition of Chekhov to which our analysis leads.

Chekhov most exhaustively treats the types of people who are not
given "full expression," who are "miscarried" by life, and he does so with a
thoroughness which is rare for him. However, the lackluster quality, the
sketchiness, and the reticence of his other figures—like his "muted
baritone," fear of pathos, restraint, and concern for "exactitude" bordering
on stinginess—are conditioned not only by the personal characteristics
which I have already mentioned, but by other factors as well.

I should now like to turn to Chekhov's general world view, insofar as it
emerges from his "objective" writings, and to look at his "epoch," the
notorious and truly accursed eighties.

I shall not bother to elaborate upon the "internal politics" of those
years or upon their socio-psychological effects. Much has already been said

about this. And what can one really say about a "system" that was established by a statesman who was responsible for the famous aphorism "the people do not need an education because then they will learn to think logically!"[20]

All cultural questions were decided on the basis of this principle—as was every other problem. But although every effort was made to stop all advancement in social and cultural thought, although reactionism triumphed on all fronts and reached a degree such as Russia had experienced only at the end of the forties, the standstill to which social life had come must be explained by other than purely external reasons.

This was the time of a profound and terribly painful rift in social outlook. Chekhov himself, in his oft-quoted 1894 letter to Suvorin,[21] retrospectively formulates this change in the following way: "It seemed as if everyone had been in love, had fallen out of love, and was now seeking new passions," and, he adds, like a "patient with a fever," was now calling for "something sour."*

Only the first half of the phrase, "everyone had been in love [and] fallen out of love," applies to the eighties. There was nothing to live by...

This *negative atmosphere* surrounded Chekhov from the earliest days of his conscious life. But this statement may require some modification. As we know, Chekhov never frequented the circle of society's extreme progressive elements on whom the external and internal rift of the eighties took its heaviest toll. At that time he was writing for *The Dragon Fly* and *New Times,* and associating with the staff of the latter, as Shcheglov attests in his memoirs, where he frequently mentions that Chekhov used to call him "Jean" and he would call Chekhov "Antoine." However, although Antoine did associate with Jean, he nevertheless differed from him and those like him. We should stress that hardly any trend of thought has ever had as universal an influence as populism. Produced by the dissolution of serfdom, this current, having been modified and splintered into thousands of nuances and gradations, was able to leave its mark on the entire range of progressive thought from the utopian socialism of *Notes of the Fatherland* to the "broad popular liberalism" of *The Week* and even *New Times.*[22] Even nowadays "pirates of the pen" resort to the "ideas" and the rich lexicon of the populist epoch, so what can one expect of the old days, of the eighties themselves? Furthermore, it was not the extreme elements who were involved in the "reevaluation" at first. They tried to preserve at least the practical scheme from which the vital theoretical spirit had already

---

* The *tone* in which Chekhov discusses this painful historical drama is characteristic of him: it exhibits the same "restraint" displayed in a letter cited by Bunin where he discusses not a historical drama but a personal and, moreover, joyous event: "So, then, Ivan Alexeevich, allow me to expect you on Strastnaya. Be so kind as to come! I have changed my mind about getting married, no longer want to, but nevertheless, if that seems a bore to you, then all right, I suppose I will."

departed; they achieved feats of "desperate heroism" in keeping up, as Tikhomirov remarked ironically, "the holy flame." It was other, more moderate and intermediate elements which escaped into "Tolstoyism," "decadence," and the preaching of "small deeds." And, doubtless, considering his temperament and lack of pathos, his upbringing and contacts, it was most natural for Chekhov to attach himself to these elements, although there is no direct evidence of the fact. In essence Chekhov belonged precisely here—among the ranks of these moderate "reappraisers," who opposed the recently prevailing theories.

"Everyone had been in love and fallen out of love." Chekhov did not participate in the love affair between the Russian intelligentsia and the people: no hint of any kind of attraction to populism is found in his juvenile writings. He experienced only "a hangover at someone else's feast," only the denouement of the affair, only the disappointment and skeptical attitude toward the former passion. If we begin to search for any traces of ideology in his writing we shall find only a few faint hints of a temporary allurement to Tolstoyism. In "Good People" the writer who escapes life's most difficult problems through his feuilletons is contrasted to his meditative and sincerely thoughtful sister, the doctor. She disclaims his "ideological" work, constantly talks about "non-resistance to evil," and abandons her brother and the capital for the country in order to help in "the vaccination against smallpox." "And Vladimir went on writing his articles, laying wreaths on coffins, singing "Gaudeamus," and busying himself over the Mutual Aid Society for the staff of Moscow Periodicals," for which he was fittingly punished by being "completely forgotten" the day after he died.

The following passage from the arguments between brother and sister is interesting:

"It seems to me," says the doctor, "that contemporary thought has settled in one spot and stuck firmly to it. It is prejudiced, apathetic, timid, afraid to climb a high mountain; it is conservative." This innovator—and perhaps Chekhov at this point as well—sees the "wide, titanic flight" to consist in non-resistance to evil and service to the people, be it only in the form of "vaccination against smallpox."

We should note here both the obvious striving toward a "reevaluation of values," i.e., the clear "oppositional" tendency, and the following, typically Chekhovian situation: the hero of the story spends his life writing feuilletons in which, Chekhov tells us, he critically analyzes various belletristic trifles in the most routine manner; it is clear that he has a very limited capacity and thus cannot serve as a target for attacks upon "contemporary thought" in general—no matter how defective this contemporary thought is, that would be doing him too great an honor. On the other hand, the doctor is apparently attracted by Tolstoy and his teaching of adopting a "simple life"; but here the "vaccinating against smallpox," i.e., medicine, interferes, for Tolstoy always opposed medicine, and cultural work in general in the village is completely uncharacteristic of the Tolstoyites. Such ideological or programmatic vagueness is quite typical of Chekhov: he no sooner touches upon some ideology than this sort of thing occurs.

In the above-mentioned letter to Suvorin, Chekhov himself admits that for a certain while he was attracted to Tolstoyism, but as if justifying himself, he adds that he was won over not so much by Tolstoy's ideas themselves as by "Tolstoy's manner of expression, his good sense and probably his special kind of hypnotism." "Now something inside of me protests," he continues. "Economy and justice tell me that there is more love for man in electricity and steam than in chastity and abstinence from meat. War and the courts are evil, but it doesn't follow from this that I should wear bast sandals and sleep on a stove together with a worker, his wife, etc." In point of fact, Chekhov did assimilate certain elements of "Tolstoyism," and they never left him. They manifest themselves first and foremost in a disparaging attitude toward most of those forms in which, to quote from the tale of Ivan the Fool, the "work of the mind" is carried on today; a disparaging attitude toward all those "government jobs" and "activities" which exist within the framework of the present structure. In Chekhov's stories there appears a whole series of public prosecutors, investigators, judges, and administrators. Apparently in agreement with the hero of "My Life," Chekhov places their "mental labor"—which "does not demand the slightest effort of thought, talent, personal abilities, or creative arousal"—"lower than physical labor, (Misail) despises it, and does not think that it can serve even for a moment as a justification for an idle, carefree life, since it is nothing more than deceit, just another form of the same idleness."

In the story from which these words are taken, the writer's temporary attraction to "Tolstoyism" is expressed more clearly than anywhere else and in a manner which is quite unique to Chekhov and characteristic of him: there is no trace here of Tolstoy's ideological sweep, and of all his deep and consistent lordly "penitence" there remains only a repulsion toward the privileged "work of the mind," a repulsion toward the commotion, falseness, and idleness inherent in so-called "cultured life." It is *boring* for the protagonist to live in this society and so he becomes a house painter. Fear of pathos, restraint, sincerity, and a simplicity of heart which leads to the final rejection of any ideology whatsoever and to the denial of ideas— these are the basic traits of the hero of "My Life." He is truly "poor in spirit." And it is worth noting that this is Chekhov's only hero whose "direction" is not undermined by reflection, not destroyed by the arguments of those around him, and not disproved by life itself: for all the trials and tribulations which befall him, he remains true to himself to the end, i.e., seemingly correct from the author's point of view. This is a rare thing in Chekhov.

Such is Chekhov's attitude toward the one ideology, the one "program of life" which captivated him for a while. All other theories and programs somehow did not exist for Chekhov. We can say that the era of reevaluation and disappointment in recent "programs" had inculcated in him a skeptical attitude toward theorizing about life in general, toward attempting in any way to systematize and grasp its *essence* and *meaning* in one, totally orderly theoretical scheme. It was as if in every religion of life he suspected *dogma,* and skeptically and fearfully avoided it, as if afraid to lose his "personal freedom," his *"precision* and sincerity of feeling and thought." Every theory appeared to him under some "extraneous" aspect, belonging to everyone, to the entire external and "deceptive" world, and he, monk-like, tried to save himself from the "temptations of intellect" in his inner world, a world of direct, "precise" experiences and moods. This is really something like the Christian *asceticism of thought,* so to speak, and Bulgakov actually could have referred to this quality of Chekhov's in order to justify his fervid proselytism, but of course it would have been greatly to his disadvantage to do so.

Chekhov expresses his disbelief in "theories" many times in his fiction. One recalls the figure of Likharev, described with such sad humor in the marvelously poetic piece "On the Road." He has squandered his entire fortune on "ideas": "Half my life I lived as a nihilist and an atheist... I became hooked on nihilism with its proclamations, its Black Partitions, and its tricks of all sorts,"... "I went to the people, served as a factory hand, greased axles, hauled barges," then (the chronology, we note, somewhat falsifies actual history) "I came to love the Russian people to distraction, loved and believed in its God, its language, its creativity. And so on and so on." "In my time I was a Slavophile and bored Aksakov with my letters... Five years ago I forfeited all my property; my most recent faith was non-resistance to evil." Now he is fussing over his nervous and capricious daughter and is on his way to work as a factory manager to earn a crust of bread. In the course of a single conversation on a nasty winter night, his physically strong, congenial, and absorbing nature and his "new faith" in women almost win over the young woman landowner who meets him at the roadside inn. Likharev is described gently and lovingly. But the author's intentions are evident: this is a satire on all the theoretical infatuations of our intelligentsia, which Likharev asserts, "cannot live without faith." The chronological muddle and the chronologically inconceivable combination of all the intelligentsia's questings in the image of one man reveal how alien all these theories were to Chekhov and underscore his ironically negligent attitude toward them.

An even more specifically hostile and clumsy treatment of "ideas" is manifest in "The Story of an Unknown Man," which in terms of plot is not very successful. The tubercular hero of the first-person story is apparently a terrorist who becomes the servant of a minor official with the intention of

killing his father, an important dignitary. But when a convenient opportunity presents itself, he feels nothing in his soul, no "hate": "His old, sad
face and the cold brightness of the stars evoked in me only petty, cheap, and
superfluous thoughts about the transitoriness of everything earthly, about
oncoming death... There was no doubt about it: a change had taken place
in me, I had become different." He has become "different" and lets slip a
convenient opportunity. But he has still not repudiated his former faith and
he preaches it to Zinaida Fyodorovna, the young woman whom he "saves"
from her unfaithful loved one. She had abandoned her husband for this
lover, for this official whom the "unknown man" serves, and now, when the
latter opens her eyes and simultaneously discloses his own "disguise," she
goes abroad with him, attracted by his preaching. But here, intuitively, she
quickly recognizes the essence of his being:

> "Vladimir Ivanovich, for heaven's sake why have you been insincere?" she
> continued, quietly approaching me. "When I dreamed aloud all these months, when I
> was in a fever, carried away by my plans, when I was rearranging my life in a new way—
> why didn't you tell me the truth instead of keeping silent or encouraging me with stories
> and behaving as if you completely sympathized with me? Why? Whatever for?"
> "It is difficult to admit one's own bankruptcy," I declared, turning around but not
> looking at her. "Yes, I do not believe, I have grown weary, fallen in spirit... It is difficult
> to be sincere, terribly difficult, and so I kept silent. May no one experience what I have
> experienced."

This, it goes without saying, is supposed to serve as a symbolic
debunking of the "ethos of the seventies" and of its unfortunate followers to
whose lot fell the "heroism of despair," a debunking of the "generation
cursed by God," as the poet of this generation, P. Ya.,[23] called it. But the
devices used are truly "clumsy." The hero's absurd act of becoming a
lackey, his love for Zinaida Fyodorovna, his tuberculosis, and his physical
and moral impotence—all of this so muddles the question that almost
nothing is left of the spirit of "opposition." Like Katya in "A Boring Story,"
Zinaida Fyodorovna point blank raises the question of what she is to do.
And the hero, like the professor, has no answer to it. All of this is directed
against the radical ideologues of the seventies.

Besides the above-mentioned story "Good People," moderate liberalism is attacked in the person of the professor of "A Boring Story...."
Unfortunately this wonderful piece suffers from the same drawback which
appears whenever Chekhov attempts to depict "ideological" people. For all
its artistic merit, the story's culmination, the final scene between Katya and
the professor, quoted above, is compromised—again because of the
author's awkwardness: he has shown Katya to be such a turbulent,
hysterical creature, passing from romantic enthusiasms to a passion for the
theater, and so on, that, truly, anyone who had even the most steadfast
"general idea" would have been at a loss in the professor's place, would
have been unable to answer the question: what should this Katya do? And if

you take all this into consideration, it turns out that the story is written not in praise of a "general idea," the absence of which renders any reasonable life unthinkable; rather it is a simple description of the gradual decline of life's forces in a sick and tired old scholar, a decline which leads him to hopeless skepticism.

Most condescending of all was Chekhov's attitude toward the line taken by the journal *The Week* toward the theoreticians of "small deeds." In a story filled with poetry, "The House with the Attic," the following dialogue occurs between the landscape artist and Lida, the landowner's daughter who has devoted herself to the local school and to curing the peasants with "powders": "You go to their aid with hospitals and schools, but you don't free them from their fetters by that. On the contrary, you enslave them even more, for by introducing new prejudices into their life, you increase the number of their needs, not to mention the fact that they have to pay the local council for their blister-flies and their books, and so are obliged to do even more back-breaking work." This is said by the artist, an ardent champion of high, abstract science who at the same time is apparently a Tolstoyan: he sees the solution only in one thing—that "all people should agree to physical labor"—otherwise they will remain "fettered by a huge chain" to which dispensaries, schools, pharmacies, and libraries add only "new links." Lida, however, answers firmly: "I can tell you only one thing: one must not sit idly by. True, we are not saving mankind and, perhaps, are mistaken in much that we do, but we do what we can." The artist, in love with Lida's sister Zhenya, comes to grief: under pressure from her sister, Zhenya leaves him.

I shall not dwell on the fact that this Tolstoyan landscapist represents a rarely encountered combination, that his theories (with their Tolstoyan, Nietzschean, and perhaps even revolutionary notes) are most strange. He is as strange and as *clumsily* conceived as Likharev and the "unknown man"; as Doctor Astrov in *Uncle Vanya,* the prophet of "nature's impoverishment" who nevertheless dreams of that beautiful life which will come within two or three hundred years; as Lieutenant-Colonel Vershinin in *The Three Sisters,* who dreams of the same thing; and as a host of other characters. All of the excerpts which I have cited adequately reveal Chekhov's vague and none-too-subtle treatment of all our ideological currents and camps, as well as his inability to understand them. These excerpts were necessary to prove Chekhov's *atheoretical nature,* his estrangement from all social theories and his general mistrust of all theories and ideas, his skepticism toward all of them. I should mention two other pieces which provide particularly broad and clear illustrations of the latter assertion: the hopelessly skeptical "Ward No. Six," a work of high artistic value, and the fantastic story, "The Bet," with its strange plot. In the former, two world views collide head-on. On the one hand there is the passive, quiescent optimism of the director of the hospital, Andrei

Yefimovich. He has reached a state of complete apathy and inaction, based on the assumption that "prejudices and all of life's vileness and abominations are necessary," since over the course of time they are reworked into something useful, just as "manure is transformed into black earth" and that "nothing is good on earth which was not originally vile." To this doctor is contrasted the official Ivan Dmitrievich Gromov, a man who reacts deeply to all evil and is constantly ready to protest. When the story opens, the latter already suffers from a "persecution mania" and is a patient in "Ward No. Six." I do not see any other idea in this story. Surely we are not supposed to see a naive sermon to negligent doctors, a reprisal for indifference, a "punishment for vice" in the cruel retribution which the hospital guard metes out to the doctor who neglected the hospital and winds up in it. Both figures may be interesting as psychiatric types, but the ideologies which they represent are again somewhat strange, arbitrary, and arbitrarily juxtaposed. In "The Bet" a cultured man wagers a banker four million rubles that he can sit in solitary confinement for fifteen years. The bet has almost been won. The next to the last day of the fifteenth year has arrived but the prisoner, who during this time has read huge numbers of books in all fields, particularly history and philosophy, and lately has been reading only the Gospels, escapes that night to prove his disdain for all life's blessings and for life in general. A somber *de profundis* to all theories is obviously intoned here, too...

Is it surprising then, after all we have said, that Chekhov "did not notice" the new currents in our social and ideological life, that he remained deaf to them, and that he hardly reflected them in any of his later fictional characters (if one discounts the beautiful, but only lightly sketched, pale figure of "The Betrothed" in the story by that name, and the absurd and completely confused student Trofimov in *The Cherry Orchard*)? Ideas and theories have again been rehabilitated in our life. The enormous upsurge of social forces, the springing up of new parties, the appearance of democratic classes—all of this, necessarily, was seeking formulations and theoretical banners expressing the new needs and ideas. But Chekhov remained on the sidelines: a true son of the eighties, he really would have had to wait for the moment "when even the blind gained sight" in order to renounce his mistrust of ideas and programs, and his "philistine" skepticism toward them. "Philistine," as the French say, "c'est le mot." Chekhov's negation of ideas and his *atheoretical nature* limited his ideological horizon precisely to the point of philistine narrowness. And perhaps the tragedy of Chekhov's life lies primarily in the eternal conflict, the endless contradiction between a refined aesthetic nature, which hated philistinism to the point of pain and repulsion, and this philistine narrowness in his scope of thought. If I were Bulgakov writing an essay on "Chekhov as a Thinker" I would have limited myself to five words: *Chekhov was no thinker whatsoever.* In this sense, he stands utterly alone in the entire pleiad of our major writers. Perhaps only Goncharov, as the author of "The Servants" and the commentaries to *The*

Precipice, can be placed beside him...

We have now come to grips with *the most interesting problem presented by Chekhov's work,* which we have already partially formulated.

A gloomy, skeptical attitude toward all "theories of progress" and toward all of mankind's slogans as it struggles for its dignity and happiness, a seemingly cheerless, pessimistic attitude toward life itself, a narrowly limited horizon together with broad artistic generalizations and works full of genuine poetry! Such is the "antinomy" which Chekhov's work contains within it.

In concluding our "first acquaintance" with Chekhov, let us track down in his writings his *positive* tastes and sympathies. I feel that I have excessively prolonged this "first acquaintance" and that in particular I have dwelled too long upon demonstrating the philistine bias in Chekhov's world view; but it has seemed necessary to go into certain details here insofar as I diverge from the majority of Chekhov's critics on this point. And Chekhov's *positive* sympathies, in my view, completely confirm the opinion which I have offered on him.

Like Maupassant or Likharev (the hero of "On the Road"), "amidst the hypocrisy of our day and the banal vulgarity and all kinds of prosaicness," amidst the wasteland of all of our life's tormentingly absurd or cruel conditions, Chekhov found only one oasis—the pure and spontaneous feminine soul. All of the female characters whom he depicts sympathetically are the unhappy victims of surrounding conditions; all of them are first and foremost sincere and forthcoming. Such is the figure of Lipa, the victim of the inhuman atmosphere of the petit-bourgeois "ravine"; such are Zinaida Fyodorovna in "The Story of an Unknown Man," Katya in "A Boring Story," the heroines of *The Seagull* (Nina Zarechnaya), *Uncle Vanya* (Sonya), *The Three Sisters* (all three of them), and so on and so forth.

Positive male types also exist in Chekhov. There are several good-natured and bashful men "in the pink of health," such as Doctor Samoleykin in "The Duel" or Likharev. Then there are a number who are wretched and unhappy, very sincere but "poor in spirit," like the hero of "My Life," probably Uncle Vanya, the landowner Bragin in "The Wife," and the "unknown man" himself. To them one can probably add the whole series of "men without pathos"—martyrs of reflection, who are also sincere and with whom Chekhov clearly sympathizes. And there are also a few intellectual figures who are *engulfed by their milieu,* such as Ivanov, Doctor Astrov in *Uncle Vanya,* the "teacher of literature," and so on. It seems that is all.

The "positive" is just not Chekhov's element. He did have tastes and moods, but they were largely negative, *passive.* In essence they were purely *aesthetic,* devoid of any vital, active feeling, lacking pathos, and stemming primarily from a sense of decency and beauty. But these tastes and moods were not rationalized, they do not reach the status of "generalized" feelings, ideas, and principles. This is why, as I have mentioned, attempts at *philosophical* criticism, at interpreting *Chekhov-the-thinker,* have totally missed the mark. Shestov's failure is especially interesting in this regard. He tried to extend all of the "segments" of ideas in Chekhov to their point of intersection. And brought to their logical conclusion, these ideas have yielded a philosophy of such gloomy and universally dismal skepticism that the melancholic Shestov himself was horrified! Shestov was horrified, but if Chekhov had chanced to read such a description during his lifetime he would merely have grinned. "It must be good," he might have said, as does Bunin in his memoirs, "to be an officer, a young student, to stand in some crowded place and listen to cheerful music."

To Lvov, who numbers Chekhov among the democrats, Chekhov would have answered something like the following; "I very much like culture and tidiness, I like the decency in all facets of life that one finds in the Germans for example. I enjoyed this decency during the last days of my life in Badenweiler.[24] I cannot bear what is wild, coarse, false, and vulgar— this is my entire program."

Probably he would have agreed only with his "Jean," in an article by whom one finds the following assertion: "Chekhov's philosophy? Is it really not absurd to raise the question of philosophy to a writer in some of whose small stories there is more philosophy than there is in the fat tome of an authorized philosopher! Chekhov's philosophy is the philosophy of common sense!"

The only theories which Chekhov firmly preached were theories of medicine. The authors of reminiscences cite opinions of professional doctors to the effect that Chekhov was a talented diagnostician. In his well-known short autobiography Chekhov himself maintains that his medical knowledge was very often useful in his artistic activity. Whether this knowledge helped or hurt him in the field of art is, in my view, a big question. But that medicine could not enrich him with ideas, could not broaden his philosophical horizon is an undisputed fact. Medical positivism, barren in content yet nonetheless pretending to have complete possession of the truth, very often constitutes the world view of doctors. Such positivism seemingly played a certain role in the development of Chekhov's atheoretical and aphilosophical outlook. What a mass of distressing questions must have constantly arisen in his consciousness under the pressure of his enormous keenness of observation and aesthetic exactitude! All of these questions found not even a hint of resolution in his world view. His positivism and fanatic devotion to *exactness* more likely than not impelled him to stifle these questions at their very conception. This must have led to a constant psychological dissonance, a depressing psychic disturbance, which resonated in Chekhov's skeptical and pessimistic thematics.

And God knows to what extent the figure of Dmitry Petrovich Silin in the story "Terror" is a product of *objective* creation, and whether the agitated words placed in his mouth are actually all that foreign to the soul of the author himself:

> I do not understand life and I am afraid of it, my dear boy. I don't know, perhaps I am a sick, deranged person. It seems to a normal, healthy man that he understands everything he sees and hears, but that "seeming" is lost to me, and from day to day I am poisoning myself with terror. There is a disease, the fear of open spaces, but my disease is a fear of life. When I lie in the grass and watch a little bug which was born only yesterday and understands nothing, it seems to me that its life consists of nothing but fear, and in it I see myself.

Perhaps the constant "restraint" and "mysteriousness" noted in Chekhov by those who knew him, apart from his natural disposition, can be explained by just such a psychic disturbance. And can one such as he "pour out his feelings!" Very characteristic of people who suffer from this kind of psychic disturbance is a passion for solitude, for quietude, and for the kind of meditative, yet unthinking mood which fishing engenders. Chekhov, as is known, loved this sport. Even more characteristic is a love of contact with children, which also gives these people "respite." Biographers stress Chekhov's love for children and his ability to make friends with them. Finally, the best and most potent medicine is, of course, nature. Whoever has read just one page of "The Steppe" or the marvelous description of a summer evening in the story "In the Ravine" will not doubt Chekhov's passionate love for nature. I think that *this was his only "pathos."*

I have always felt that much of *The Seagull* is autobiographical and personal. Shcheglov, who often had dealings with Chekhov in those years, confirms my conjecture. And in Trigorin's declarations about his "writer's happiness" I hear in part Chekhov's own confession:

> I love this water here, the trees, the sky. I can feel nature, it arouses in me a passionate, irresistible desire to write. But, you know, I'm not just a landscape painter, I'm a citizen as well. I love my country and its people, I feel that if I am a writer it is my duty to write about them, about their sufferings, about the future, science, the rights of man, and so on and so forth. And so I write about everything. I hurry, people urge me on from all sides, get angry at me, I dash back and forth like a fox brought to bay by the hounds; I see that life and science keep moving farther and farther ahead, while I fall further and further behind, like a peasant who has missed the train and, in the end, I feel that I only know how to paint landscapes and in all the rest I am false—false to the marrow of my bones.

Remove the final, excessively sharp notes of self-reproach from this tirade and you have several features of Chekhov himself. Remember, by the way, that like Chekhov, Trigorin also passionately loves fishing.

On this note I conclude our "preliminary acquaintance" with

Chekhov. I think that it gives us a certain clue to Chekhov's work. At the base of it lies a profound dissonance. Psychologically this is a dissonance between an innate, typically *comic* gift and a melancholy perception of life—a dissonance which found expression in the *radiant* laughter and the lackluster, *muted* voice which biographers have noted. Ideologically, this is the dissonance between, on the one hand, enormous aesthetic sensitivity and feeling and, on the other, a narrow world view, resulting as much from a nature that was devoid of pathos as from an epoch which lacked ideals—the "negative" eighties. The widely accepted opinion that Chekhov was only the *objective* chronicler of the spirit of the eighties is, in my view, an incorrect one. In his work, as in all genuine creation, there are many subjective elements. He himself was a true son of his era, its product and its *victim*. These years clipped his wings, made him a *wingless poet*.

I should like to provide this essay with a postscript of sorts. As only the first chapter of a larger work on Chekhov which remained unfinished, this article hardly exhausts the complex question of Chekhov's creative work. In particular, it only touches in passing upon the purely aesthetic side of Chekhov, yet it is precisely this side of him which has determined his enormous position in our new literature and his right to immortality. I shall now try in a few pages to fill at least partially the gaps left by my article, at least somewhat to fill in the perspectives I see opening up from these points of departure.

Let me begin with aesthetics. First of all I should note a peculiarity of Chekhov's work which sets him completely apart from the *school* of Russian fiction which was created as early as the fifties. Chekhov's work had as its main, if not its only source an aesthetic sensibility, an organic need for contemplation and reconstruction. His art was a value in itself. "Creation from the void," Shestov said of Chekhov in the article which I have mentioned. Yet Shestov forgets that the primary source of any artistic work is this "void," specifically an aesthetic yearning which seeks gratification. Among the great writers Chekhov embodies this phenomenon in an unusually pure form. Through his work he proved how powerful this source is in and of itself, almost detached from other subsidiary sources of creation—moral and philosophical.

In this sense Chekhov's writings are of enormous interest to critics and psychologists of art. Many times he himself gave artistic form to the theme of the self-worth of creative work. Refracted through the prism of weary skepticism, this theme emerges in Trigorin of *The Seagull* and in his words about the "obligation to write and write." The same need and obligation inspires the tailor Merkulov in the short comic sketch "The Captain's Uniform": he sews civil uniforms for which he is not paid, disdaining "profitable" homespun coats. "I'd rather die than sew homespun coats."

Finally, somewhat complicated by the theme of the artist's relation to the crowd, the same thought pervades the charming story, appropriately entitled "The Work of Art," about the loafer Seryozha who is creating a "Jordan."

Chekhov was always aware of this source of his work. He loved and stood by it. It even led him to create a corresponding theory, nearly the only one (besides theories of medicine) which this atheoretical man professed. He always defended the principle of *free* art with great conviction: "I fear those who look for tendencies between the lines," he wrote to Pleshcheyev in 1887. "I am not a liberal, not a conservative, not a gradualist, not a monk, not an indifferentist. I would like to be a free artist and only that."

On this score he was an innovator, and he "opposed" the ideas of the previous generation profitably and victoriously. Specifically with Chekhov there begins a turning away from the former restrictive, civic, and ideological theory of art which was preached both by our writers (except perhaps Turgenev) and our critics, beginning with Belinsky (in his final period). Specifically with Chekhov there begins a new phase of our art, a transition from moral and publicistic concerns to more expanded horizons, to an art which has primarily aesthetic and philosophical concerns. Chekhov represented the first stage for this transition, albeit only formally, because ideologically he was even narrower than his predecessors. But he understood the principle of free art, the possibility of filling it with a broadened content, and he affirmed and gave life to it through his writings. Along with Chekhov, the mystics, "idealists," and decadents raised their banner of protest against the former theories. But while they were only exchanging one form of slavery for another, switching from moralistic fetters to the fetters of "pure art"; while in their literature the artist's personality was being entirely engulfed by purely technical problems, by "playing the artist," by images as an end in themselves, by *rhyme and rhythm for their own sake;* and while the vital meaning and value of their works were disappearing along with the artist's personality, Chekhov was remaining true to the serious, sacred, life-giving traditions of our literature. His theme was life, real life in as much of its diversity as was accessible to him. This is why this *innovator* still falls within the organic, time-honored mainstream of our literature, continuing the work of the Turgenevs and Tolstoys.

Chekhov's unceasing and loving attention to art as a value in itself prompted him to develop and sharpen his literary devices such that his work attained a refinement and beauty heretofore unknown in Russian literature. None of his predecessors attained such simplicity and precision of style, such polish, precision, pictorialness, and richness of language. The language which the characters of his stories and plays speak radiates with all the colors of life's rainbow, it has a color and nuance for every profession, calling, and position. He embodied the principle of *artistic balance and economy of artistic means* in his stories with such care and sensitivity that they are truly classical. One can say that Chekhov created not only the genre of the "comic sketch" in Russian literature but the genre of the short story in general—to such perfection did he bring this form. Continuing what Tolstoy had begun and following in the footsteps of Maupassant, whom he knew and valued as did few others, he cultivated in Russia the *impressionism* of literary painting and the *dramatic method of narration* (his characters are not described but are revealed, so to speak, "in practice," by their actions and speeches). Finally, in the realm of the theater (if I am not mistaken, under some influence from Hauptmann),[25] he created in Russia the *drama of mood*—the drama of increasing lyricism which does not translate into action.

Depth, seriousness, and breadth of conception grew in Chekhov's work in accordance with the maturation and development of his talent—and increased until the very end. If at first his stories were fragments of life, a kaleidoscope of minute, brilliantly perceived psychological strokes which exposed now one, now another cranny of Russian life and allowed the reader to peer into the soul of the gray people who inhabited these crannies—then toward the end of his career Chekhov was trying to synthesize, to embrace the lives of entire strata and groups and to take stock of them. From this time on, beginning with his stories "The Man in a Case," "Gooseberries," and "In the Ravine," his traditionally *realistic* devices are increasingly interspersed with elements of *symbolism*. This is particularly evident in his *swan song, The Cherry Orchard.* In this respect Chekhov was the son of his time, keeping pace with all art—both Russian and European. Need one speak of the influence of Chekhov and his style on the latest writers of Russian fiction? In recent times, considerable confusion exists as a result of the enormous uncertainty in Russian art with respect to life and ideology; consequently our contemporary writers' connection to Chekhov is not so obvious and perceptible. But the direct ties between him and Gorky and Andreyev (especially in their early period) are clear to everyone. As for the realist portrayers of everyday life such as Kuprin, Veresayev,[26] and Artsybashev,[27] there is no question of a connection there.

Such are the achievements engendered by that aesthetic gift which was Chekhov's basic trait and which, with the force of fate, compelled him to meditate and reproduce—in the endless game of art as an end in itself. And the invariably serious, I would say *religious* attitude toward this art, which caused Chekhov to see in his experiences and in the experiences of people in general the sole object worthy of his art, resulted in the fact that Chekhov did more for Russian life and culture than any of his coevals. None was a better spokesman of the epoch and none better summed it up. And here one must speak positively of Chekhov's skeptical, atheoretical nature and of the *dissonance* between his ideological poverty and aesthetic richness, which I said was the key to the problem of his art as a whole.

Is an ordered world view a blessing or a curse, a plus or a minus, for an artist? In the general scheme of things there can be only one answer: it is a blessing and plus, if by world view one means a definite religion of life, a harmony between one's disposition and one's attitude toward life. A fixed dogma and rational scheme of things which do not flow from a direct perception of reality deaden, debase, desiccate, and practically kill an artist's work. But a genuine religion of life can only deepen and broaden his work, it can only give him wings. As I understand him, Chekhov completely lacked such a religion, he was a *wingless* poet. But he lived at a time when the populist religion of life, which had just recently prevailed in the hearts and minds of men and given them "wings," had exhausted itself and died out, and history had not yet worked out a new one to take its place. The spirit had left the old religion, and it had turned into a mere shell, into a fixed scheme and dogma: for an artist to profess it meant practically to condemn himself to sterility.

Let me cite an observation made by the *populist* Korolenko (from his reminiscences of Chekhov), which, for all its indecisiveness and ambiguity of tone, adequately confirms my thought.

"The need for a certain 'reconsideration' before setting out on the road to further strivings was felt in the air...and therefore Chekhov's very 'freedom' from the current 'parties,' coupled with such great talent and sincerity, seemed to me then a certain advantage. It doesn't matter, I thought, it won't be for long."

Chekhov's lack of ideology proved useful to him. Being himself without an ideology and, in the ideological sense, almost a philistine, he was able to understand intimately and thoroughly that milieu which in those years was left without ideology and religion. And he reproduced it like no one else. Granted that the active elements which were scattered in the thick of life even in the eighties never entered his field of vision. Granted that in the nineties he remained blind to the newly-emerging types, the new currents, the new *urban* epoch of Russian culture. Still *his* epoch, the epoch of the liquidation of *rural* culture, the epoch of the decomposition of the peasant-master structure he understood and felt in all its pain and anguish, in all its repellent and seemingly hopeless immobility, and he described it in exhaustive and immortal pictures. Although he focused upon only one positive type—the "sweet person," sincere but weak-willed and poor in spirit—although he almost always seemed to suspect men of deed and action, although the realm of the *positive* is not his forte at all (except, perhaps, when it comes to his constant attraction to *culture* and his yearning for it), he depicted and embraced the *negative* aspects of his negative epoch in generalizations which will always remain monuments to that epoch and, perhaps, a *threat* and a lesson to other ones.

I have spoken about Chekhov's most powerful generalization before, but I will allow myself to repeat those lines here: "The loss of personality, generated by an order which has as its motto 'each to his own appointed task,' reaches its limit either when the individual is transformed into some sort of wooden mechanism after it finds itself a place in life and becomes rooted to this 'appointed task' ("The Man in a Case," the professor in *Uncle Vanya,* etc.), or, if it does not find a place in life, when it is transformed into a shadow of a personality, a sort of ghost, glimpsed fleetingly. 'Without' faith, without love, without a goal, like a shadow I loiter among people,' says the hero of *Ivanov.* In the fine story "On Official Business" the figure of the auxiliary policeman, who all his life does not know for whom he has been delivering packages, is transformed in the doctor's dream into a symbol of peasant, but not only peasant, existence: 'We go on . . . go on . . . go on.' Where? Why?—there is no answer."

Likharev ("On the Road"), both heroes of "Ward No. Six," Katya in "A Boring Story," Treplev and Nina in *The Seagull,* Uncle Vanya, and so on—all sing this leitmotif.

"If only we knew, if only we knew," exclaim the intelligent heroines of *The Three Sisters* with a cry of despair. "We are not here, there is nothing in the world, we do not exist, and it only seems that we exist . . . And isn't it all the same?" the intoxicated doctor Chebutykin answers them.

Anisim's "each to his appointed task" and Chebutykin's "we are not here" are the poles of the axis around which revolve all of the life dramas which Chekhov depicts.

Maxim Gorky in his reminiscences about Chekhov very nicely formulates the publicistic significance of Chekhov's work. "A great, intelligent man, attentive to everything, has passed by the boring inhabitants of his country and said to them: "It is a shame to live like this."

The publicistic and in general the *real-life* significance of his writing was and will remain enormous, yet Chekhov neither taught nor preached and was as alien to publicist writing as anyone could be. He submitted only to his need to create and reproduce reality, moved by his *aesthetic martyrdom,* and always basing himself upon a *quest for contradictions,* a method which was inherent in him as an artist with an innate gift for the *comic.*

Two words about this method and this "martyrdom" and I can conclude my postscript.

I mentioned Chekhov's "quest for contradictions" not only in his purely comical pieces but also in his "gloomy" stories and dramas. One recalls here the "famous" professor of "A Boring Story," who for all his scholarly grandeur is pitifully impotent in the face of life's questions; one recalls the millionaire factory owner in "A Woman's Kingdom," who almost marries a poor working man in order to escape the meaninglessness of her life, and another, similar millionairess in "A Doctor's Visit" with its picture of the enormous enterprise which exists only so that the proprietess' lady companion "can drink tasty wines"; one recalls the "happiness" of the celebrity Trigorin, whom Nina Zarechnaya envies in *The Seagull,* and his confession; one recalls the juvenile aestheticism of the owners of the *Cherry Orchard* and their failure in life, and the sad confessions of Lopakhin—vital, very "solvent," but eaten up by the worm of doubt over the meaning of his existence—and so on and so forth. The *lever* which Chekhov uses to approach all phenomena—everywhere the same and formally comic—is the search for contradictions. And despite his lack of all social and ideological inducements, he often, by means of this lever, revealed huge contradictions and sores which lay deep within the social structure.

With regard to his *aesthetic* martyrdom, there is a remarkable confession in Chekhov which proves that even his aesthetic enjoyment was attended by a feeling of torment and sadness. Here are several lines from his story "Beauties," in which he summarizes his impression of a meeting with a beautiful Armenian woman at an inn: "I felt her beauty rather strangely. It was not desire nor ecstasy nor enjoyment that Masha aroused in me, but a painful though pleasant sadness. It was a sadness as vague and undefined as a dream. For some reason I felt sorry for myself and for my grandfather and for the Armenian, and for the girl herself, and I had the feeling that all four had lost something important and essential to life, which we should never find again."

The encounter with the Armenian woman is a youthful recollection, but when he describes a blond girl with a purely Russian beauty whom he sees only fleetingly much later, the impression left by her is the same; it contains that same, incomprehensible "painful though pleasant sadness."

And actually, could the feeling of beauty be any different in such a marvelous, aesthetically gifted artist whose fate it was to contemplate Russian life and Russian reality, and who, being *without wings,* did not hope for any outlets or escape from the "ravines" of this reality?

Chekhov, with his aesthetic giftedness, amidst Russian reality—this is exactly the antithesis which appears in his works. Never, it seems, in the entire history of the artistic word was such horrifying raw material vested in such a fragrant and enchanted form.

Notes

1. Lvov's article appeared in *Obozrenie (Survey)*, 1905, Nos. 10, 11 and 12.

2. Mikhailovsky, Nikolai Konstantinovich (1842-1904). Russian critic and social thinker, and beginning in 1892, one of the main editors of the popular thick journal *Russian Wealth (Russkoe bogatstvo)*. It was in this journal that Mikhailovsky published several articles on Chekhov, as well as some interesting pieces on Tolstoy and Dostoevsky. His major work on the latter, *Dostoevsky: A Cruel Talent* (1882) is now available in English (Ardis, 1979).

3. Bulgakov, Sergei Nikolaevich (1871-1944). Religious philosopher and critic. Nevedomsky is referring to Bulgakov's essay "Chekhov as Thinker" ("Chekhov kak myslitel'," 1905).

4. Nicodemus was a Pharisee and member of the Sanhedrin whom Jesus addresses as "the teacher of Israel" in the Gospel of St. John.

5. Shestov, Lev (pseudonym of L. I. Schwarzman, 1866-1938). Philosopher and literary critic, many of whose writings have been translated into English. The essay to which Nevedomsky refers, "Creation From the Void" ("Tvorchestvo iz nichego," 1905), was issued in 1966 by the University of Michigan Press in a volume entitled *Anton Chekhov: Creation From the Void and Other Essays*.

6. Merezhkovsky, Dmitry Sergeevich (1865-1941). Poet, novelist, critic, religious thinker, philosopher, and one of the leading figures in Russian literary matters in the early twentieth century. Merezhkovsky wrote important articles on Gogol, Dostoevsky, and Tolstoy (available in English). The work to which Nevedomsky is referring is "The Vulgarian of the Future: Chekhov and Gorky" ("Griadushchii xam: Chekhov i Gorkii," 1906).

7. Protopopov, Mikhail Alexeevich (1848-1915). A Russian critic with populist leanings.

8. Skabichevsky, Alexander Mikhailovich (1838-1911). A literary critic and historian of literature. Nevedomsky is referring to Skabichevsky's article "Does Chekhov Have Any Ideals?" ("Est'-li u Chekhova idealy?," 1895).

9. Volzhsky (pseudonym for A. S. Glinka). For more information on Volzhsky see the next article in this collection. Nevedomsky is referring to Volzhsky's book *Sketches on Chekhov (Ocherki o Chekhove*, 1903).

10. Batyushkov, Fyodor Dmitrievich (1857-1920). Philologist, literary critic, and editor of the thick journal *God's World (Mir bozhii)*, 1902-1906. Nevedomsky is probably referring to Batyushkov's article "Chekhov's Dying Legacy" ("Predsmertnyi zavet A. P. Chekhova," 1904) in which the critic claims "Chekhov increasingly predicted the coming of a better future."

11. The Social Democratic Party (or S. D.'s) was a Marxist-Socialist party organized in 1898 by Lenin and Plekhanov.

The Cadets (or K.D.'s) were Constitutional Democrats (organized in 1905) who constituted the major liberal party.

12. Gornfeld, Arkady Gregorievich (1867-1941). Highly prolific literary critic who as late as 1939 wrote an excellent essay on Chekhov, entitled "Chekhov's Endings" ("Chekhovskie finaly").

13. "Antosha Chekhonte" was the most popular of several pseudonyms used by Chekhov during the early years of his literary career, when the young writer/medical student contributed scores of comic sketches to various journals and magazines, such as the ones Nevedomsky mentions here.

14. Shcheglov (pseudonym of Ivan Leontyev, 1856-1911). Playwright and novelist for whom Chekhov had great respect, but who ultimately failed to live up to it. For more information on Shcheglov and on Chekhov's entire milieu, see Simon Karlinsky and Michael Heim, *Letters of Anton Chekhov* (New York, 1973).

15. A character in Griboedov's comedy in rhymed verse *Woe from Wit* (*Gore ot uma,* 1824). The lines Chekhov invariably quoted are from Act IV, Scene VI:

> We met by chance just now, and talked all kinds of tattle!
> Most interesting! We just discussed a vaudeville.
> The vaudeville's the thing—and all the rest is nil!
> We two—our tastes—we're just such kittle-cattle.
>   (Trans. Sir Bernard Pares)

16. Leikin, Nikolai Alexandrovich (1841-1906). A writer-humorist whose comic sketches had some effect on the young Antosha Chekhonte. Leikin's writing tended toward cliché and caricature.

17. Kuprin, Alexander Ivanovich (1870-1938). A literary realist and one of the leading novelists and short story writers of the early twentieth century. Kuprin's memoir about Chekhov is known for its warmth and objectivity.

18. Kuprin and Nevedomsky are referring to the increasing amount of social and political activity and the emergence of political parties (reflecting the continuing dissatisfaction with the Tsarist regime) which began seriously to emerge in the 1890s and which culminated in the Revolution of 1905.

19. Here, as elsewhere, Nevedomsky exhibits considerable perception into Chekhov's poetics. The theoretical interest of which Nevedomsky speaks is the subject of a recent study of Chekhov, and one of the two or three best books on the writer's art, A. P. Chudakov's *Chekhov's Poetics* (*Poètika Chekhova:* Moscow, 1971; English translation: Ardis, 1983).

20. This infamous statement belongs to Konstantin Petrovich Pobedonostsev (1827-1907), who, as Ober-Procurator of the Holy Synod of the Russian Orthodox Church, came to be associated with the most reactionary elements of Russian social and political life in the 1880s and 1890s. A friend of Dostoevsky's in the 1870s, Pobedonostsev was, quite fittingly, labelled the "Grand Inquisitor"; he finally retired from office in 1905.

21. Suvorin, Alexei Sergeevich (1834-1912). Conservative journalist and editor of the newspaper *New Times (Novoe Vremya),* remembered today chiefly as Chekhov's publisher and most frequent correspondent.

22. These are some of the leading journals of the mid- to late-nineteenth century. *Notes of the Fatherland (Otechestvennye zapiski)* was edited by the poet Nikolai Nekrasov (q.v.) and Nikolai Mikhailovsky (see note 2), and enjoyed the frequent support of Saltykov-Shchedrin (q.v.). *The Week (Nedelya)* was a weekly political and literary newspaper, published in Petersburg from 1866-1901.

23. P. Ya. (Yakubovich, Pyotr Filipovich, 1860-1911). Revolutionary writer and poet who belonged to the "People's Will." Although popular in its time among young radicals, P. Ya's civic poetry is totally forgotten now.

24. Badenweiler is the German spa where Chekhov died of tuberculosis on July 2, 1904.

25. Hauptmann, Gerhardt (1862-1946). German writer many of whose plays were translated into Russian and enjoyed considerable popularity with the reading public.

26. Veresaev, Vikenty (pseudonym of V. V. Smidovich, 1867-1945). Novelist and short story writer whose major work of fiction is a novel about the Russian Civil War, *In a Blind Alley (V tupike,* 1923).

27. Artsybashev, Mikhail Petrovich (1878-1927). Novelist and short story writer whose most famous work is the crudely written novel *Sanin* (1907), which advocates free love and gratification of various sexual desires. There is hardly a serious connection with Chekhov here.

3

A Survey of Some Themes in Gorky's Work

A. Volzhsky   (1878-194?)

Volzhsky (pseudonym of Alexander Sergeevich Glinka) was a prolific literary critic and scholar whose career began around 1900 and spanned forty years. Although he reviewed several books by symbolist writers and wrote some of the most elaborate pieces of his time on the critic-philosopher Vasily Rozanov ("V. Rozanov's Mystical Pantheism," 1904-1905) and the poet-philosopher Vladimir Solovyov ("Przybyszewski and Solovyov on the Idea of Love," 1905; "Man in Solovyov's Philosophical System," 1906), Volzhsky specialized in pre-Revolutionary realist prose writers. To him belong about a half dozen articles on Leonid Andreyev, a long piece on Vladimir Korolenko, a major essay of over eighty pages entitled "Religious and Moral Problems in Dostoevsky" (1905), and the article on Gorky included here. His book Sketches on Chekhov (Ocherki o Chekhove, *1903) contains some insightful discussions on Chekhov as seen against the background of his early contemporaries, the poet Semyon Nadson and the short story writer Vsevolod Garshin. In 1919 Volzhsky published* Socialism and Christianity (Sotsializm i khristianstvo), *and seems to have remained totally silent for the following fifteen years until a last flurry of activity occurred between 1934 and 1940. During these years he was primarily engaged in writing about, and editing the works of, Gleb Uspensky (1843-1902), the populist writer whose prose often deals with the hardships of Russian peasant life.*

A Survey of Some Themes in Gorky's Work*

A doubter of everything, Nietzsche also questioned man's need for truth. Having embarked on his enormous attempt to reappraise all values, he naturally raised *the question of the value of truth itself.* "Let us assume," he says, "that we did want the truth. But why not falsehood, uncertainty, and even ignorance? How is truth better than falsehood?" Gorky also doubts the actual value of truth, as well as man's need for it. "It is impossible," says a hero in one of Gorky's most philosophically oriented stories, "to call a lie harmful, to revile it in any way and to prefer the truth. . . . Why, it's still unclear what the truth is anyway; no one has seen its passport, and the devil knows what it'll turn out to be if it ever does produce its documents."[1]

Gorky's entire *oeuvre* is pervaded by a peculiar philosophy of the lie; his poetry is the poetry of "lofty deceit," of beautiful illusions, charming inventions, fantasies, and "golden dreams." Through the honeyed tongues of his heroes Gorky draws complex artistic designs which constitute an alluring apologia of the lie. At times these designs are very elegant and subtle. Sparkling with the luxuriantly rich colors of Gorky's lush artistic palette, they bear traces of profound thought; yet at times, crude and tasteless, they bristle provocatively and irritate the eye with their awkwardness of form, their blemished colors, and their gaudiness. Let us call to mind a few of these designs.

Here are the words which Gorky has his Reader address to the Writer: "Your pen scratches feebly at the surface of things, pokes gently among life's trifling circumstances; as you describe the commonplace feelings of commonplace people, *you may teach them many base truths: but can you create for them even the smallest deception capable of elevating the human spirit?*** No! Are you sure it is so important to rake through the garbage of daily life where one finds nothing but dismal crumbs of truth proving only that man in himself is evil, stupid, impotent, and pitiable?" And the same Reader goes on to say: "We long to indulge once again in pretty fancies and daydreams and to find quaintness and difference, for the life of our creating is dull, colorless, and boring! Life, which we were once so passionately set on changing, has crushed and broken us. Well, then, what are we to do? Let us see—perhaps the imagination can help man to rise above this world, if only for a brief space, and locate his lost place in it. For he has lost his place in it. He is no longer lord of the earth but a mere slave of life."

Gorky's "Rogue" says the same thing, only incomparably more frankly and cynically: he speaks with self-rapture, savoring his philosophizing—a trait which is characteristic of many of Gorky's heroes, who

* "O nekotorykh motivakh tvorchestva Maksima Gorkogo"—published in *Zhurnal dlia vsekh,* 1904, Nos. 11 & 12, pp. 49-56 and 109-116.

** Unless otherwise noted, the italics used throughout the text are Volzhsky's.

love to look at themselves admiringly, often at the most inappropriate moments. "Being able to lie is a great delight, I tell you. If you lie and see that people believe you, you feel elevated above them, and to feel higher than other people is a rare pleasure. *Perhaps, every lie is good, or, conversely, everything good is a lie.* There is hardly anything in the world more deserving of attention than people's various inventions, dreams, fantasies, and the like."[2] In *The Philistines*, Terenty Bogoslavsky concludes that the very value of goodness stems from its false origin. It is falsehood which makes goodness possible. The need and value of the lie when true life fails to satisfy, when it is boring and colorless, is defended by Konovalov,[3] Varenka Olesova,[4] the ardent idealist Benkovsky,[5] the deacon in "Creatures That Once Were Men,"[6] Aunt Anfisa in *Foma Gordeyev*,[7] Yakov in "The Three"[8]: all revel in beautiful fantasies. The pitiful little siskin in the fairy tale "About the Siskin Who Lied and the Woodpecker who Lived for the Truth"[9] lies for the sake of the beauty of invention, in the name of arousing faith and hope. The story "Boles,"[10] like the character Nastasya in *The Lower Depths*,[11] is built entirely on the idea of the healing, life-giving force of the lie, and the same theme is sounded in the wonderful story "Twenty Six Men and a Girl." But the apotheosis, the culmination of Gorky's philosophy of the lie, its best spokesman, is the complex figure of the wanderer Luka in *The Lower Depths*.

When he appears in the lower depths, Luka collides head on with life's terrible tragedy. Before him unfolds a series of hopeless situations from which there is no escape—at least under the existing conditions of social, spiritual, and, generally speaking, earthly life. Under the existing power of reality and its laws there is no individual escape for any of the people concerned with their one life to live...The tragedy which pervades the external circumstances of the flop house's inhabitants, who have plunged irreversibly into life's lower depths, is reinforced by an atmosphere saturated with philosophical problems, with concern over life, over justice, over man, over God.

Here people suffer from hunger, from life's disorders, from neglect and uselessness; but even more, they suffer from spiritual hunger, they are tormented by an unquenchable ideological thirst to comprehend the meaning of life, by a longing for truth and moral quietude, by spiritual emptiness, by a tormenting, gnawing awareness of the absurdity of life in general. Gorky's fallen people, like his tramps in general, are by and large philosophers. It is right in the thick of these distressing, unresolved, and painful philosophical problems, right in this abyss of accursed questions that the wanderer Luka lands. The author consciously places him in this most crucial of all positions. And Luka approaches the sphinx bare-handedly; he hopes to handle the enormity of his task in a very simple manner: by means of the lie, the lulling, caressing "good lie which rubs you the right way." Lacking the real means for struggling against the power of fact, against the terrible force of cruel reality, Luka wants to outsmart this power, he wants to create another reality, the reality of dream, fantasy, legend, deceit, and self-deception. He wishes to transport unhappy, suffering man, who is hopelessly crushed by life, to a world of visions, beautiful illusions, and happy fantasies, he wants to have him live on his dreams and reveries in this new world, where he wishes to make the impossible possible, the desired real and the real an illusion, a phantom. Luka attempts *to falsify reality,* to paint it in bright colors, to color it with dreams and illusions. Luka creates for the actor a fantastic world, a dream-hospital, "only half a mile from the end of the world"; there his cure and a new life await him. For the dying consumptive Anna, Luka opens up a dream world, but it is a totally different one. "Death alleviates everything. It is tender to us." "And what about *there*—is there suffering there, too?" asks the dying woman. "There will be nothing. Nothing. Believe me! There will be peace and nothing else. You'll be called before the Lord and He'll be told: look, God, your servant Anna has come." And Luka recounts in detail how Anna will be received in the Lord's household. Luka also tries to envelop the lives of the other inhabitants of the flop house in the optimistic haze of bright illusions. He welcomes the rainbow-hued fantasy which the unfortunate Nastya creates for herself from the book *Fatal Love,* as she tires of coping with horrible reality. "I believe you. Yours is the truth and not theirs. If you believe that you had a real love then you had one. Yes, you had one!" He doesn't forget to envelop even the policeman Medvedyev—although he does so by means of the crudest deception, by constantly calling him Officer...

But upon examining his behavior, pondering his glib, smooth speeches, sayings, and catch-phrases, we experience the urge to fathom Luka's holy of holies, to pierce the outer shell of his tireless, ceaselessly edifying lie, to penetrate the heart of this complicated old man, to lay bare his soul, to understand the meaning and truth of his lie.

What, in fact, does "every lie is good or, conversely, all that is good is a lie" mean? "Listen old man, does God exist?," Vaska Pepel asks him point blank. *"Luka is silent and smiles."* Pepel repeats the question. "Well? Does He? Speak up!" "If you believe so, He exists; if you don't—He doesn't. Whatever you believe in, exists." This highly significant formula, which negates and destroys the very object of faith, considerably broadens the sense of Luka's lie. Whereas with regard to the actor, Anna, and Nastya his lie is provoked by the character of the situation and is similar to the lie of a doctor at a bedside of an incurable patient, in his response to Pepel about God and faith, Luka's lie is prompted by incomparably broader philosophical grounds...

In the final act, when Satin rises to Luka's defense, he reveals the meaning of the wanderer's teachings and behavior. As we shall see below, Satin's point of view, his eloquent, intelligent, and proud words not only have nothing in common with Luka's doctrine, but directly contradict it. Luka's lie contradicts Satin's truth about man at every turn. Satin explains Luka's lie as follows: "The old man's no fake. What's truth? Man! Man— that's truth! *He understood this*—you don't! You're as dumb as stones! *I understand the old man*—yes. He lied, but lied out of pity for you, God damn you! Lots of people lie out of pity for their fellow human beings! I know!... Some lies bring comfort, some lies bring reconciliation. A lie can justify the burden which has crushed a worker's hands.... and condemn those who are starving to death. I know what lying means! *The weak in spirit and the parasite*—they need lies. Some are supported by lies, others take refuge in them. But he who is his own master, who is independent and doesn't suck another's blood—he needs no lies! Lies are the religion of slaves and masters. Truth is the god of the free man."

Luka "understands the truth"—it lies in man; Satin "understands the old man"—he lied for man's sake, out of "pity" for him. But those who are "weak in soul" and those who "suck another's blood" need lies. The lie is "the religion of slaves," it is for *those other people* who suffer hopelessly in life's lower depths, for *humanity,* whom one can only envelop in a golden dream. This is not Satin's or Luka's lot: their truth is the god of the free man; they are able to look boldly into life's terrible eyes...

Thus there runs through Luka's words and deeds a peculiar double standard, which recalls the double standards of Nietzsche and Dostoevsky's Raskolnikov: one morality for oneself, for the select, for the "man" or superman, and another for them, for the crowd, for everyone. The Nietzschean element in Luka's philosophy of the lie, the dual character of his morality, the split of his exalted cult of "man"—all of this manifests itself in the nature of his views on the meaning of human life.

The riddle of human existence has long occupied Gorky's attention; he has long been searching in his works for the meaning of man's life, he has long desired to understand its aim. Let us review some of his attempts. "The meaning of life lies in man's perfecting himself," says the Rogue ironically. "Well, I just don't understand that; the sense of perfecting a tree is clear: it is perfected until it can be used suitably for something—for a shaft, for a coffin, or anything else that is useful to man." Foma Gordeyev in his yearnings and wanderings, unable to make sense of man's life and losing himself in conjectures, at one point reasons as follows: "A river flows so that you can travel along it, a tree grows so that people may use it, a dog guards the house. You can find some justification for everything in the world. But people are like cockroaches, totally superfluous on earth!... *Everything exists for them* but what do they exist for? Huh? What is their justification? Ha, ha!"

There are times when Gorky, unable to find any more sensible aim in life, believes that it exists in the very power of one's strivings... "One day I asked him," Satin says of Luka, "grandpa, what do people live for?" And he replied, "Why, my dear, people live for the sake of something better. For instance, let's say there are carpenters and all of them are trash. But one day a carpenter is born—and there's no equal to him, he's head and shoulders above the other carpenters. His whole brilliant personality is reflected in the trade—and all at once the trade advanced twenty years. And this is true of other artisans—smiths, shoemakers, and other workers—and all the peasants—and even the masters, they all live for the sake of something better. Each person thinks he's living for himself, but it turns out that he's living for the sake of something better. A hundred years or more they live for the best man... " Man as an independent, moral value is *superceded* here; the Christian, democratic idea of all mankind is replaced by the Nietzschean, aristocratic idea of the best, of the Übermensch, who is born every now and then and for whose sake people live a hundred years or more. "I teach you the superman; man is something which must be surpassed," Nietzsche confesses. Presented with the idea of "the best man" as the ultimate aim and highest value, Foma Gordeyev could no longer, with the malicious delight born of despair, have compared people to cockroaches.

Satin's words about man being the truth mean something entirely different, but by some strange confusion of ideas, the author and the majority of critics believe that Satin, in uttering these words, is somehow explicating the old man's crafty teaching. Previously, in other works of Gorky, the concept of man being subordinated to something more elevated, to something which stands higher than him, to some super—or suprahuman value, emerged even more sharply and decisively. Indeed, in echoing Nietzsche, Gorky, be it consciously or unconsciously, touches base with him in the most negative, shopworn points of his philosophy, in his doctrine of the superman.

Nietzsche wanted to secure and rest content with a life-loving optimism, he wanted to create a cult of the man-God and exalt him through the beautiful hues of his poetic philosophy. But this great martyr of the mind did not succeed in obtaining the conciliating tranquility he sought so passionately in the ideational world which he created; the man-God, the deliverer, only tortured him, and in no way reconciled him to life: the majestic optimism which was to result from the divine calm of the amoral condition beyond good and evil only tantalized his weary imagination but was never granted to him. To Gorky, however, this optimism and reconciliation to elemental life and this rapturous worship of the man-God are granted more easily.

In the character of Luka, Gorky is certainly close to Nietzsche, but not to the stern Nietzsche who flaunts his cruelty and, as he agonizingly parades it, enjoys the pain. Here Gorky is, so to speak, a compassionate Nietzsche, but one who in his compassion nevertheless turns man into a means, a bridge to the "best man"; as with Zarathustra, man and humanity are superceded. To be sure, for all the golden vistas he paints, for all the broad horizons he envisions of the future which is vouchsafed to the "best man," Luka does not forget immediate, concrete humanity: he cares for mankind solicitously. Because he respects him, because he values his human worth, Luka deceives man; such is the bitter irony of his actions as opposed to his words. Respect out of pity! "You've got to respect man! Not pity him, not demean him by pity, but respect him," says Satin, explaining the meaning of Luka's teaching. Yet one cannot help but feel that he is mocking him. And then there is Luka's story—a story which I feel awkward listening to on the stage or even reading—his account of how he forced two hungry tramps to thrash one another! This is supposed to illustrate the general principle that "When you pity a person at the right time much good comes of it." "You've got to respect man!" Actually you should merely spare the reader's taste and not corrupt it with such melodramatic scenes. It is quite astonishing that even now, at the height of his fame, Gorky is still not free of these unartistic taints...

If a painter wanted to depict symbolically the essence of Gorky's idea of "the lower depths," he would have to draw, on an utterly dark background, a black dungeon and in it place the figure of a tortured man symbolizing humanity: all possible earthly torments and agonies, all possible affronts are inflicted upon him, yet the face of this anguished and humiliated man, this victim of torture and outrage, does not bear a martyred or painfully twisted expression, but rather a joyous, blessed smile of inner light: his sensitivity has been eliminated; he is sleeping, enveloped in the atmosphere of the lie, he is sleeping and dreaming golden dreams.

Substantially diverse and often contradictory elements meet and coalesce in the intricate weaving of ideological threads which make up the philosophical fabric of Gorky's works. While several sonorous chords of Gorky's work happen to harmonize with the themes of Nietzsche's artistic philosophy, it is also true that in the features of Luka there is something which recalls the figure of Dostoevsky's Grand Inquisitor. Luka approaches the moral and philosophical features of this character in his attitude toward truth and humanity. Of course, as regards the depth of psychological and philosophical meaning, Dostoevsky's Grand Inquisitor is beyond comparison—he is much richer in content, more diverse and complex than Gorky's character, and besides, the two authors have different attitudes toward the artistic generalization embodied in their creations. Consequently, a comparison of the two is of necessity very limited in all senses.

The Grand Inquisitor wants to soothe "tormented, suffering, stinkingly sinful humanity." In order to make men more happy he tries to overcome freedom, "for nothing has ever been more unbearable to human society than freedom." People can never be free because they are "weak, depraved, insignificant, and rebellious." Reserving for himself the freedom of negation and disbelief, Dostoevsky's philanthropic Jesuit and human despot sets three forces as the basis of the kingdom of human prosperity and tranquility which he creates: "miracle, mystery, and authority." The Grand Inquisitor attempts to found people's prosperity on material well-being, on satiety in the narrowest sense, "for nothing is more incontrovertible than bread." The edifice in which Luka and other Gorkian philosophers of the lie seek to shelter humanity is built of completely different materials. As any reader will see, its foundation is not the cult of material well-being, but rather a well-being of another kind—an idealistic, or falsely idealistic one. In his loving despotism, the Grand Inquisitor is a materialist and a realist; he is attracted to fact, to the world of tangible, perceptible, material values and tries to make people the slaves of reality. Luka, on the other hand, is an idealist or a false idealist; he is a romantic, but once again, a false romantic, a feigned and forced romantic since the direct simplicity, the artless naivete and the sincerity of genuine romanticism are lost in him.

The Grand Inquisitor wants to clip man's wings, Luka proposes that he soar in his dreams. But like the Grand Inquisitor, Luka takes much more from mankind than he gives or wants to give to it; he takes from it the courage to relate freely to reality, he dissuades it from looking squarely at life's horrors and staring into the abyss. Luka leads men off to the world of fairy tale, but he doesn't allow them to look back or down at the truth of reality, for fear of them turning into pillars of salt or hanging themselves, as the Actor does in the play. Neither believes in the truth of good nor wants to *justify* value or respect it. And neither is the slave of his lie, but rather its master. Both privately *endure* the horror of the truth, the horror of unbelief, of atheism; they carry within themselves the terrible secret of their lack of faith, allowing people to believe out of pity and compassion. Both are atheists, both are Jesuits, but their Jesuitism is complex, profound, and subtle. Each in his own way loves man and both degrade him...

Both the Grand Inquisitor and Luka represent an expression of extreme pessimism, an expression of lost faith in the truth, in its very existence and in its value and necessity for man. But the Inquisitor's lack of faith reflects a truly essential condition—terrible, sinister, full of torment and horror; therefore, he is a majestic and genuinely tragic figure. In Luka's lack of faith one senses qualities which are predominant in Gorky's work as a whole—self-admiration, self-esteem, and a self-satisfied relishing of one's own comforting words. "You'll never say it better than I do," Luka tells Pepel, and his entire character is strongly colored by this enamored opinion of his own good. Every truly terrible and deeply tragic experience can be depreciated and minimized by this self-esteem which verges on rapture at tragic moments. A pessimism which admires itself and delights in itself is no longer a sincere pessimism, but a false one; self-satisfied, exultant, and ecstatic, tragedy is no longer tragedy.

The element of self-admiration which one clearly notes in the artistic fabric of Gorky's writing and which manages quite inappropriately to creep into the most tragic nuances of his work, promotes its shallowness and coarseness.

Gorky's artistic philosophy—brilliant and alluringly beautiful in form, enchanting in its lushness of colors and richness of hues—is primarily the philosophy of a self-satisfied, self-satisfying amoralism and a peculiar, joyously ecstatic, smugly derisive atheism. Self-admiration, *contentment with one's own discontent,* rapture over one's own anguish, despair and lack of faith, and indignant protest which regards itself with delight—these are unsuppressible and persistent motifs in Gorky's artistic and philosophical world. While more intense at some times than at others, they nevertheless add a sweetly cloying, unctuous, unremittingly irritating, and boring element to the serious content of Gorky's writing. This considerably lowers both the psychological and social wrath of Gorky's work and forces his great artistic talent in large measure to be consumed in the rays of its own radiance.

However one regards the positive philosophical value of Nietzsche's writing, one certainly feels that underlying his desire to destroy the very "shadow of God," "to achieve freedom by uttering a sacred 'no' to duty," his cult of life's powerful flow, his defiant declaration of amoralism, is an all-consuming, profound tragedy of the soul, a tormenting, martyrizing experience, an unappeasable aching, an inextinguishable unrest, a perpetual quivering, an endless anxiety. Gorky's psychological experience is also great and his emotions are not without their tragic character: he also displays anxiety and indefatigable strivings, doggedly pursues the meaning of human existence, constantly attempts to fathom the terrible riddle of life. But in his disquiet there is a certain hidden quietude, in his tempests one really finds calm, in his tragedy reconciliation, even rapture, in his strivings, the joy of struggle and delight in seeing oneself in quest. He imparts strength to his impulses, beauty to his aspirations, and never fails to demonstrate a loving admiration for himself as a suffering and dissatisfied person. Of course, there is something to ponder and admire in the profound nuances of Grigory Orlov's anguish,[12] in the noble and beautiful, albeit slightly theatrical speeches of protest of Captain Kuvalda,[13] in the grim and embittered mood of the stately Teterev, and there is a unique power even in the snide cynicism of the Rogue, Promtov. But the fact that these characters themselves all too frequently notice and emphasize this fact significantly diminishes their stature, as well as that of the others like them in Gorky's work.

The intense self-admiration of Gorky's characters and the rapturous, contented, and irrepressibly mirthful expression of the author's face, which quite perceptibly emerges from behind the general background of the stories and the heroes' speeches, do not strengthen the reader's admiration of them, but quite the contrary, weaken and spoil it. Grigory Orlov, for all the significance of his psychological motives, so openly and naively delights in his own torment and restless discontent that at times one feels somewhat embarrassed for him. Kuvalda simply revels in his own speeches and in his heroic role as a dissenter; he is hypnotized by his own words: "He spoke more than the rest and this gave him an opportunity to think himself better than the rest." The writer himself submits to these charms, as one cannot help but feel when reading "Creatures That Once Were Men." The Rogue relishes the audacity of his impertinences and negations and at times he is transported with delight by his own eloquence and profundity of thought; this is why the cynicism of his speeches lacks depth and severity—one senses something insipid in them, one feels a lack of pungency and causticity...

In the overwhelming number of cases one can generally say that Gorky's tramp, whether it be Kuvalda or Orlov, Kyzka in "Anguish,"[14] or Seryozhka in "Malva,"[15] is pleased with and proud of himself. Although this satisfaction may take on an aspect of discontent and anguish, of resentfulness and abuse, the tramp views himself with genuine delight, admiring and constantly showing himself off. And the author himself, both covertly and overtly, delights in his creations and takes pride in them; through his vagabonds he *censures, threatens,* and *intimidates.*

In Gorky's intemperate audacity, in the boldness of his negation, in the utter resoluteness of his protest, and in the extreme quickness of his onslaught, one occasionally senses something intimidating, bellicose, and militant. This quality of Gorky's writing makes him a tremendous socio-philosophical agitator. Of course, the significance of this corrosive ferment, of this giant social battering ram beating with gusto against the stone wall of bourgeois vulgarity, routine, and decay is substantial, and to a certain degree it can be evaluated independently of any particular meaning underlying Gorky's ultimate ideals or apart from the final purpose and higher value in whose name he acts. "No work goes as smoothly as destruction," Gorky writes in "The Affair of the Clasps,"[16] and indeed he performs this kind of work with inspiration, animation, and rapture. But even here he does not forget, with an ecstatic smile of self-satisfaction, occasionally to look at himself admiringly or to have his heroes do the same. "I love this vagrant's life," says one of Gorky's affable tramps. "It's a cold and hungry life, but it's entirely free. There's no boss standing over you. You're the master of your own life. You want to cut off your head— nobody can say a word to you. Fine. I've been real hungry lately and real angry... but now I'm lying here looking up at the sky. The stars wink at me as if they're saying; 'No matter, Lokutin, travel the earth without letting things get to you, and don't submit to anyone.' Yes, and now my heart feels good." Such is the poetry of physical and spiritual vagabondage. Gorky's heroes speak about it beautifully and inspiredly, and one could quote many similar speeches extolling the ferment of vagabondage.

But to really make sense of Gorky's destructive work, one needs to understand the ultimate goal in whose name it is accomplished and the aim which gives it its fascinating luster, as well as its value and significance. In order to comprehend the meaning of this fermentation, spiritual vaga-bondage, and incessant wandering, and the significance of Gorky's negation, protest, and indignation, we need to go back to the sources of the ideas and moods, the passions and impulses from which all of this seeking and repudiation flows. In the midst of this swiftly moving, perennially changing, perpetually upsurging current—a current which, though always dissatisfied, always dismally and angrily seething, is at bottom quite content with itself and with its raging anger and dissenting anguish—one wants to single out something stable and unshakably solid, to detect some permanent point of support, to understand the very meaning of this *constant* change, this *avowed* negation, this self-subduing turbulence.

What may best bring us to the heart of the matter is the tormenting, upsetting question with which Gorky's Reader so agitates and confuses his interlocutor, the Writer, when asking: "Who is your God?"

The Writer hangs his head in silence, not knowing what to say; in his heart there is no genuine or worthy reply to this fatal question "which any man of our times who is honest with himself would find difficult to answer. Who is your God? If only I knew!"

However, with the author's help, the Reader himself answers this question. "There are those who blindly search for something that will set their minds soaring and thus restore their faith in themselves. But often they wander away from the place where God dwells, and the eternal verities uniting all mankind are hidden. Those who wander off the path of truth are doomed to perish. Let them! Do not intervene or waste your pity on them—there are lots of others in this world. The important thing is the longing to find God, and as long as there are souls which yearn after God, He will manifest himself unto them and abide with them, for what is He but the eternal striving after perfection?" The endless striving after perfection presupposes a conception of perfection, but no such concept is disclosed in Gorky's work. And it is often difficult to imagine just who Gorky's writer supposes God is... Living for Gorky's heroes means "to think, to be agitated, to burn with desire," while to move means first and foremost to move constantly, ceaselessly. Gorky's heroes spend their lives searching, often for the sake of searching; this process of perpetual restlessness gives them stability and tranquility. The fascination of flight is expressed by the brave Falcon, who serves as a "proud summons to freedom and light."[17] "Forward," the "Siskin Who Lied" calls to the birds. "That is the only way to live," says Makar Chudra. "Move from one place to another, and never stop long in one place—and why should you? Just see how day and night are always on the run, chasing each other round the earth; in just the same way you must run from your thoughts about life if you would not lose your

zest for it." This is the meaning or *almost* the meaning of Luka's teaching.
"We are all wanderers on earth," he says. "I have heard it said that even our
planet is a wanderer in the universe!" If Luka does not preach the endless
striving toward perfection, inasmuch as one may or may not believe in the
truth of perfection, at least he propagates the *illusion* of this endless striving
toward perfection, i.e., the semblance of a movement toward perfection.
He may not preach the real God, but he does sermonize about an invented
one...

But alongside Gorky's growing desire to comprehend the meaning of
life and consciously define the purpose of man's existence, his God, and his
ideals, there clearly exists in his work, particularly in his early writings,
another tendency—the tendency to answer these questions by eliminating
them or by avoiding them by devious means. This tendency is what I call
Gorky's amoralism, and it is in this more than in anything else that he
recalls Nietzsche. The internal contradictions into which Gorky falls by
proceeding along this devious path are explained first by the fact that, as
critics have shown, he has a poor understanding of his own philosophy and,
second, that systematic amorality and atheism, taken to their final
conclusions, are unbearable to a living consciousness. They bring about
self-destruction, but a living person wants to go on living, he needs a moral
ideal, he needs God. And so Gorky deviates from his formerly chosen path,
at the cost of contradiction...

The Rogue Promtov, even in recent editions, continues to say: "What
business is it of mine what is moral and what isn't? You will agree that it
isn't any of my business!" "The wolf is right," the Narrator still thinks.
"You know," Promtov goes on, "I learned early on and somehow
imperceptibly the simplest and wisest philosophy: no matter how you live,
you die all the same; *why fight with yourself, why drag yourself by the tail
to the left when your entire being pulls you to the right? And it is the people
who tear themselves in two whom I hate most of all.*" Promtov finds
trampdom delightful because he sees it as a basically amoral and natural
condition. "In a life such as this one there are no duties—that's the first
good thing; the second is that there are laws other than the laws of nature."

Of course, it is Gorky's *protagonist,* the Rogue, who says all of this,
and the author cannot really answer for his words. True, the narrator's
rejoinders, such as the above-cited "the wolf is right," as well as the tone of
the story, do say something about the attitude of the author. But even here
we are dealing with a fictional narrator and evidence such as this is always
insufficiently precise. The Reader, a character who is much closer to the
author, thinks that the meaning of life lies in the beauty and strength of
one's striving after some goal. Here the cult of beauty and strength denies
the independence of any moral value. This same respect for power, for the
"beauty of strength," permeates Gorky's entire poetry of trampdom, but in
this case isolated passages are less telling than the general spirit and timbre

of Gorky's *oeuvre* as a whole. Mayakin and the Gordeyevs essentially give voice to this idea, and it is also brought out by Gorky's intellectuals, who are crushed by their own impotence. In the final analysis it is not crucial for us to know what Gorky himself thinks; what is important for us as readers is to understand the basic themes of his fiction.

Philosophically transcendent, otherworldly elements are completely alien to Gorky's fiction, which is devoid of all mystery and mysticism. His work is immanent; it is strongly rooted in the real world, in the here-and-now. Despite an unremitting attraction to ascend into the magical world of lofty deceits and an intense striving "to fabricate" life and adorn it with the poetry of golden dreams, Gorky remains deeply loyal to reality; he is a sober realist who always remains in the power of *this* world, within the limits of empirical existence. Therefore "heavenly flights," idealistic enthusiasms, and the romantic impulse are for Gorky *always* a mere deception which amuse his soul, a fabrication invented specifically as a result of his respectful awareness of the terrible power of reality and a conscious desire *to intoxicate* himself so as to diminish his sensitivity to the power of fact.

In concluding his tale "About the Siskin Who Lied and the Woodpecker Who Lived for the Truth," Gorky writes: "Having read this, you of course will note that the Siskin is noble, but lacking in faith and therefore is poor in spirit." Like the Siskin, the wanderer Luka also "lacks faith": at most, like Dostoevsky's Grand Inquisitor, *he has faith in faith,* he believes in its practical, appeasing, healing quality. Ideals are valuable to the philosopher of lofty deceits only as an agitated, elevated state of intoxication, as a more intense manifestation of reality itself. Ascending and revolving in the magical world of artificially idealistic eddies allows you to live more vigorously than in the flat, boring plane of reality.

Gorky's artistic philosophy is alien not only to the transcendent but also to the transcendental. Morality, God, the ideal do not exist for Gorky *a priori* as autonomous values, independent of all empirical content; he values such concepts only as beautiful fabrications invented to embellish and brighten up life. Refusing to acknowledge an autonomous value which transcends the empirical content of life and which is independent of the arbitrary play of the dark, blind forces of life's elemental process, Gorky, like Nietzsche, idolizes life as a totality, deifies nature in its "complete harmony" with itself and worships the strength and beauty of its endless movement, eternal change, and unceasing, perpetual striving after goals, toward an unknown perfection. Outside of this intensely beating pulse of vigorous elemental life Gorky finds nothing dear, holy, or valuable. Morality, and any moral ideal, is arbitrary, something that melts away into the rays of the "beauty of strength," in the creative power of life itself. Nothing is binding or required here; there is no higher or more valuable thing than life itself. Life *itself* provides its own higher sanction, it sanctifies and justifies itself; all is permitted to it. The religious idea of God, of duty, of moral law is drowned here in artistic amoralism. This worship of force, spontaneous feeling, and the harmonious power of beauty comes to the fore with particular vividness in such fantastic figures as the old woman Izergil, who never ceases to love; the individualist Larra;[18] the enemy of society, Orel's son; the daredevil Danko;[19] the handsome songster Loiko; the proud Radda; the Khan and his son; and many others. Although somewhat weaker, this cult of life's creative principle is still perceptible in the philosophical position of Luka. Life *in itself* is so powerful, beautiful, and bountiful that it has no need of any unshakeably firm, independent, or external truth. What is of real importance is the summons to "life's creative work," "the vigorous words which give wings to the soul."

Gorky's is a peculiar, inverted teleology: it is not reality which is assessed from the point of view of the ideal of truth; rather, the truth of ideals is assessed according to how practically, how vitally necessary this truth is to reality. Yet as it turns out, the lie possesses great value. In his article "Nietzsche and Gorky,"[20] Gelrot is totally correct in noting that the "small man" in Gorky's story "The Reader," as well as Mayakin and Konovalov, talk about a personified life which must be enriched, to which man must contribute, and from which those who serve no purpose in it must be eliminated. The result is a totally original teleology: not life for man, but man for life. In other words, instead of the question of the value of life, Gorky poses the question of the value of man. As the reader will recall, Mayakin likens life's treatment of man to man's treatment of his own trousers: he doesn't pay any attention to them—just wears them out and throws them away.

Gorky's worship of life's force and power, of beautiful strength and healthy, harmonious wholeness, serves as the basis of his unfavorable criticism of the intelligentsia. Intellectuals are pictured as sad and mournful creatures; they are lifeless, sickly, spiritually impotent, and corroded by all kinds of contradictions; they have no living spirit, no strength, none of life's harmony, beauty, joys, or contentments. To this group belong the assistant professor in the sketch "Varenka Olesova," Ezhov and Lyuba Mayakina in *Foma Gordeyev,* the protagonists of "The Mistake"[21] and of the unfinished story "The Peasant,"[22] the journalist in "The Mischief-Maker,"[23] Ivan Ivanovich in the tale "Still More About the Devil,"[24] Tatyana and Pyotr in *The Philistines,* and many others. Their inner worthlessness, imbalance, limpness, and rottenness are intensified firstly by the inner wholeness, harmoniousness and vitality of Gorky's various vagabond heroes, who have achieved spiritual tranquility in their endless and agitated questing, which proceeds stably in its uninterrupted movement; and secondly by the personification of elemental spontaneity and primitive, half-animal inner harmony displayed by such characters as Varenka Olesova, the Rogue, "my travelling companion"[25] the princeling Sharko, and, finally, the fantastic figures of Gorky's fairy tales. Artificial, labored, and invariably confused in their world of emotional contradictions, Gorky's intellectuals are castigated and repudiated for lacking the elemental spontaneity and free will, the harmony and inner balance of the natural state—primitive, coarse, and half-animal though they may be. In "The Peasant" the hero rebels against the hypertrophy of the intellect. The intellect and the intelligentsia, with all of their valuable qualities, are rejected in favor of the lost paradise of harmonious existence... Gorky's critique of the intelligentsia may have some serious foundations, and his quest for the harmoniously beautiful as a respite from tormenting weariness and oppressive, cheerless emotions may be psychologically justified. But his inspiration, which yields completely to the power of these indefinite, vague, and purely formal guiding principles, often culminates in the idolization of the primitive aspects of harmony. In his cult of beauty and strength and in his desire to see in man a majestic demi-god, mighty, beautiful, and harmoniously integral, Gorky sometimes fixes his gaze upon a powerful beast, upon primitive animal forms of harmony, which he takes to be supreme, ideal, and divine. Instead of God, he worships nature, and demeans man for its sake. This is the traditional, classical error of many, and often very fine, critics of civilization, the traditional error inherent in any kind of return to a simple life, be it on a large or small scale, covert or overt.

Thus the moral underpinning of Gorky's work is in large measure a denial of morality, or at least a denial of its independence. Moral value is subordinate to the amoral features of strength, beauty, etc. Religion is reduced at best to an understanding of God as *"endless striving toward perfection,"* without any definite conception of *perfection* or, more accurately, with a conception that is obscure, indefinite and vague. The writer entrusts his morality and his religion to the endlessly moving and changing flow of life!

In Gorky, as in Nietzsche, we have the morality of amoralism, the religion of atheism. An apt psychological explanation of this ecstatic, triumphant amoralism and this calm, joyous atheism is given in Dostoevsky's *The Idiot:*

> He has reached the shore, he has found the land and he rushes to kiss it. Russian atheists and Russian Jesuits are the outcome not only of vanity, not only of bad, vain feelings, but also of spiritual agony, spiritual thirst, a craving for something higher, for a firm footing, for a fatherland... *It's easier for a Russian to become an atheist than for anyone else in the world.* And Russians do not merely become atheists, but they invariably come to *believe** in atheism, as though it were a new religion, without noticing that they are putting faith in nothingness. So great is our craving!

* Dostoevsky's italics.

Our craving for a religion is indeed great, but it is very often satisfied by surrogates of religion. The conditions of Russian life are particularly propitious for this.

Yet if the so-to-speak *theoretical* aspect of Gorky's artistic philosophy contains many negative elements, this need not diminish the significance of the *practical* aspect of its poetry of will and movement, and its call to struggle and protest. We have already mentioned that with regard to their social significance Gorky's works represent a truly powerful ferment, a strong reagent, but that its effect is in the highest degree indefinite, undirected, and *fraught with all kinds of possibilities, both positive and negative.* Rich in internal contradictions, Gorky's artistic philosophy harbors the possibility of the most diverse practical conclusions. Many of Gorky's critics tend to hear in his work the very distant voice of an awakening consciousness which loudly and boldly comes out in defense of its moral rights. They see here a protest of the personality against the social body which opposes it, a challenge hurled at society by its "lower depths," by the bottom of the social pyramid, by its "basement," the angry protest and indignant ramble of a humanity eliminated from active participation in life, the rumble of the coming storm. Eliminated from participation in life, this part of humanity asserts its *right* to life, its claim to life's joys and happiness. This theme is supposed to give Gorky's work enormous social import. Unfortunately, this is much truer in the conditional than in the indicative mood.

As one who rose from the horrible and mysterious lower depths of life which, in any case, were no secret to Russian literature even before Gorky, and after having roamed every inch of them, Gorky extracted from the experience not only enormous psychological knowledge, not only the philosophy of the bottom, but also a deep and strong feeling of sympathy and love for those who remain there. He has brought from the lower depths the protest of the neglected human personality, rejected by, and itself rejecting society. And by exposing the lower depths to the entire reading public through his mighty talent, Gorky is accomplishing something of enormous significance.

However, one should not forget that in its basic themes Gorky's work represents less the ideology of historically real trampdom as a social class than an expression of *spiritual* trampdom, with its peculiar philosophy and psychology. Furthermore, it is wrong to see in Gorky's work a vindication of the human personality in general. It is rather a defense of the *strong* individual or even of certain properties of human personality, such as strength, beauty, etc. This idolization of the beauty of strength, this touch of false romanticism considerably weakens and obscures his apologia of the human personality. The value of the individual and of the personality as such is diminished here by life's superior power over man, by the value of life itself. It is also diminished by the ugly distortion of this very individual through a morbid concentration on honor, as well as an extremely individualistic glorification of one's own "I," to the point that it inevitably encroaches upon the "I' of another, different personality and, consequently, upon all human personality. The concern of Gorky's tramps with honor often assumes acute, awkward, and painful forms of tension. Psychologically this over-emphasis of one's own "I"—in the narrow, crudely empirical sense—is quite understandable. It is curious that Gorky's tramp does not arouse the reader's conscience or awaken in him a passionate sense of moral responsibility and voluntary or involuntary guilt, as does Dostoevsky's or Uspensky's poetry of consciousness. Rather, Gorky seeks to provide honorable indignation, to extol the tramp's enviable self-will, and to make the reader envy his free spirit and lack of restraint. Gorky's tramp does not represent reproach, but rather indignation; full of anger and satisfied with his state, he demands not justice, but power, authority, and domination, and he himself will seize all of this when he so desires...

Besides the strengths upon which it must rest, the personality which rises up against society seeks its rights, the justification and the religious and moral sanction for its revolt. The mere fact of rebellion does not, and in essence cannot, justify itself. It is not the force of desire or of the half-starved "I want" which is important, but rather the truth of "the desire," the moral right to want.

To be sure, in Gorky's work the theme of protest assumes a variety of different colorations; his works represent an entire gallery of protesting people of various types. There are those who in their protest and in their revolt against society come forth with purely naked desire, devoid of any moral sanction, which they both reject and shun. There are those who vaguely feel the necessity of idealistic foundations for their revolt against society, but who do not know where to seek them; it is they who raise the question of the moral right to protest. "As a person who once was a man, I must obliterate in myself all feelings and thoughts which were once mine. That is very likely true. But with what will I and all of you arm ourselves if we abandon these feelings?" asks an early philosopher of trampdom, Kuvalda. And his words do not remain without a response. Although the philosophy of trampdom and protest in Gorky's works does not furnish a definite and resolute answer, what is valuable are the very impulses of the protesting individual (the amoral tendencies in Gorky's works notwithstanding) to base himself in his strivings not only on a blind and slippery "I want," or a naked act of will, but a conscious and firm belief in the moral right of his claims as well. Providing a *genuine* ground for the rebellious personality through the power of such huge talent as Gorky's would really have been a matter of enormous social and moral importance, but in its present dimensions this task could be carried out only on the basis of religious and moral premises alien to him.

There is much in Gorky's work which we have barely touched upon here, and much has been left completely untouched. But we wanted to speak about only some of Gorky's themes, essentially the negative ones. For much has already been said about the positive ones.

Notes

1. From the story "The Reader" ("Chitatel'," 1898).
2. From the story "The Rogue" ("Prokhodimets," 1898).
3. From Gorky's story "Konovalov" (1897).
4. From Gorky's story "Varenka Olesova" (1898).
5. A character in "Varenka Olesova."
6. Gorky's story (Russian title: "Byvshie lyudi") was published in 1897.
7. Gorky's first and, to most readers, best novel was published in 1899 and is dedicated to Chekhov.
8. Gorky's tale "The Three" ("Troe," 1901) is of novel-length proportion, running over 200 pages.
9. This tale (Russian title: "O chizhe, kotoryi lgal, i o dyatle—lyubitele istiny") was published in 1893.
10. This story was published in 1897.
11. Gorky's second and most famous play, *The Lower Depths (Na dne)*, which is arguably his best work, was published in a separate edition in 1903. It was produced by the Moscow Art Theater in December of 1902.
12. From the story "Orlov and His Wife" ("Suprugi Orlovy," 1897).
13. From "Creatures That Once Were Men."
14. Gorky's story (Russian title: "Toska") was published in 1896.
15. "Malva" was published in 1897.
16. Gorky's story (Russian title: "Delo s zastezhkami") was published in 1895.
17. From the story "Song of the Falcon" ("Pesnya o sokole"), 1895.
18. From the story "Old Izergil."
19. From the story "Old Izergil."
20. M. Gelrot's article, "Nietzsche and Gorky," was published in *Russkoe bogatstvo (Russian Wealth)* in May of 1903. Gelrot saw Gorky's Nietzscheanism as a protest against "a determinism which undermines faith in the creative role... of the personality."
21. In Russian the title of this story, published in 1895, is "Oshibka."
22. In Russian the title of this story, published in 1900, is "Muzhik." The work consists of several sketches ("ocherki," which Gorky uses as a subtitle) which were never completed.
23. In Russian the title of this story, published in 1897, is "Ozornik."
24. In Russian the title of this story, published in 1899, is "Eshche o cherte." The piece is a sequel to "About the Devil" ("O cherte"), published a month earlier.
25. From the story "My Fellow Traveler" ("Moi sputnik," 1894).

4

Ivan Bunin

Abram Borisovich Derman (1880-1952)

Before moving into the field of literary criticism, Abram Derman worked as a foreman in a coal mine and studied law at Moscow University. He published several stories in the early years of this century and as late as 1941 was writing fiction; in 1912 he made his debut as a literary critic. To Derman's pen belong many critical articles on Korolenko, Leo Tolstoy, Sholom Aleichem, Gorky, Bunin, and others, but his most lasting contribution to literary scholarship are his numerous articles and books on Anton Chekhov.

Ivan Bunin*

The remarkable thing about Bunin as an artist is that he is *divisible,* and in this sense he constitutes a rare exception. Try, for example, to divide Pushkin or Lermontov or, among our contemporaries, Sologub, into poet vs. prosaist. Such a division would be purely formal and highly detrimental to understanding the essence of their work; it would be cleaving in half a live and unified entity. You might need to do this for a specifically literary purpose, but beyond this it is intolerable and unnatural.

Bunin is different. His poetry and prose are completely autonomous. The critic divides Bunin not for his own benefit, but rather because Bunin himself, for his own internal "convenience," has split into two, thereby forcing us to deal separately with his poetry and prose. Of course, common devices, a common lexicon, even common objects of observation and reproduction exist in both; but Bunin's poetic and prosaic perceptions, the tone and spirit of his poetry, the feelings and thoughts which are embodied in each mode of his creative output, are totally different.

Dividing Bunin into two realms is significant because this phenomenon is becoming more pronounced. You find little difference between the first collection of Bunin's stories and his early poetry. On the contrary, reading these stories you feel the arbitrariness of their form; you feel that "Silence," "The Crossing," "The Bonfire," and many others are the fruits of the author's poetic inspiration. The difference between these pieces and Bunin's verse is only one of form, of their rhythmic qualities.

But soon this similarity begins to disappear; Bunin's poetry and prose split apart. Actually, his poetry has changed little: its coloration and thematics are fixed and constant. His prose, however, has more and more persistently taken on its own peculiar traits and as a result it more clearly differentiates what had previously been indivisible and unified in the author's soul. Essentially no common ground exists between Bunin's recent poetry and stories.

In his poetry Bunin expresses enchantment; in his prose—disenchantment. Perhaps it is just this possibility of ordering his perceptions and giving vent to each without mixing them up which has led to the perfection of a process wherein his poetry is transparent and clear, while his prose is dark and joyless. Here we will speak only of the latter.

Disenchantment is the theme of Bunin the prose writer. One generally gets this impression reading his latest works on the heels of his early ones. Take one of his earliest stories—"The New Road." The author is traveling along a new road past the most God-forsaken villages. "Lost in the woods, the sparse settlements of the dreary and despondent forest people grow

* "I. A. Bunin," published in *Russkaya mysl',* 1914, No. 6 (II), pp. 52-75; and "Pobeda khudozhnika," published in *Russkaya mysl',* 1916, No. 5 (111), pp. 23-27.

dark. Sometimes several men from these little towns stand at the train station—paupers in torn sheepskin coats, dishevelled, infirm, but meek and with such innocent, almost *childlike* eyes!" The significance of these attributes must be underscored: they relate not to a specific face, but to the peasant's face in general. Take another of Bunin's earliest stories, "Kastryuk." An old peasant, laid off from his job due to ill health, pines away. He dreams about his work as something great and joyful, and when his son yields to his entreaties and allows him to accompany the children and feed the horses—Kastryuk is happy. "The happy old man spread out his coat by the boundary strip and with a pure heart and genuine reverence stood on his knees and prayed to the dark, starry, beautiful sky, to the glistening Milky Way, to the holy road to Jerusalem."

These are the contours and tones of Bunin's early depiction of the peasant. In order for us to have a general feel for the road which Bunin has since traversed, let me speak of where he currently stands. We have just seen an instance where prayer was offered with genuine reverence to the sweetness of work. In "A Nighttime Conversation" the author personally stresses the peasants' "unexpected, absurd but unshakable logic, the patness of their accepted truths, their coarseness and generosity, their capacity for work and *their hatred for it.*" In his last volume, describing a moment of prayer in the fields, he notes: "The group bowed and crossed themselves, pressing their fingers firmly to their foreheads; this was the one time of year when they prayed passionately, with all their soul." This obviously calculated prayer is completely unlike the thanksgiving prayer of Kastryuk. Finally, note the following description—quite characteristic of Bunin's current perceptions—of a group of paupers, so markedly different from those "paupers, with such innocent, almost childlike eyes." "During the mass these horrible people stood in two columns inside the church fence, all the way to the church porch! In its thirst for self-torture, in its aversion toward restraint, work, and normal life, in its passion for all kinds of guises—tragic as well as buffoon-like, in its dark, criminal desires, in its impotency, eternal uneasiness, misfortunes, grief, and poverty—Russia forever and anon has given birth to these people." There then follows a description of the people whom *Russia engenders in its aversion toward work,* a terrifying description which stands beyond the boundaries of art, for it evokes in the reader not a psychic, but rather a physiological reaction of disgust ...

If we limit ourselves to the simple juxtaposition of the peasants with childlike eyes and Kastryuk on the one hand, and the selfishly praying peasants—those lazy, disgusting monsters who hate work and whom Russia endlessly brings forth from her depths on the other, the existence of Bunin's disenchantment is undeniably established.

Incidentally, I suspect that the word "disenchantment" does not fully characterize the change in Bunin's views toward the peasant. But it is unquestionably precise vis-à-vis the evolution of this writer's view toward another social group which he frequently depicts—the nobility. Here we have genuine disenchantment because preceding it there exists a seductive charm which never existed in his relations with the Russian peasantry.

Many Russian writers have devoted their attention to the area of life which we can designate by the collective and classic term: "a nobleman's nest." But not all who have depicted these nests have loved them. One nearly always finds here a certain bookishness or love for an ideal state rather than for the phenomenon as such. Bunin's love for the nobleman's nest is genuine. It exudes a poetry and sweetness which come directly from the estates and parks of the gentlefolk themselves, and not from the pages of a book where everything is refracted through someone else's thoughts and sensibilities—through a Pushkin or Turgenev, for example. You believe Bunin when he looks back on his childhood and writes: "With sadness you remember grandma, her polonaises and quadrilles on the clavichord, her langorous reading of *Eugene Onegin*. And a strange dream-like existence rises up before you, as if it were alive.... Fine girls and women lived back then on noblemen's estates! Their portraits stare at me from the wall; their aristocratic and beautiful heads with their old-fashioned coiffures tenderly and femininely lower their long eyelashes or their sad and soft eyes.... Could all of this not help but perish immediately when confronted with a new life?"

Bunin's pictures of aristocratic life depict the individual components of the stock formula: "the past, the confrontation between the old and the new, and the consequences of this confrontation." And all of these scenes are permeated by a genuine love—sad, painful, occasionally morbid—for the "nobleman's nest." Read such stories as "Antonov Apples," "Babaiki," and even "Sukhodol"—the obvious constant in all of them is the feeling of melancholic love for an obliterated way of life.

But only this is constant. The view *itself* of the past, the entire way of its evaluation has changed most abruptly in Bunin's eyes. The love has remained, but it is now poisoned and partakes of hatred and bitterness.

To appreciate the acuity of this disenchantment one need only compare "Antonov Apples" or "Babaiki" with "Sukhodol." Strictly speaking, there is destruction in all of these stories, and "Babaiki" depicts not only ruin, but genuine poverty, just beyond which lies beggary. But depicting all of this in his early stories, the author shows no indignation: he does not seek any culprits, or judge. In the forefront are the facts themselves and not their national or sociological significance. In "Su-khodol" we have exactly the opposite. The entire weight of the piece lies precisely in a national philosophy, in the author's generalizations in relation to which the artistic facts serve as "eyewitness proof," arguments, and illustrations. With merciless frankness the author discloses and underscores the complete unadaptability to life of that social order to which he belongs: "The Sukhodolians were not capable of rational love, rational hatred, or rational attachments, nor of normal family life, or work, or communal life.... The Sukhodolian chronicle abounds in absurd and terrible legends. In Sukhodol's past we recognized its soul. And its soul is what makes it the place it is. More than in the present, its truly Slavonic traits, which fatally separated it from the soul of common humanity, stood out in sharper and clearer focus."

And so, this is not a momentary pessimism, but a historical one, penetrating to the very heart of the nation. With profound bitterness the author abandons the enchantment and lyricism of the past. He rejects and reevaluates his former relationship to it...Bunin characterizes the psychology of the Russian landowning class as he had characterized, we recall, the horrible paupers to whom Russia has always given birth. Now we have the "horror of life," then—"eternal uneasiness"; now "the thirst for self-destruction," then—"the thirst for self-torture"; now "the incapacity for work, for communal life," then—"an aversion toward work and normal life." A complete similarity! And, of course, not an accidental one: it is founded upon a disappointment over the national soul, common both to the proprietors of Sukhodol and the horrible paupers who exhibit their festering wounds.

Nevertheless, contrary to reason, Bunin's poisoned love for Sukhodol and its inhabitants remains: not in defiance of the elements, but in obedience to them, for this is a love which itself is an element that is equally blind and strong. Mercilessly exposing the Sukhodolians, the author nonetheless feels "a terrible closeness to them," and in the sharpest outlines he etches the irresistible attraction to Sukhodol of all who come into contact with it, although besides evil it apparently yields nothing else. "It was not attachment, but something much deeper, much stronger," notes the author, without specifying the feeling. It is, of course, blind love.

We should not forget that this is a love specifically for a particular way of life, for its disappearing forms which constitute an odd mixture of the pitiful, the cruel, the poetic, and the dramatic, and nothing more. There is no love for the national soul here, not to mention for man in general, and this is all the more closely revealed when we analyze Bunin's attitude toward the other strata of Russian life—whose forms differ, but whose national essence is, of course, the same.

I said earlier that Bunin never endured disenchantment with the peasant, since there was never any enchantment to begin with. In terms of intimacy of tone, Bunin never wrote anything about the peasant which compares to "Antonov Apples." Peasants with childlike faces are only episodic. In and of himself, Kastryuk does not contain anything lyrical or uplifting; he seems a morally elevated character only in comparison with Bunin's later peasants. And it is a noteworthy fact that during his phase of disillusionment Bunin devotes almost all of his prose to the peasant, whereas when he relates neutrally to this class, he writes very few stories. Bunin's interests have not lain in the direction of the peasant: he has been indifferent to him. In fact I think in general *man* occupies second place in Bunin's scheme, in his *artist's* soul. Bunin's remarkable veracity, sincerity, and openness, as well as the above-mentioned lyricism of his early stories, allow us to base our opinions on the author's own rather telling statements.

As is usually the case, Bunin's sense of alienation from his surroundings has an immediately social tinge: " 'To what country do I belong,' I thought, 'I, a Russian intellectual-proletarian, wandering alone in my native land? What do I have in common with this forest backwater? It is endlessly vast, and can I ever understand its grief or help its people?' " Here Bunin speaks of "us," meaning the intellectual-proletarians. But one hardly needs to prove that the substance of this doubt is least of all typical for the Russian intellectual-proletarian. The question, "To what country do I belong?" belongs solely to Bunin, and it is no accident that it arose during his youth.

A bit later he notes: "I am completely alone . . . I don't know where I am or why I exist." Finally, at a later date he writes the sketch "Silence," in which there are two very characteristic moments. Together with a friend the author is sailing in a boat on Lake Geneva, far from human habitation. "Where is happiness?" inquires the author's companion. "You know, it's so wonderful here that I wonder whether it's right in front of us. Perhaps it lies precisely in tranquility. Now, for instance, it seems that I shall one day merge with this everlasting silence on whose threshold we are now standing, and that happiness will be found here. Now we are still among people. But there, just beyond these hills, is the promised kingdom of another life."

"Now we are still among people"—consequently there is no happiness. This is exactly what these words mean. Do they express, if not the opinion, then the sense of the author also, or does he feel differently than his companion? I think that he feels similarly, although he does say something seemingly contradictory. "From afar, generally speaking, man's life seems beautiful, interesting, seductive. But nearby it is different. How many low and base thoughts and feelings, how much pettiness, stupidity, and bestiality, how many vulgar and offensively ugly people! And we have just been on the threshold of nature's kingdom. But here, on this blue lake and in our mountain-top wanderings—everywhere, the same fleeting, enticing, and changeable female image has floated before us, and as in the past the same longing for persons, the same yearning for human life, the same desire to share with others what the beauty of eternity has aroused in our hearts."

Bunin's friend is content with solitude; Bunin himself "longs for people"—but this contrast is only apparent. First, the person for whom he longs is a woman; second, Bunin does not need this person in and of herself, but as a confidante with whom he can share those feelings which the beauty of eternity arouses. Call it a loftily utilitarian view of man, but it is utilitarianism nonetheless. If the writer needs man only in order to share, then his interest in and attention to him count for precious little. Only "from afar, generally speaking" does man's life seem beautiful, interesting, and seductive to Bunin; it immediately loses its attractiveness as soon as he draws close to it.

All of Bunin's disenchantments are *simple consequences of his drawing close.* As long as he fails to immerse himself in the human element of Russia, but instead, so to speak, describes it from without, frequently as an ornament, a background for his intimate lyricism—it occasionally attracts him, or at times leaves him indifferent; but in any case it is unobjectionable. But when he does immerse himself in it, it suddenly exposes him to a whole sea of "low and base thoughts and feelings, pettiness, stupidity, and bestiality, and offensively ugly people." As stated above, the lyricism of the noblemen's nests has survived this catastrophe, although it has changed color. But I stress that Bunin's is specifically a poetry of nests, of structures, and of forms of life, and not a poetry of human souls.

Where these forms of life have not existed, total human deformity begins. But before I speak about this, I want to indicate, albeit *en passant,* one peculiarity of Bunin which in yet another way illustrates his indifference to man: the absence of children in his artistic gallery. In this regard he constitutes a rare exception among major Russian writers. There is only one small sketch which deals with the child's life and psychology— "Numbers"; two others which touch closely upon this motif, "The Well of Days" and "The Dream of Oblomov's Grandson," have a mixed character. The latter is more concerned with the landowner's way of life and "The Well of Days" is more a retrospective look at childhood (an interesting detail: everything in the story is colored by the depressing and horrible aura of death). But even this solitary story "Numbers" is so unlike the enormous treasure house of child psychology in Russian literature! There is absolutely none of the poetry, emotion, or tenderness which we find in Tolstoy, Turgenev, Goncharov, Dostoevsky, and Chekhov. What we have is a *self-satirizing,* autodidactic sketch in which intelligence and precision cannot replace love and tenderness, without which it is impossible to depict children.

If Bunin does treat children in his other stories then he does so only episodically or expediently; they do not attract him for their own sake. And this is very natural and characteristic: more than anyone, children require selfless attention and genuine, spontaneous love. This is not a beloved woman or a subtle and understanding friend with whom Bunin would like to share his rapturous contemplation of solitary nature...

Indifference toward man is a bad school for comprehending his soul. The struggle with idealization is no better a school for impartiality. But the imprint of both lies on practically all of Bunin's prose. The question arises as to what impels the artist incessantly to analyze the life of people to whom he is indifferent.

The only assured answer to this question is an extremely subjective one. I would take the following angle. The past years have been characterized by the increasing disappearance of those forms of aristocratic, manorial life to which Bunin is bound genetically and, so to speak, poetically. The last remnants of that singular existence, which is so dear to Bunin, are fading. This is the theme of "Sukhodol." But one notes in "Sukhodol" the indisputable connection between the aristocratic style of life and the popular style, in the broad sense of the word. This "cogwheel" of causal dependence has seized Bunin... The writer is indifferent to Russia, but its fate and the events which it endures arouse him unwillingly. Forcibly attached to Russia, he is required to investigate the reason for its fate as well as the milieux where this fate occurs. But this forced attention is already poisoned at its core, for it is from the very start an analysis which is colored by the irritation of "captive thought," and not an explanation which is dictated by the free attraction of the heart.

We need still to pay attention to the unique and special nuance of all of Bunin's impressions and to the distinctive character of his perceptions.

The most unmistakable artists are those who see the external and internal sides of a phenomenon with equal clarity. The writer A. K. Tolstoy almost exclusively sees the lines, colors, and forms of things externally, leaving the reader himself to see the internal connections. Fyodor Sologub almost equally exclusively sees (perhaps because he only looks at) the internal. Especially exceptional in the latter category was Dostoevsky, the difference between whose qualities of vision was exceptionally enormous. Bunin belongs to the type of artist with a hypertrophy of vision directed to the externals of an object, but with the above-noted attraction toward depicting the object's inner essence.

The quality of Bunin's artistic vision appears literally in almost every line. It is manifested first and foremost, i.e., more graphically and conspicuously, in the striking abundance of nuances of shading and color. If we were to list the epithets dealing with various shades and tints found in just one of Bunin's stories, for example "The Bird's Shadow," this is the gamut of colors we would find: "blackish violet," "violet ash," "pale malachite," "bluish yellow," "faded red," "golden blue," "pinkish yellow," "blemished bay," "lilac brown," "yellow bay," "lilac grey," "bloody violet," "dirty slate," "silvery blue-grey," "rust red," "silvery stannic," "ceramic orange," "translucent opal," "purply velvet," "greyish green," "greyish yellow," "bluish violet," "smokey malachite," "light steel," "lilac grey," "ash blue." If one notes here that these semi-tones are frequently repeated, that even more exist in this story, and that there are as many tones as semi-tones, then it is clear that we are not encountering mere chance, but one of Bunin's definite attributes.

Let us explain the dimensions of this quality. Bunin enjoys the firm and deserved reputation as a glorious landscapist, and I will not begin to cite examples of the marvelous scenes which enrich both his early (e.g., "The Pines") and late works. Bunin's feel for Russian nature is subtle; he loves it tenderly. But we cannot deny that his landscapes are frequently encumbered by hues which are difficult to perceive. For brevity's sake I will take an example which is not the most characteristic for my argument: "The hills of Moab were like the southern sea in fog, a delightful *violet-lilac*. But the *grayish lilac* desert of St. John was fading. The sky was a *cold, pale blue*. The ashes, falling upon the city, became a *rosy blue-grey*. And everything was like a pastel." Even the last generalization doesn't save the picture from the obvious defect which hampers its contemplation: its piling up of semi-tones. The power of visual impressions is so strong in Bunin that he submits to it involuntarily, often to the detriment of the overall style of the narration...In the story "The Dream of Oblomov's Grandson" the author depicts a child's dreams filled with images which both in form and content are thoroughly childlike: "He would visit the farm and live however he liked....He would make himself gruel, sleep on a strip of felt on the threshold of his favorite part of the house, and would awaken when the *greenish-silver* dawn would just begin to glimmer." But the perspective here is greatly spoiled by this extremely un-childlike and highly deliberate literary epithet.

The technique of capturing the reader via visual impressions has enormous significance, and perhaps one which determines the nature of Bunin's entire outlook. Bunin sees the world as a series of pictures which he values not because of their *content,* in the broad sense of the word, but because of their function as a *motif,* as an excuse for accumulating colors in his peculiar say; as a pretext for arranging figures and projecting lines. He is aroused not by history, but by the style and power of its images. He is moved not by religion, but by the radiant beauty of religious images. He is not sympathetic or endearing to nations, tribes, and people, but to the forms of their social structure. Ruminate the following excerpt from Bunin's travels: "Yes, I had never experienced anything akin to the feelings of Orthodox Christians on my visit to Jaffa this morning. I had almost an animosity toward them. Thousands upon thousands wept and kissed the shores. Have these simple-hearted pilgrims, educated in the Orthodox faith, ever thought about the simple, genuine life which once existed on these shores? Did they feel that there really once was, there really once existed a living Jesus—thin, well-built, bronzed, with shining black eyes, with darkish violet dry hands and thin sunburnt legs? Only momentarily, only forgetting about their Christ, did my heart shudder from the closeness to Him, whose name animated and humanized me when I looked at the shores of His homeland."

A wonderful admission—which is entirely in character with Bunin.
First, the tone and spirit of alienation: Christ's image revives in him as a
result of his rupture with the Christian world, as a result of his
obliviousness to people, and not through his fusion with those like himself.
Further, there is the doubt whether the simple pilgrims have felt the living
Christ. Of course, they have experienced Christ with more considered
clarity and spirit, untouched by the destructive work of abstract, critical
thought. After all, stigmata are observed not among writers, but among
simple folk. But Bunin has his doubts. Why? Because the living Christ is
unquestionably he who has briefly appeared precisely to Bunin's imagination, he, with the "darkish violet hands." And Bunin feels the spirit of
Christ only when he has seen with his own eyes the "genuine life," the
nature, the landscapes which surround Christ; his heart shudders with
religious palpitation only in this tangible panorama, *accessible to the eye*.
And this is understandable: Bunin can be touched by "visual religiosity"
and no other.

This is why Bunin can be touching and tender only when he is an
observer of human affairs, and not an active participant in them. This is
why he recalls with pleasure that Russia remains in the distant past. People
may surround him, but only as accessories in pictures of nature who don't
demand either involvement or attention from him—as, for example, in the
streets of Constantinople, where "multicolored streams of a multilingual
people flow uninterruptedly past one another," where this very human
throng and the atmosphere of a warm southern evening "seizes the body
and soul with a hot rush of life and draws one into fusing with the whole
world's being." In his native land, where this fusion should not come about
via aesthetic uplift, where the *picture* of the human crowd is always
complicated by a *content* which has certain rights on those who contemplate it, people again will be alien to Bunin.

For this reason, although they originate from similar impulses,
Bunin's foreign and domestic impressions are assessed completely differently. With what unpoetic serverity Bunin notes in his peasant stories the
remuneration for clerical services—something pitiful always permeates
these moments; in Turkey he "even like(s) the ancient Eastern haggling
with the mullah for the right to enter the Hagia Sofia"—for that's a genre
picture! With what trembling he describes the filth and barbarity of
Russian villages and peasant huts; yet in that same Constantinople, not far
from the Hagia Sofia, in a little narrow street, he notes especially (and
rightly, with a smile!) that "in the sun *it reeks* of dried garbage."

Bunin has never depicted worshippers in Russia with such tenderness
and affectionate, graphic power as he has the Moslems in "The Shadow of
Birds," the description of whose every genuflection is filled with profound
insight. To be sure, one can look at their praying as at a picture—
contemplating it and nothing more. But when the peasant prays, you look

at him and unwittingly begin to consider what he is praying about—and then the *picture* falters, becomes complicated, and produces anxiety: it seems as if the peasant prays sincerely and passionately, but for selfish reasons.

Only by admitting that the one inherent element in Bunin's work is the element of visual impressions can we explain the abrupt change in Bunin's attitude toward the peasant from compassionate tenderness to passionate censure: both are of rational origin. Organically derived impressions do not undergo evolution. Neither Dostoevsky's evolution from Fourierism to Orthodoxy nor Tolstoy's evolution from Orthodoxy and aristocratism to a struggle against the Church and a desire for simplification shook their elemental love or elemental hatred for one or the other order of things. At their most basic and essential, the Dostoevsky of *Poor Folk* and *The Brothers Karamazov* and the Tolstoy of *Childhood,* the *Sevastopol Stories,* and of *Resurrection* and *Hadji Murat* did not change, but rather became stronger, for a writer's soul does not change—only thoughts change.

The world of man's soul does not constitute the innate and cherished sphere of Bunin's interests; he has never loved it and thus it is essentially closed to him.

A subjectively honest and zealous observer with a sharp eye and an incorruptibly severe attitude toward the word and toward the exactness and polish of the artistic work, Bunin is externally precise and, based on what *he* has seen, he depicts a series of facts and phenomena of Russian life. But he has passed this off as Russian life itself. It may be that this life does contain everything that Bunin describes, but his writing lacks what is most essential in it and what his eye does not see. "I look at everything like a dead man," Tolstoy complained to his wife about his ailing condition. "I see what there is to see; I understand, imagine, but I don't penetrate fully with love, as I did before."

And when, having read these astonishing words, I encounter in Bunin, for example, a depiction such as the one of a hanged dog: "Its dark violet tongue was jutting out, its coral gums opened to form a grimace, the day's light, reflected in its extinguished wine-colored eyes, began to grow pale"; and when I recall that in the same tone and often with a touch of disquiet Bunin depicts suffering people, I distinctly feel that Tolstoy's words apply to him, to his manner of perception, and to his examination of the world of man's soul.

Thus the reader of Bunin, taking the writer's facts and descriptions with a grain of salt, is required to approach his conclusions and generalizations with particular caution; often he must do with his facts what Tolstoy felt was necessary: to look at them independently, but "fully, (and) with love."

* * *

I have never been a great fan of Bunin's prose, and my attempted critique of it in *Russian Thought* led me to the distinct conclusion that his work was flawed by a coldness toward people (insofar as they were people and not just living "matter" for his dispassionate canvasses), combined with an inclination to depict their inner world. This combination fatally led the author to the one-sided depiction of human vices, to a certain embittered subjectivity, to a position of exposer of the dark sides of Russian life and its rotten core.

The purely graphic side of these early stories was never weak; nonetheless the pieces as a whole left me somehow unsatisfied. The author's irritation was irritating; there was too much negative—at times unjustifiable—trivia, which Bunin was never squeamish about exposing. Legitimate and admirably perspicacious though they may have been, these dark spots were never accompanied by a sufficiently broad or deep perspective; the reader never quite knew what to do with these negative data which had been piled up tediously before his eyes.

Reading "The Gentleman from San Francisco" one unwittingly wants to exclaim: you have triumphed! One can only rejoice when, through stubborn and systematic work on perfecting his talent, an artist takes such a giant step forward, being able to strengthen even those qualities of his authorial persona which heretofore have assumed the kind of negative forms which I analyzed in my above-cited critique.

"The Gentleman from San Francisco" requires one to seek analogies in Tolstoy, and if it weren't so similar to some of Tolstoy's pieces we would undoubtedly have a genuine masterpiece before us...

The similarity of Bunin's story to certain works of Tolstoy is unquestionable (there can be no thought of imitation here; people who imitate are either talentless or very young talents): it is found both in the story's design and in its execution, in its style and in its moral sense.

Two words about its plot. A wealthy, fifty-eight-year-old American, a certain "gentleman from San Francisco," sets off with his family for the Old World to enjoy what his wealth entitles him to. The agenda of amusements is varied and vast, but it comes abruptly to an end: no sooner does the gentleman from San Francisco complete his voyage across the ocean on the ominously luxurious boat "The Atlantic" and set foot on Italian soil to partake of its delights, then death overtakes him in an opulent hotel on Capri, and the American's body in the hold of the same ominously magnificent "Atlantic" returns home to the New World.

The American's life and its meaning are put to the test by death. This is the theme which is characteristic of the works of Tolstoy, who under the sign of death reviews all values and his own in particular, as well as human existence in general, with the accompanying psychology of this process—

beginning in "Three Deaths," through *War and Peace,* and *Anna Karenina,* and on through "The Death of Ivan Ilych" and "Master and Man," and beyond. The joy of wealth, luxury, earthly pleasures, and sensual delights exposes its transparent, empty, and pitiful essence at the moment of death. This is the usual theme in Tolstoy, with its customary corresponding devices that often elevate the hero to great "earthly" heights so that his fall into the abyss of death will be all the more striking and tragic.

We find the same device in Bunin. One must read and re-read these few pages, so thickly saturated in imagery, where the author describes the interminably refined cult to luxury and pleasure which the American serves, and the general readiness to satisfy his smallest desire, which he doesn't even notice, in order to feel how the above-mentioned style permeates everything. The similarity with Tolstoy extends even further, to comparisons of a social nature, as if in advance of the characters' own exposés there appears before the reader's eyes the threatening, lurking instability of this sinful earthly life of splendor, based on slave labor: "The siren, suffocating in the fog, wailed in mortal agony; the watch up in the crow's nest froze in the cold, their minds reeling from the unbearable strain on their attention. . . . The giant furnaces roared with laughter as, with their blazing maws, they devoured ton after ton of coal, flung down them with a clatter by men drenched in pungent sweat, dirty, half-naked, and purple in the glow of flames. While up there in the bar, legs were flung carelessly over the arms of chairs, brandy and liquers were sipped at leisure, clouds of aromatic smoke hung in the air." In the spirit of Tolstoy, with that mercilessness of open contempt which exposes stupidity and haughtiness behind the veneer of impeccable civility, and ugliness behind the cheerful veneer of external radiance, there follows a description of high society on the Atlantic, the famous hotel on Capri, etc. "There was a world-celebrated beauty and an elegant pair of lovers watched by all with curiosity, who made no secret of their happiness, for he danced with no one but her, and all this was so exquisitely and charmingly performed that no one but the captain knew that the couple was hired by Lloyd's to play at love for a good wage, and had been sailing on the company's ships for a long time." "Every word he uttered was echoed by the maitre d'hotel in tones of the most varied pitch, all of which, however, had one meaning: that the rightness of the gentleman's wishes could not be doubted, and that everything would be carried out to the letter." Particularly characteristic of the author's contempt for the transparently opulent forms of life is an excerpt from his description of Capri with its ruins of Tiberius' palace: "On that island two thousand years ago, there lived a man who got hopelessly entangled in his foul and cruel deeds, who for some reason rose to power over millions of people and who, losing his head from the senselessness of this power and from his fear that someone might thrust a knife into his back, committed atrocities beyond all measure. And mankind remembered him forever, and those who with combined effort are now ruling the world with as little reason and, on the whole, much more cruelty as he did, came here from all over the world to look at the remains of the stone house where he lived."

In this outline of power and its seduction, as in the above-quoted excerpts, the similarity between Tolstoy and Bunin goes beyond purely artistic devices; there is a resemblance of views on the meaning of life in the face of man's inevitable death. The artist unambiguously hints that first and foremost it is necessary to remember our mortality and then to impart to our lives a meaning which death cannot destroy. This religious-moral idea, embodied in a form where social injustice manifests itself in moral obtuseness, and moral obtuseness leads inevitably to the senseless death of the areligious being, typifies Tolstoy's world view and is adopted in Bunin's story.

"What did the gentleman from San Francisco feel, what did he think about on that night that was to be so momentous for him (i.e., shortly before his sudden death, A. D.)? Frankly, nothing in particular, for the whole problem is that in this world everything seems too simple." Of course, simple not for everyone, but for those who do not seriously ponder life and its meaning. Significantly, when the image of death suddenly appears in the opulent hotel it produces the impression of a wicked scandal committed by someone's negligence. "No one could make out what had happened because to this day people find death the most amazing thing in the world, and they flatly refuse to believe in it." And suddenly everything changes: those "refined" enjoyments for which the gentleman from San Francisco set out for Europe seem somehow insignificant and even vulgar, for they were utilized vulgarly. Only death brings the American that quality of beauty of which his openly egotistical and self-assured existence does not even hint, despite all of its impeccable external polish. "And slowly, very slowly, before the eyes of all of them, a pallor spread over the face of the deceased, his features grew finer and lighter, with a beauty that would have befitted him long ago"—here is that same familiar Tolstoyan trait: beauty brought about by death—"And again the hired lovers make merry before the earthly colleagues of the gentleman from San Francisco, not suspecting that the dead body of their prototype lay on the floor of the dark hold of the Atlantic, "a many-tiered and many-funnelled ship, created by the arrogance of a New Man with an old heart."

Bunin's remarkable story is permeated by Tolstoy's power and by the moral sense of his artistic works. From purely methodological considerations I shall continue the comparison further, touching also upon the issue of the dissimilarity of artistic devices in the two. In this given instance I shall raise the following question: how would Tolstoy have solved the same artistic and moral problem upon which "The Gentleman From San Francisco" is based? How has Bunin departed from the usual Tolstoyan scheme in dealing with analogous questions?

The answer to this question is complex, but nevertheless two basic lines can be singled out. One has a more artistic significance, the other has a moral character.

In the purely graphic sense, Tolstoy undoubtedly would have proceeded to portray the generalized type of American completely differently from Bunin. Bunin intentionally removed his hero from the past, from personal, concrete traits, from a specific biography: this is literally a Mr. so-and-so, a "type," generalized by comparing him socially with those who are like and those who are unlike him in, so to speak, nominal traits, but not in particulars. Tolstoy always proceeded oppositely, by way of elevating the individual, characteristic, and concrete to the level of the typical. Bunin himself does the work of comparing the American to millions of others; in Tolstoy this is always placed on the reader's shoulders.

On the moral side, Tolstoy more than likely would have given the American the time and opportunity to be horrified by his life, to curse it, "to come to his senses," to grasp (with the help of a Gerasim, an Akim, or someone like them) the meaning of life and, using it as an illumination of the remainder of his days, to reveal via this dying process the moral perspective not only of the present and future, but also of the past, all of this by aiming his blows at the hero who had strayed from the knowledge of truth. In Bunin the moral perspective is closed to the American completely and forever—only for the living does the meaningless death of the stray hero remain a threatening "memento."

These admittedly only hypothetical distinctions vis-à-vis Tolstoy provide a guiding thread for judging the profoundly interesting moment of Bunin's literary evolution which his new story represents. The reader sees that Bunin first and foremost remains true to himself to the end: of course there is no love for a concrete person in "The Gentleman from San Francisco"; it would be hard to be more merciless to one's protagonist than Bunin is to the American. How, then, has the author evolved? In the range of his feelings. His lack of love for the American does not contain a shadow of irritation; this is extraordinarily and fruitfully set aside. With a certain solemn and just sadness the artist has drawn a powerful image of enormous evil—an image of sin in which flows the life of modern, proud man with an old heart, and the reader feels here not only the legitimacy, but also the fairness and beauty of the author's coldness toward his hero. Here the author's disillusionment is objectified and raised to great heights. And if love for a concrete person is lacking here, then there is still a broad range of feeling in his affrontery before those forms of life which man has created for himself, but which are unworthy of him.

There are in the story, although only slightly hinted at, images of a different, sensible human existence—the Abruzzi singers, who are simple people close to nature, and with a soul that is uncorrupted by the sin of idle pleasure. But the story's pathos lies not in them, but in the American and the "Atlantic."

It is impossible to judge by the isolated citations given above how powerfully the story is written. Remarkable are not only the story's saturated and unforgettable details, those "red-coated Negroes with eyeballs that looked like shelled hard-boiled eggs," or the "golden snakes, gliding away from the lamposts on the quay, (which) came floating on the subdued waves which gleamed like black oil"; the entire style of the story is amazing: the measured, metallic music of its flawless, austere sentences, so much like the deep sound of low ringing bells; the simultaneous richness and purity of the words—not one too many and not one too few.

We cannot help but note that this wonderful story will serve as an argument in the debate about the importance of ideological content in artistic creation. This debate has temporarily been silenced, but has not ceased. And when it flares up again it will be possible to say that here is an artist who knew the value of color and word as such, who constructed on the old idea of social injustice a story in which this idea is not only unconcealed, but is actively emphasized. Indeed this story is the strongest piece of Russian fiction during the last ten years and the best work of this artist in general.

5

Summing Up Russian Symbolist Poetry*

P. Gurev**

When Russian symbolism first made its appearance in the early 1890s under the name "decadence," it was completely out of harmony with the prevailing mood in literature and criticism. The total lack of public-spiritedness of its adherents, their declaration of the principles of pure art, carried to the limit—the limit in versification and style—all of this was so out of step with the prevailing atmosphere in the literary world that the decadents were looked upon as charlatans, the followers of some sort of eccentric fad which could not last long. People explained the appearance of the decadents as a blind imitation of French decadence, without admitting even the thought that, possibly, the conditions for the appearance of a similar tendency had ripened in Russian society. A hail of jibes descended on the decadents; disconcerted critics and readers dismissed the very possibility of a serious attitude toward such poetry. The extremism and pranks of its practitioners concealed the essence of decadence from everyone and long deprived it of serious attention on the part of critics and society. Decadence, it was decided, was a soap bubble destined to be short-lived. But Russian criticism was wrong in denying a future to decadence: the past two decades of Russian poetry have indisputably proceeded under the banner of the decadents, whose acknowledged leaders were Konstantin Balmont, Valery Bryusov, and Fyodor Sologub, followed by Vyacheslav Ivanov, Alexander Blok, and Andrey Bely.

Likewise there was nothing abrupt or unexpected in the appearance of symbolist poetry, as it might have appeared earlier. Setting aside extremism in expression and verse, and directing our attention to the ideas and moods of symbolist poetry, we see that the major motifs of symbolist poetry had already been established and even elaborated in the work of

---

* "Itogi russkoi simvolicheskoi poèzii," published in *Nachalo: sbornik statei* (Saratov, 1914), pp. 29-62.

** To the best of my knowledge, no information about this Marxist critic exists in any source available in the West.

Dostoevsky, as well as in the poetry of Fet,[1] Tyutchev,[2] and Vladimir Solovyov,[3] and that it is only because of the general public's unfamiliarity with these poets and its incomprehension of Dostoevsky's profundity that the decadents seemed to be opening a new world. The entire cycle of moods and ideas of Russian symbolism is contained in the poetry of Fet, Tyutchev, and Solovyov, as well as in the novels of Dostoevsky. The symbolist poets continued their tradition, merely taking the poetry of symbols out from the rural byways of literature onto its "highway." Let us first note the influence of Dostoevsky.

First of all, symbolist poetry is related to the fiction of Dostoevsky by the fact that the City has left its indelible and peculiar impression on them both. The hopeless isolation of Dostoevsky's heroes, their wild fantasies, their warped psychology, their boundless exaltation of their "I," their profound degradation in an abyss of sin and voluptuousness—which does not destroy their craving for heavenly purity—the union in one heart of the ideal of Sodom and the ideal of the Madonna: all of this found an echo in the verses of Balmont, Bryusov, and Sologub. Parallel to the apologia of the hero who can in conscience allow himself a crime (Raskolnikov) and to the Karamazovian "everything is permitted," we can set Balmont's line: "The laws are not for me, since I am a genius!" Both in Dostoevsky and in the decadents one must note a morbid love of evil, of torments, of moral anguish, in which Dostoevsky's heroes find a peculiar voluptuousness. Even the "revolt" of Ivan Karamazov, his non-acceptance of the world, is echoed in certain lines by Balmont, particularly "The world must be entirely justified in order for it to be possible to live." The work of Dostoevsky was not understood by critics and society in all of its psychological and philosophical depth. Not having understood Dostoevsky, they also could not understand the decadents, who to a significant degree were his spiritual offspring. And although some critics (for example, Skabichevsky)[4] noted at the time the important circumstance that Dostoevsky was the first major artist of the city, they did not further investigate this profoundly important peculiarity of his work. Not having elucidated the social foundations of Dostoevsky's work, they forfeited an understanding of decadence as well.

From Fet the symbolists inherited one of his central motifs, the aspiration to break loose from the fetters of coarse reality, from the "blue dungeon." The influence of Fet is particularly detectable in Balmont's verses of his first period; the two poets are similar both in their withdrawal into a region of azure dream and in their airiness, elusiveness of color, and transparency of outline. In *Notes on Fet,* Strakhov[5] depicts Fet's muse in this manner: "But whether the world is a phantom or reality—isn't it all really the same? It is importunate, it embraces us on all sides, it will not give us peace and draws us to itself, sometimes caressing and lulling but more often tormenting us. Where is there salvation, where is there sanctuary? In song, answered Fet to himself, and he was right: those songs which he sang all his life were his actual salvation, his liberation from the world." The poetry of Fet particularly evinced the aforementioned duality of existence, which was taken up by the symbolists. Fet allowed man the possibility of looking into that "secret crucible in which the prototypes seethe." Such glimpses were provided by inspiration and in ecstasy. The ideas of "contact with other worlds" and of the transparency of this world were expressed in Fet's notable lyric, which begins his *Evening Lights*. We cite it in its entirety, as it also expresses the philosophical essence of symbolist poetry:

> I am exausted by life, by the perfidy of hope,
> When I yield my heart to them in battle,
> And day and night I close my eyes
> And somehow strangely at times I recover my vision.
>
> The gloom of everyday life is still darker,
> As after a bright autumnal flash of lightning,
> And alone in the sky, like a friendly call,
> There shine the golden eyelashes of the stars.
> And so transparent is the endlessness of the fires,
> And so accessible the whole abyss of ether,
> That I look straight out of time into eternity
> And your flame I recognize, sun of the world.
>
> And motionless on the fiery roses
> The live altar of the universe burns,
> In its smoke, as in creative visions,
> All force trembles, and all eternity appears in a dream.
>
> And everything which rushes along the abysses of ether,
> Each light, corporeal and incorporeal,—
> That is only your reflection, o sun of the world,
> Only a dream, a passing dream.
>
> And in the universal flow of these dreams
> Like smoke I arise and involuntarity melt away,
> And in this recovery of sight and in the forgetting
> It is easy for me to live and not painful to breathe.*

A poet with such a perception of the world could not obtain wide renown during the heyday of civic motifs in literature and poetry. Fet had, both in life and after death—until most recently—an insignificant circle of readers.

In another early poet, Tyutchev, we find the same basic motifs that were subsequently elaborated by the symbolist poets, the same consciousness of the duality of existence and "contact with other worlds":

---

* Translation from Richard Gustafson: *The Imagination of Spring—The Poetry of Afanasy Fet* (New Haven, 1966), p. 20.

> O my prophetic soul,
> O heart filled with disquiet,
> How you flutter on the threshold,
> As it were, of two realities.

Another poem contains a proud summons to the solitude which is inescapable because we are powerless to reveal our soul to another person.

> How will the heart express itself?
> How will another understand you?
> Will he understand what it is that you live by?
> A thought that is spoken is a falsehood;
> By stirring up the springs you will cloud them:
> Drink of them and be silent.

Love of evil, which is strewn invincibly everywhere, recognition as the world's essence of something irrational, acknowledgement of the "chaos" which "stirs" behind the visible forms of the real—these are the fundamental motifs of Tyutchev's poetry, and this is what makes Tyutchev a great symbolist. "Tyutchev stands as a great master and progenitor of the poetry of allusions" (Bryusov, *The Far and the Near*). At the same time as Baudelaire (and even earlier than he), yet completely independently from him, Tyutchev was concerned with the same themes as the French poet.

Vladimir Solovyov is a poet-philosopher. The small volume of his lyrics is closely and vitally related to his philosophy. Solovyov's mysticism and his cult of Beauty as a superterrestrial essence powerfully influenced the work of two symbolist poets, Blok and Bely. All of Solovyov's poetry is a passionate surge toward "unearthly shores," a surge having for him all the palpability of the real. His profound mysticism and religiosity were peculiarities of Solovyov's psychological make-up, which left a particular imprint on his whole life and activity. The penetration into the beyond and the intuition of it were, according to Solovyov, the only suitable subject for "pure lyricism." In Solovyov's works, poetry of worldly, earth-bound sensations is almost completely non-existent; these, in his opinion, stand outside true poetry. Despite the originality of his philosophy, as reflected in his lyrics, Solovyov is similar to Tiutchev and Fet in his postulation of "other worlds" and "unearthly shores."

Let us take this poem of his as an example:

> Oh sovereign-earth! To you I bowed my head
> And through your fragrant shroud
> I felt the fire of a kindred spirit
> And heard the quivering of earthly life.
> Passionately voluptuous, the shining heavens
> Descended in noon's rays,
> And the flowing river and noisy forest
> Gave their melodious greeting to this quiet splendor.

And in the explicit mystery I see again the union
Of earth's soul with an unwordly light,
And from love's fire human suffering
Escapes like fleeting smoke.

And this fragment:

Not believing this deceptive world,
I felt the imperishable purple
Under the hard core of matter,
And recognized the divine light.

In Solovyov's view, the artist depicts each object and phenomenon "from the point of view of its ultimate status in the light of the future world."

These forerunners of symbolism in Russia point to the fact that the emergence of symbolist poetry was not an unexpected occurrence—and here we observe that same continuity of literary trends which is a phenomenon common to the entire history of literature. To deny the influence of French symbolism or that of the poetry of Edgar Allan Poe is certainly impossible, but it is also necessary to note that Balmont was influenced not only by Baudelaire and Poe but also by Fet, while Bryusov fell under the influence equally of Verlaine and Verhaeren and of Tyutchev's poetry, and Blok and Bely were shaped to an immeasurably greater extent by Solovyov than by Western European symbolism.

But these precursors of Russian symbolism were isolated phenomena against the backdrop of Russian literature. They clearly acknowledged their estrangement from the general trend and sensed the "unseasonableness" of their work. They stood in the shade, enjoying fame only among a small circle of readers, and did not create schools around themselves, nor did they attempt theoretically to substantiate the principles of their creative work. In short, during their lifetimes they did not set a trend in literature. Symbolism as a trend arose only in the 1890s when Balmont and Bryusov came forth with their verses—when they, together with Merezhkovsky,[6] proclaimed a new "credo," a kind of "aesthetic manifesto." The question quite naturally arises, why did symbolist poetry, which heretofore had been a hidden, unnoticed, and, as it were, an underground current in Russian literature, turn into a broad and noisy current, beginning with the 1890s? It is obvious that this poetry, previously almost unknown to the broad circles of Russian society in the verses of Tyutchev and Fet, had found its reader; obviously, in certain strata of this society a psychological dislocation had occurred, and the interests, ideas, and moods of the symbolists became congenial to these strata. The burgeoning of symbolist poetry's influence can be explained only by profound, gradually swelling changes in the socio-economic sphere, viz. a rapid development of urban life and the rise of the Russian bourgeoisie, hence, of the bourgeois intelligentsia, and of the intelligentsia in general, uniting within itself segments of various social classes. These factors created both the readership with whom symbolist poetry had an affinity[7] and the poets who cast in sharper relief the motifs already noted in the poetry of Tyutchev, Fet, and Solovyov.... In comparing Russian symbolist poetry with Western European (mainly French) poetry, it is necessary to observe that in Russian symbolism the motifs of decadence and decline do not so exclusively and wholly predominate; Russian symbolism is healthier than Western European symbolism. If we take the work of Balmont and Bryusov as a whole, without spurning or overlooking a single lyric, then amidst the motifs of decline and renunciation of life we encounter creative impulses, love of life, and a radiant acceptance of life. In Russian symbolist poetry there are "flowers of evil," but there are also Balmontian hymns to the Sun; there is the refined, intimate mysticism of Maeterlinck, but there is also a Pushkinian clarity and love for the earth. One need merely recall such lines of Bryusov's as:

> The years go by. But I am ready,
> Like a boy, to breathe
> My love with the inevitable power of fiery verse.
> As before, I childishly believe
> In the joy and truth of changing dreams.
>
> I only dreamed the past;
> Life's solution is ahead;
> The soul still wants to search,
> The heart quivers in the chest.

And again, from Bryusov:

> What a fate is destined for me—
> To be spent in noisy storms and quiet,
> But my spirit is whole, and the treasures
> Of my soul are not wasted.

But one should not overestimate these features of symbolist poetry either. Later we shall see that though there is indeed a wholeness in the symbolists' work, it is unquestionably the wholeness of "decay." Our symbolist poets frequently strive to overcome the decadent within themselves, but without success or hope of success. Yet, if the words of Georges Rodenbach,[8] "Art is a means of forgetting life," can fully be applied to the work of the French symbolists, with respect to Russian symbolism they can be accepted only with some reservation. The healthier atmosphere of Russian symbolism suggests the thought that it was created by social conditions not quite corresponding to those in Western Europe.

The characterization of symbolist poetry as exclusively urban raises no doubts whatsoever. The coutryside stands completely outside this poetry. True, in it one frequently encounters non-urban scenery and descriptions of nature, but to the symbolists nature is merely a pretext for purely lyrical and mystical utterances. The city has left its heavy mark on their poetry. But in precisely the same way as with nature, the life and struggle of the proletariat have remained utterly foreign to symbolist poetry. It originated in the bourgeois strata of society, and the entire cycle of its ideas and moods does not overstep the bounds established by its bourgeois origin... If the non-aristocratic intellectuals of the 1860s and 1870s characteristically aspired to tie their fate to the peasantry, the bourgeois intellectuals—for whom the way to the *muzhik* was psychologically closed, while their own class, the bourgeoisie, displayed the flabbiness and weakness of a dying order—had but one way out: to bury themselves in the realm of purely personal experiences and cultivate those feelings, moods, and ideas which develop in an environment of solitude and estrangement. Whereas the non-aristocratic intellectual characteristically aspired to merge with the life of the people, to dissolve in the sea of the populace, it is characteristic of the bourgeois intellectual to escape into himself and only there find that world in which it is possible to live. "I closed my eyes, and the world was inside me." Reality offers no interest; it cannot capture and fill the soul with its content, for everything in it is worthless, empty, and ugly. "I hate mankind and run swiftly from it; my only fatherland is my desert soul" (Balmont). "I do not see our reality, I do not know our age, I hate my native land, I love the ideal of man" (Bryusov)...

The theme of solitude is the fundamental motif of symbolist poetry. In all the experiences of the symbolist poets, we encounter, either directly or in reflected form, the fact of their estrangement not only from the life of groups, but also from the life of another individual, even their beloved. Solitude is by turns extolled as the delight and happiness of life—it alone remains to the man not wishing to mingle with the crowd—and cursed: he strains to break out of it, seeks salvation among people, in love for a woman, but in vain. He remains alone and alienated from all. A complex internal process begins in his soul—the adaptation of the whole psychological apparatus to the basic fact of solitude. In the novels of Dostoevsky we more than once encounter a depiction of the rebirth which is undergone by a solitary man who has escaped into himself. One need only recall Raskolnikov, Kirillov *(The Possessed),* and the hero of the tale "White Nights." All the forces of his soul recede deep into the individual; his surroundings interest him less and less, and he separates himself from life, as it were, with a translucent screen through which everything seems to him less real, phantomlike. The real world loses something in palpability and weight, and reality comes to resemble a dream; but, in exchange, the images engendered by the soul acquire the brilliance and force of actuality.

Dostoevsky demonstrates how such a solitary man is susceptible to all that is fantastic and wild, how it is easy for him, no longer feeling the fetters of life, to come to the most terrifying conclusions and to believe in their incontrovertibility. Thought does not come into conflict with life, is not regulated by it, and roams unchecked, feeling itself omnipotent. This loss of the sensation of the real to a greater or lesser degree pervades all of symbolist poetry. The unreality and illusoriness of human life is the main content of the work of several of its representatives. Sologub can serve as an outstanding example; for him, all of life is the fruit of his "I." He carries through his negation of life, his acknowledgement of it as an illusion, more consistently than all the rest. "There is no way of life nor are there any customs, there is only an eternal mystery being acted out. There are no plots or intrigues, and all beginnings have been long since begun and all denouements long since foretold.... What are all the words and dialogues?—A single, eternal dialogue with the questioner answering himself and thirsting for an answer. And what are the themes? Only love, only death. There are no different people, only one "I" in the whole universe, willing, acting, suffering... and saving itself from the savagery of a terrifying and hideous life in the embrace of the eternal consoler—Death" (Sologub).

In endless variations, reality is depicted now as a dream, indistinct and mysterious, now as a nightmare, terrible and wild, or gray and soiled. The boundary between dream and reality is effaced; the symbolist poets often dwell in some sort of novel, half-illusory, fantastic world, where fantasy and life are strangely and whimsically intertwined. Here is a lyric of Bryusov's which vividly depicts such a state:

> Each day and night I have roamed
> 　　in the country of my dreams;
> Like a sick moth, I have hung
> 　　on the stalks of flowers.
> Like a star on high, I have shined
> 　　and lay on a wave;
> This world of my dreams I have kissed
> 　　in a half-sleep.
> Now I roam all day, I roam
> 　　Like an invalid;
> All day, like a star on high,
> 　　I am apart from people.
> And in all that surounds,
> 　　in the light and in the dark,
> There is only dream, only dreams
> 　　without end appear.

Such a perception of life through the translucent shroud of dream and reverie lends a nuance of etherealness and incorporeality to the symbolists' pictures of nature; rather than pictures of reality these are diffuse dreams, vague reveries.

Left to themselves, the symbolists know only their own "I": this is the alpha and omega of their existence. The entire sphere of their sensations and moods is limited by the bounds of their "I"; for them it is difficult, nigh only impossible, to reconstruct the spiritual life of another person, since they do not like people at all and are not interested in them. Even when love for a woman is concerned they are infinitely more fascinated and carried away by their subjective experiences and the nuances of their feelings than by the soul of the beloved. Despite the fact that the symbolists devote much attention to love, they have rendered almost no clear female images. All the forms and nuances of love—from tender, half-childish infatuation to nearly bestial passion—have been described by these poets, but in all of these descriptions we see only their "I"; the images of the beloved women are indistinct, indefinite, and frequently lacking altogether.

But it would be a mistake to think that their work displays a striking enthusiasm for the individual, that they are preachers and apostles of individualism. This one cannot say. Their individualism loses a significant degree of its value because their personality is deprived of wholeness and unity: it is dissolved in the passing moment. Individualism is the proclamation of a powerful, whole, and harmonious personality; but a personality cannot become such if every instant swallows it whole and each moment is regarded as equivalent to any other. The individualism of the symbolists lacks energy. An individualism pervaded by a contemplative attitude toward everything inevitably leads to the idea of the equivalence of all moments and denies the necessity of sacrificing one moment for the sake of another. With the symbolist poets, the center of the personality vanishes and its disintegration draws near. The aspiration to engrave one's soul in the given moment is quite characteristic of the symbolists. "I put only the transitory into verse," says Balmont. There are such verses of his as:

> We are thrown into a fantastic world
> By some powerful hand.
> For a funeral meal? A battle? A feast?
> I do not know. I am always another.
> I am confused with every passing minute.
> I live only in betrayal.
> Not in vain am I incarnated here.
> And while awake—I sleep.

> We always change—
> Today "no," tomorrow "yes"—
> Today me, tomorrow you.
> All in the name of beauty.

In his early articles, which were supposed to constitute the *credo* of the new school, Bryusov even attempted to make the "moment" the cornerstone of its creative work. "And it is not man who is the measure of things, but the moment," he pronounced, amending the celebrated dictum of Protagoras. Of course, such assertions cannot be taken entirely seriously—this is impossible psychologically—but the tendency to subdivide the personality pervades the symbolists' work to a considerable extent. In their theories and in certain poems individualism is carried to the absurd, to the point where the personality disintegrates. It is for this reason that these poets cannot be regarded as Nietzschean, although Nietzschean motifs are not uncommon in their verse. Nietzsche considers man as something which must be transcended; each man is but a bridge to the Superman. The ideal that Nietzsche thus places before man imparts strength and integrity to his individualism. Here we find not only the subordination of one moment to another, but the subordination of a whole life to a high ideal. Nothing like this is possible where the "moment" reigns over the personality and where an ideal of the personality is out of the question.

The declaration of the supremacy of the moment is the limit beyond which it is impossible to go, beyond which non-existence begins; here individualism abolishes itself. The dominion of the "moment" is the most graphic and significant expression of decadence. In reality, of course, it could not be expressed in poetry—this would have brought about the death of poetry as well. Such a harsh formulation of the subdivision of the personality as in fact exists in the symbolists' poetry was obviously intended by them as a challenge to realism and to tendentious art, which advanced the demand that art be subordinated to a particular idea. One senses a lone personality alienated from society throughout the work of the symbolists. Such a personality always has a propensity for purely aesthetic experiences, which by their very nature *are ineffectual yet fully accessible* even if the personality has totally withdrawn from life and people. The cult of pure beauty, art for art's sake—these principles lie at the very basis of symbolist poetry.

Of the "eternal" triad of Good, Truth, and Beauty, the symbolist poets recognized only Beauty. They are indifferent to good and are sooner prepared to extol evil, since it has more of that poisonous, delicate beauty which entices the broken soul. Paeans to Evil are far from rare in the work of the symbolists:

> I am happy there is suffering on earth;
> I weave it into a fabulous pattern,
> And I make dreams out of others' fears.
> Deceit, madness, disgrace,
> Senseless horror—these are sweet to see.
> Dust and litter I twist into an ornate tempest.
> —Balmont

And again:

> I love my own debauchery.
> It is sweet to fall from grace,
> Insane blossoms live
> In the hollow gaps of recklessness.
> —Balmont

The symbolist poets are amoral and profoundly indifferent to the grief and joy of other people. This significantly narrows the scope of their creativity; they are psychologically unable to respond to everything, being solely preoccupied with their "I"—here they achieve genuine virtuosity in the description of all the subtleties of their own experiences. But their "I" is not an inexhaustible source, and symbolist poetry has, not without foundation, been reproached for the poverty of its content. Life in all of its manifestations is not reflected in the symbolists' work, and this makes symbolist poetry a poetry for the few.

The symbolist poets do not seek truth, because for them it has already been found: it is that which exists inside them, and inside them reign "moments"—today "yes," tomorrow "no." Truth and good are nothing special; they are closely bound up with mankind and they become fully tangible only through participation in human life, struggle, efforts, and downfalls. Outside of this context, truth and good are merely pale and bloodless concepts, utterly foreign and therefore unnecessary.

The spiritual order of the symbolist poets has been shattered once and for all. They are hopelessly bereft of inner harmony, and utterly lack simplicity and clarity. In complete accord with this is the fact that we never encounter laughter, humor, or irony in their work. It seems that these votaries of the beautiful never smile, so it is hard to believe in their sincerity when they extol the joy of life or the happiness of love. Everything bearing the stamp of sociability and interpersonal relations is alien to them. Laughter—that radiant god—appears only among people, in the crowd, amidst friends; by its very nature laughter is social and inaccessible to those solitaries who have withdrawn into themselves and renounced life. In the symbolist poets' most joyous hymns one senses a psychological breakdown, for instance in the hymns and invocations of Balmont. There is none of that redeeming clarity and radiance of spirit which infects us with love for life more strongly than the most multicolored and magnificent rhetoric. Behind the symbolists' invocations and hymns, insofar as these are to be found in their poetry, one senses the painful process of a struggle undergone with their own estrangement from life; although the struggle has ended in a sort of victory, the victor is left maimed forever. Not love for life but an impotent striving to fall in love with it—this is what one finds in their most radiant works.

Everything which is not their "I" touches the symbolist poets but little.

This explains the exclusively lyrical character of their poetry. It is the lyricism of a modern, devastated soul, the poetry of a solitary heart. Even if they undertake to write an epic, they prefer to select subjects from long-past eras; they withdraw, in Bryusov's expression, "into mysterious, bygone ages." Here there is greater scope for fantasy, here they are free in their quest after beauty; they are uninterested in the past destinies of humanity—its battles, victories, and defeats—but hope to find here glimmers of unusual beauty as yet unexperienced and unknown. They are drawn either by a thirst for novel aesthetic experiences, a craving which, in a person deprived of all other life, can take on extraordinary proportions and intensity. It is possible to create the beauty of the past even while remaining in one's "ivory tower"; for this, it is unnecssary to go among people. It is easier and far less disquieting to reproduce, from books and monuments, antiquity, the middle ages, and the era of minuets and powdered wigs than to plunge into actuality, where one inevitably will collide with living people and their sufferings, struggles, victories, and defeats. Not for nothing did Bryusov write at one point: "I do not see our reality, I do not know our age." This is quite true with respect to symbolist poetry as a whole.

But the more decisively the symbolists cut their ties with truth and good, the more strongly they bind themselves to beauty: it is as if their spiritual energy, liberated from the power of good and truth, is entirely spent in the quest and contemplation of beauty. Indeed, what remains for the bankrupt, solitary soul? Only the cult of beauty. In the symbolists' hymns to beauty, their idolization of it as a sort of superhuman, superterrestrial essence, their poignant impulses toward this absolute which they themselves have created, one can feel how irrevocably and hopelessly they have withdrawn from life and from living relations with people. On the other hand, it is clear that beauty is their only refuge, that it alone enables them to endure a life deprived—for them—of any other content.

> I know only the whims of my dream,
> All I give for the creation of joy
> And of the sumptuous inventions of beauty.
> —Balmont

Sundered from the communal life of people, they cling with all the strain of desperation to that which is left them. In their worship of beauty they are capable of such monstrous assertions as, for example, we find in the French symbolist Mallarmé: "The world exists to provide material for beautiful books." Bryusov expresses the same thought in the lines: "Perhaps everything in life is but a medium/For vivid and melodious verse."

The quest after beauty—this is the driving spirit of symbolist poetry. But how do the symbolists understand beauty? There are two distinctive elements in their conception of it: above all, the absolute character of beauty, beauty conceived metaphysically. For them beauty is an absolute concealed within the objects and phenomena of life and bearing the stamp of the beyond. As an absolute, beauty never lends itself to full elucidation, and this imparts a tragic character to the symbolists' quest after beauty. They are not averse to applying to themselves Baudelaire's verse about "the sphinx Beauty, against whose stone breast poets bruise themselves."[9]

We find a similar notion of beauty in Fet, Vladimir Solovyov, and also in Dostoevsky, in the utterances of his heroes (Prince Myshkin: "Beauty will save the world"). Connected with this absolute conception of beauty is the symbolist poets' exaltation of beauty above all else; in their work beauty truly is located "beyond good and evil." They view it as absolute and emancipated from good and truth. It would be possible to cite many corroborating examples; even Merezhkovsky, that failure as a symbolist poet, has exclaimed:

> We break all laws
> And cross all barriers
> For our new art.

In Bryusov and Balmont one frequently encounters a readiness to extol everything in view of the equivalence of everything from the perspective of beauty.

> I strangely loved the haze of contradictions,
> And greedily did seek fatal intrigues.
> All dreams are sweet, all speech is dear,
> To all the gods I dedicate my verse.
> —Bryusov

> I only know the whims of dream,
> And I'd yield all to happily erect
> The beauty of sumptuous inventions.
>
> . . . .
>
> The whitest flowers grow from slime.
> Blood's the reddest flower on the scaffold
> And death a lovely theme for painting.
> —Balmont

In order to set off the symbolist poets' conception of beauty more clearly, let us compare them to the old Russian poets. Russian literature from the time of Zhukovsky is full of beauty, but beauty was never the purpose of creative work; at least it was never understood as such. It appeared of its own accord when the poet created his images and pictures. We cannot at all imagine Pushkin, for example, writing a hymn to beauty, even though his work is saturated with it. Russian poets did not separate beauty from life; being fond of it, they depicted life with palpitating love, thereby revealing beauty as well. For them beauty merged organically with life, and love of beauty for them was love of life. One must stand completely outside of life in order to extract one element from the living whole, elevate it into an abstract principle, and make all of poetry serve this abstraction.

The often one-sided aspiration to find beauty everywhere sometimes leads the symbolist poets to a complete poverty of inner content. A great many of their lyrics are bereft of all meaning, and a serious attitude to them is unthinkable. They frequently lose all sense of proportion and in their urge to transform the world aesthetically they incline to empty mannerism. It turns out that it is not possible to put *every* "transient moment" into verse. Carried away by the purely external beauty of the verse, by the richness of the rhyme, by the music of consonances, the symbolist poets repeatedly destroy the harmony of content and form, most often in the sense that their content is much poorer than the form in which it is invested; this gives many of their verses the character of beautiful trinkets. Richness of form—this, it seems, is the generally acknowledged merit of symbolist poetry. The symbolist poets not only further developed the old forms of Russian versification, they also created much that was new in this area. Perfecting the old and creating the new, they acted in full accord with the content of their poetry; the new content required the perfection of old forms and the creation of new ones. The exceptionally lyrical character of their poetry, its extreme subjectivism, demanded a greater variety of forms to reproduce the slightest nuances of a refined soul; the poetry of vague moods and sensations required a greater musicality of verse. A certain abstractness and elusiveness of words were necessary because the symbolist poets were attempting to convey the feeling of their own "contact with other worlds," their insight into "that world where prototypes seethe," for which purpose a clear-cut and highly colored language was unsuitable.

The variety of meters and the wealth of rhythms are striking—one need only leaf through the lyrics of Balmont and Bryusov. Almost every one of their poems is written in its own meter. The symbolists were the first among the Russian poets to pay particular attention to the correspondence of the meter and the form of poetry to its content. Frequently a single poem is written in several meters because of a change in content or a shift in emotional coloration. As an example of the successful switching of meters in a single lyric, one may point to Bryusov's "Temptation."

Poetry may approximate to painting, to sculpture, or to music. The predominance in his poetry of one of these elements should not be accidental in the case of a real artist. Poetry approximates to painting in the work of the so-called landscape poets; for example, the French Parnassians[11] or the Russian poet Bunin: here distinctness of contour and vividness of color are important. In such poems there is little lyricism; in any case, the picture, the image—and not the striving to pour out one's soul—comes first. In contrast, the richer the emotional content of poetry, the more natural it is that it approach music—the ideal art of the emotions. Among the Russian symbolists one encounters in profusion verse painting and verse music—more of the latter, on account of the lyricism of this poetry. Landscapes without lyrical coloration are almost non-existent in their work. As an example of a poem where music is clearly felt and painting is almost completely absent—so indistinct and uncolored is it— one can cite Balmont's poem "Chords":

> In the beauty of melody,
>   As on a still, mirror-like surface,
> I discovered the outlines of dreams
>   Untold by anyone before me,
>   Pining and confined
> Like plants under blocks of ice.

> I gave them the power to delight,
>   I gave beauty to their birth,
> I shattered the ringing blocks of ice;
>   And, like soundless hymns,
>   Luxuriant lotuses breathe
> Above the expanse of the mirror-like water.

> And in the soundless melody,
>   On this new mirror-like surface,
> Their live round dance generates a new world,
>   Not yet fully revealed,
>   But linked to the known world
> In the depth of reflecting waters.

The musicality of the verse is achieved by means of the meter, rhythm and abundance of open vowel sounds. The symbolist poets often success-fully use alliteration, internal rhyme, and other similar devices. Here is an example of a felicitous combination of sibilants which corresponds perfectly to the mood being created:

> Ranniaia osen' liubvi umiraiushchei,
> Taino liubliu zolotye tsveta.
> Oseni rannei liubvi umiraiushchei,
> Vetvi prozrachny, alleia pusta,
> V sini bledneiushchei, veiushchei, taiushchei,
> Strannaia tish', krasota, chistota.
>   Bryusov*

---

* A translation of the poem into English would render both the poem and Gurev's point meaningless, and so I have left it in its original Russian. — S. R.

The numerous new word formations of symbolist poetry, many of which have already obtained citizenship, are directly connected with the fact that symbolist poetry aspires to "contact with other worlds." Symbolist poetry has been succinctly defined as the poetry of allusions. Reality is important for its apertures into another, concealed world—thus think the symbolists. A difficult task arises: to communicate their insights, their sensations of this other world, which, of course, they do not see, do not hear, but only vaguely feel. Hence the symbolists' complaints about the poverty of human language. Even Tyutchev had raised the question: "How can the heart express itself, how can another understand you?" and came to the hopeless conclusion that "a thought expressed is a lie." The matter seemed hopeless to Fet as well, who exclaimed, "O, if only it were possible to express oneself without words!" In order to create an "allusion" to something unearthly, a language of nuances and a certain abstractness is necessary, since this "something" is completely abstract. Thus, a distinct, definite, and highly colored language was inadequate for the symbolists. Hence, for example, arises the need for so-called "Balmontisms"—i.e., words ending in *—ness (—ost')*, e.g., *mirrorlikeness (zerkal'nost')*, *verblessness (bezglagol'nost')*, *caressingness (laskatel'nost')*, and so on.

Suffice it to compare the old poetical expression "the mirror of the waters" and the new "mirrorlikeness of the waters." Indisputably, the first image is more concrete and, so to speak, more earthy than the latter, and this springs from the fact that the ending *—ness (—ost')* is the ending of words which express abstract concepts. The Russian symbolists were the first to undertake a detailed study of Russian verse; one need only mention the scrupulous investigation of the iamb as used by Russian poets in Bely's book *Symbolism*. If we believe in the coming flowering of Russian poetry—when it will return again to externally youthful life and scoop up as much as it can hold of life's inexhaustible wealth—then all of these perfected and novel modes of expression will be grasped and still further developed by it. In this alone, symbolist poetry is a major epoch in the history of Russian verse.

Symbolist poetry is closely allied to metaphysical, mystical, and religious strivings. No other trend in poetry is so firmly and necessarily bound to philosophy. Such a solid bond exists neither in realism nor in romanticism, although it is quite possible for a realist artist to be a metaphysician in the sphere of philosophy or a religious seeker. Such, for example, was Tolstoy, but he was not prevented from being a realist by his fascination with Schopenhauer, Buddhism, or Christianity. He was a realist by disposition and no metaphysical systems could compel him seriously to doubt the realness of human life. But we cannot imagine the opposite: that a symbolist poet could be an adherent of positivism and the enemy of mysticism, religiosity, and metaphysics. This is quite understandable because symbolist poetry is based on pure metaphysics, on the assumption of the existence of two worlds; without "contact with other worlds" there can be no symbolist poetry. For the realist artist this world is too vivid and alive, it troubles and attracts him too much for there to arise in him the need to peer into "the secret crucible in which the prototypes seethe" (Fet). The realist is vitally bound to life and to people; the idea of the illusoriness of this world psychologically cannot arise in his consciousness. Only the weakening of this vital bond creates the basis for the emergence of the idea of the world's unreality and of the possibility of another, more real world. Two different attitudes come into play here: the realist senses all the reality of life; to the symbolist life seems illusory—there are less durable ties between him and life. We can quite agree with Balmont, who in his collection *Mountain Heights* says: "The realists are caught, as in breakers, in concrete life, beyond which they see nothing; the symbolists, estranged from actual reality, see in it only their dream, they look at life—out of a window...The one is still enslaved by matter, the other has escaped into the sphere of ideality."[12] One can agree with this, with the reservation that the realists see nothing beyond real life, because beyond it there *is* nothing. It is characteristic that all the most prominent Russian symbolists have also operated as the theorists of a new poetry. There even exists the opinion that they have operated and continue to operate more as theorists than as poets. "Among the leaders of Russian symbolism there are more theoreticians of what is new in the literary movement than creators. They display infinitely greater awareness that a new word is needed than strength to say this new word" (Gornfeld, *Books and People*).[13] In any case, they theorize zealously. And it is here—their creative work aside—that it becomes clear how firmly they have bound their creativity up with metaphysics, mysticism, and religion. This is not peculiar to Russian symbolism; it was so with Edgar Allan Poe and the French symbolists. Let us examine how the symbolists define poetry. One of the fathers of symbolism, Poe, says: "The origins of poetry lie in the cravings for a more insane beauty than that which the Earth can give us."[14] Baudelaire, in his noted poem, "Correspondences," regards all of nature as an array of symbols speaking to us of the world beyond. The Russian symbolists speak even more clearly, defining works of symbolism on the basis of the metaphysical systems of the philosophy of Kant and various others. According to the Russian symbolist poet and theoretician Vyacheslav Ivanov, the chief mark of symbolist art is the "consciously expressed parallelism of the phenomenal and the noumenal; the harmoniously discovered consonance of that which art depicts as external reality *(realia)* and that which it discerns in the external to be an internal, higher reality *(realiora)*." The slogan of symbolism is *"a realibus ad realiora,"* i.e., a summons from the real to something still more real which alone expresses the essence of all that exists (V. Ivanov, *Among the Stars*). Andrey Bely proceeds from neo-Kantianism in raising the edifice of symbolism (Bely,

Symbolism). Ellis asserts that the basis of symbolist art is Schopenhauer's philosophy of contemplation (Ellis, *The Russian Symbolists*[15]).

In exactly the same way almost all of the symbolist poets are involved in religious quests. And again, this is a phenomenon common to symbolist poetry everywhere. The mother country of symbolism, France, is full of such examples: Baudelaire, Verlaine—who was accorded the honor of having his later poems printed in the journals of the Catholic church—Huysmans, who ultimately became a Trappist monk. One might also note the quiet emotion aroused in Georges Rodenbach by Catholic old Bruges. And we have seen how earnestly the poets of the new school participated in the recent phase of "God-seeking" in Russia.

Almost all of the symbolist poets also lay claim to mysticism and see in mystical insight the highest form of knowledge (Bryusov). But certain writers, evidently considering themselves mystics *par excellence,* deny that the decadents have the capability for mystical experiences and find theirs to be refined, yet purely empirical. This is how Berdyaev looks on the Russian decadents (*Russian Thought,* 1907). He recognizes as mystics only Tyutchev and Vladimir Solovyov. This is not so important in our view, the mysticism of Berdyaev, Tyutchev, and Solovyov being nothing other than refined, yet purely empirical experiences; but it is characteristic of the confusion of concepts which is connected with mysticism. What is important is that the symbolists feel a need for experiences of this kind; what is important is their aspiration to peer "from time into eternity."

Be that as it may, symbolism aspires to be an integral *Weltan-schauung,* not limiting itself to the sphere of purely artistic problems, and one cannot deny the consistency and wholeness of this world view. Metaphysics and symbolism can provide a logically complete world outlook, the *theoretical* basis of which is the bifurcation of reality (the phenomenal world and the noumenal world) and the *practical,* the escape from reality into the sphere of Dream. Such a world view certainly cannot be regarded merely as the affair of this or that poet or philosopher; it becomes the common world outlook—of course, in different variations and with different nuances—of the cultural representatives of definite social classes, the ideology of the declining bourgeoisie. We see that everywhere symbolism as a literary trend has brought to the fore first-class artists of the word; parallel to this we observe a ubiquitous inclination toward the realm of metaphysics and religious inquiry. Obviously, to this tendency toward symbolism and metaphysics corresponds a general psychological change in certain classes. We have already noted the psychological basis of both symbolism and metaphysics—escape from collective life into the realm of purely individual experiences, profound and protracted inner solitude, and absence of living ties with the life, work, and struggle of the collective.

The symbolist poet, as a psychological type, is to a certain extent an extraordinary phenomenon in the history of mankind. Of course, from the midst of social groups doomed to extinction as well as from the midst of déclassé elements, there have always emerged poets and writers who have evolved similar themes and forms related to symbolism; but their experiences and feelings have heretofore lacked such acuteness and tension. Modern life is full of such lacerating discordances and is notable for such a furious rate of development that all experiences naturally are exacerbated. All of this has affected symbolist poetry as well. The close union of symbolism and metaphysics points to the profound crisis in the consciousness of the bourgeois cultural representatives and transcenders: what we behold is their capitulation in the face of life.

What, then, are the conclusions to be drawn?

Symbolist poetry has two fundamental insufficiencies. The first is its narrow scope: a vast side of life remains completely outside this poetry. The symbolist poets have little love for life and know it but little. They dwell outside life, and the rays of their poetry illuminate only the tiny world of their own "I." . . .

In their work there is precious little of "life." Can one say, perhaps, that their "I" is so completely reflected in their work and that this "I" is so rich that the symbolist's ignorance of life and indifference to it is thereby completely redeemed? Yes, their "I" and that alone is present in their work, but, knowning their attitude toward life, one may guess in advance that it cannot offer any particular riches. Of what sort is the content of their "I"? Solitude, its joys and torments; love for woman; nature, permeated by their lyricism; a vague but ardent aspiration to escape into a realm of dream and forget real life. The symbolist poets demonstrate by their own example how the human "I" narrows in proportion as its vital ties with life and with people are cut. Even love ceases to be a relationship between two beings; even the beloved woman is for the symbolists but a shadow, but a means to experience a series of instants of their own "I." It is no wonder that after all of the content that his "I" is psychologically capable of has been drained, after experiencing a love which does not give happiness, finding itself in a state of indifference to life, the symbolist poet's soul pours forth hopeless and gloomy sounds:

> A great disgust for others and myself
> Grows powerfully within and rules my fate.
> I'd love but can't; not seeking, there's nothing to expect,
> And all my dreams are false, and all desires—lies.
> Should truth reveal or not reveal itself to us,
> Should I succeed to live to ripe old age,
> Should you, of whom I always think, show me your love,
> Should I go off and wander or fail to live another day—
> It's all the same, it's all the same, if I go on at all,
> I've looked at life so long and sized it up.

I give myself to fate, just like a fallen leaf,
There's just disgust for others and myself.
                    —Bryusov

Herein lies the second major inadequacy of this poetry. The point is not that the symbolist poets are antisocial or apolitical, although indifference to the enormous social problems of our times cannot be counted as a virtue either. The important thing is that the path to experiences to which the symbolists beckon us in a fatal way grows even narrower and ultimately leads to a "great contempt both for people and oneself"—indeed, leads to the complete extinction of the human soul.

What, then, are the merits of this poetry? On what is its right to immortality based, and does it have such a right? Unquestionably it does and, unquestionably its best exponents have created much that is "eternal."

Russian symbolist poetry has its own cycle of ideas and feelings, its own content and its own style, first elaborated by the symbolist poets themselves. Consequently, we have before us a complete literary movement, which serves to express the ideology of certain social classes in a particular phase of their historical development. As such an ideology, symbolism has every right to our attention. Symbolism should also attract public interest because it is a general, European trend in poetry, and as such marks a characteristic and noteworthy evolution in the socio-economic relations of all the states having a European culture.

Symbolism, therefore, has all those rights to attention which belong to any genuine art expressing the ideology of a particular class.

But when the discussion turns to the merit of symbolist poetry, this can only be understood to mean the value of symbolism for the future culture of mankind, for the culture of the proletariat. Symbolism, as the poetry of the alienated man, is, of course, the diametrical opposite of future poetry, which will be thoroughly social and human. The poetry of weariness and renunication of life can have nothing in common with the poetry of life and struggle. It is hard to imagine that the ideas and moods of symbolist poetry could have a place in the poetry of the future. But its achievements in the area of form and style, carried out in an original way, must be incorporated into any poetry of the future no matter what form it takes. From the example of Verhaeren, we see what can be done by a poet of the popular masses and of social struggle who does not scorn all the achievements of symbolist poetry. In his work, Verhaeren provides us with a prototype of the future poetry of the masses, profound and all-embracing in content, expressive and vigorous in form. The poet of the future cannot be less sonorous than Balmont or less vigorous than Bryusov. While working out the forms of his works, he must pass through the school of symbolist poetry. Only under these conditions will the poetry of the future be able to master all the wealth of subject matter which history is preparing for it.

Notes

1. Fet, Afanasy Afanasievich (1820-1892). A major poet of the mid- to late-nineteenth century. His poetry was occasionally metaphysical in nature and celebrated nature, love, beauty, and dream. For this he was vilified by the radical critics, and it was only in the 1890s when his verse began to achieve the recognition it deserved.

2. Tyutchev, Fyodor Ivanovich (1803-1873). Russia's most important metaphysical poet whose work owes much to German romanticism with its emphasis on dualistic and pantheistic themes. Never very popular during his own lifetime, Tyutchev was rediscovered and revered by the symbolists who found in him a kindred spirit.

3. Solovyov, Vladimir Sergeevich (1853-1900). Philosopher, mystic, and poet. He inherited from Tyutchev the belief in a dualistic universe pervaded by a dark, threatening chaos. Much of his writing deals with the striving to seek unification in the Eternal Feminine of Sophia, the symbol of Divine Wisdom. His work significantly influenced Bely.

4. See note 8 in Nevedomsky.

5. Strakhov, Nikolai Nikolaevich (1828-1896). Russian critic, philosopher, and publicist of the mid/late nineteenth century. Like Fet, he was a conservative. He wrote on such major writers as Pushkin and Dostoevsky, but his best writing is a series of essays on *War and Peace,* the author of which became his close friend and frequent correspondent beginning in 1870.

6. See note 6 in Nevedomsky.

7. For an enlightening and comprehensive study of readership in late-nineteenth/early-twentieth-century Russia, see Jeffrey Brooks, "Readers and Reading at the End of the Tsarist Era," in William Todd (ed), *Literature and Society in Imperial Russia, 1880-1914* (Stanford, 1978).

8. Rodenbach, Georges (1855-1898). Belgian writer and one of the leading exponents of European decadence.

9. Although Gurev uses quotation marks, he is actually paraphrasing Baudelaire's "La Beauté."

10. Zhukovsky, Vasily Andreevich (1783-1852). An important poet before Pushkin and one of the best translators in Russian literature.

11. The Parnassians were a group of poets originating in France who stressed technical perfection and aesthetics as such ("l'art pour l'art") as opposed to social responsibility and duty, which was advocated by the civic poets. Among the major representatives of this group (which derived its name from the Greek mountain Parnassos—considered holy in ancient times), were Leconte de Lisle and the young Mallarmé and Verlaine in France, and Fet, Apollon Maykov, and Yakov Polonsky in Russia.

12. Balmont undoubtedly has in mind here Mallarmé's important programmatic poem "Les Fenêtres."

13. *Books and People* (*Knigi i lyudi,* 1908) is a collection of Gornfeld's essays on practically all of the leading literary figures of early twentieth-century Russia.

14. As in the case of Gurev's quoting of Baudelaire, this line from Poe is actually a paraphrase (and not an entirely accurate one) of a passage from Poe's essay "The Poetic Principle."

15. Ellis (pseudonym of Lev Lvovich Kobylinsky, 1879-1947). Russian poet, critic, and theoretician of symbolism.

6

Estranged: Toward a Pyschology of Sologub's Work

A. S. Dolinin (1883-1968)

A. S. Dolinin (pseudonym of Arkady Semyonovich Iskoz) is regarded as a distinguished scholar and critic, known particularly for his work on Dostoevsky. A graduate of Petersburg University, he lived in that city (now Leningrad) most of his life where, before the Revolution, he was a member of the famous Pushkin Seminar, directed by Professor A. S. Vengerov. Dolinin began his career as a critic of contemporary literature, writing on such authors as Remizov, Merezhkovsky, and Boris Zaitsev. His article on Sologub belongs to this period. After 1917 Dolinin turned his attention to nineteenth-century Russian prose, examining works by Pushkin, Belinsky, Herzen, Gogol, Turgenev, and Chekhov. But his most lasting contribution to literary scholarship is unquestionably his very fine work on Dostoevsky, whom he spent almost fifty years studying. Besides writing numerous articles and books on almost every facet of Dostoevsky's life and works— particularly on his novels, Dolinin served as editor of the monumental four-volume collection of Dostoevsky's letters, published between 1929 and 1959. His critical methodology tends to stress the psychological and biographical elements of the literary persona, examining the importance of these elements in the literary creation. His piece on Sologub is typical of this approach.

Estranged: Toward a Pyschology of Sologub's Work*

> "It is his fate to remain unrecognized—
> not *to act* or *to live,* but only *to see.*"

> "With all the words he can find he speaks
> about one and the same thing. His summons is
> always the same."

I.

Belinsky[1] instructed that when entering the creative realm of an artist we are supposed to forget him, ourselves, and everything else in the world; we are supposed to leave behind all demands, prejudices, questions, dispositions, and, even more so, all predispositions, conceptions, and preconceptions. This holds all the more true in the case of Sologub. No one is easier to repudiate than Sologub; no one shuts himself and his world off from us with a more impenetrable wall. There are hardly any tried-and-true well-beaten paths which would allow us to enter the soul of this writer. Nor do Russian literary tradition or present trends provide much assistance. For Sologub is outside of all schools and traditions; he does not fit into any established and customary framework. He is an exceptional artist in the highest sense: solitary, narrowly focused, and constantly following his own road. He "does not live, does not act" with and among us; he is able "only to see" himself, his inner world and nothing more. He is complete in himself, like a circle; he confines his creative material exclusively to his own persona and finds his laws solely within himself. All of his creations—even *The Petty Demon*—are projections of his individual "I," statements about his own soul, which knows its past and conjectures about its future, but which never lives in the present, and which always resides somewhere outside of immediate reality, outside of this world—in the literal sense of the word. In this respect Sologub is, of all writers, the *most estranged* from life, more so and more profoundly than anyone who has broken with the "objects of the objective world."

I say "the *most* estranged" because every artist must possess this quality to a certain degree, every artist must be able to look at life in a somewhat "detached" fashion . . . But whereas this estrangement always manifests itself purely spontaneously in every other artist, apart from his will and consciousness, in what I would say is a certain innate ability, quite independent of him, to see, hear, think, and feel in a positive way, in Sologub it is complicated by his *conscious* detachment from life, his conscious withdrawal from it. He was the first to *realize* his estrangement,

* "Otreshennyi—K psikhologii tvorchestva Fedora Sologuba"—published in *Zavety,* 1913, No. 7, pp. 55-85.

as it were, the first to perceive its necessity and to come to love it fully and tenderly, to raise it to a principle, to its apotheosis. And he not only became estranged, but also *actively renounced* and deliberately rejected his place in life. Cursing at the outset all of life's boundlessly rich colors, lines, and forms, as well as all of its constantly changing "guises and masks,"[2] Sologub recognizes only one compulsory law for himself, a kind of categorical imperative: "not to act," not to live with and among us, always to move in reverse motion, toward himself, toward the center, toward the "I." Life in its bustle demands that we exert all of our emotional energy toward utilitarian purposes, it forces us to perceive only what is bound up with our own actions and behavior, and thus conceals the world's true image. Therefore, down with life and its diurnal behests; let night and twilight reign with their mysterious specters and dreams—night, when man's "active" will, which is always directed outward, subsides together with life, when the voices of the subconscious become audible and the visions of hoary chaos are more perceptible. This is the leitmotif of Sologub's work; this is the "intimate become universal"[3] in him; these are the "direct" commands which he addresses to us.

However, the catalyst here is not consciousness alone, no matter how strong it is in Sologub. His is not the kind of estrangement which is the product of reflection and philosophy. Rather it seems more likely that the starting point is a peculiar *type of will*—it can exist even in simple mortals—which I would call *centripetal*. People who possess it *organically* shun life and reality; they are doomed to inertia *from the start*. They lack what is called *dynamism;* they lack our usual urge to move, work, build, destroy—in a word, to enter into any kind of contact with the surrounding world. Their external appearance is usually morose, intense, or coldly indifferent. Nothing and no one outside of them is interesting to them— they are always occupied with themselves and their own experiences. This is not the same as egocentricity. The latter in no way excludes customary manifestations of self in life and among other people—it merely presupposes the advancement of *the self* to the forefront, as well as an ever-present sense of the exclusiveness of *one's I and its primacy* over the environment. But what I have in mind here is an almost total absence of any kind of interest in surrounding life. People of this sort simply do not see or notice life. They are ordinarily taken for weak-willed; in point of fact, their will can be quite strong, only it does not manifest itself in the usual fashion, the way ours does. It manifests itself *negatively* in estranging these people from their surroundings, and *positively* in *powerfully* and *intensely* directing their intellect toward the only place left for it to go: the realm of the inner world.

By the nature of his will, Sologub quite closely approximates this type of person. His will is also *internally* focused; it does not extend outside the limits of the circle he has drawn for it, does not extend beyond the boundaries of his own soul, and spends itself entirely within him as it were. It is largely consumed in the intensive workings of his consciousness, in the constant pressure of his intellect upon his emotions, in the continual struggle between his victorious reason and vanquished feelings. (Not for nothing is he so conscious, so rationalistic, one feels like adding.) It must be said here that nature has lifted only one part of her veil before him, namely that part which separates us from our own selves, which screens the depths of our soul from our consciousness. On the other hand, she has kept closed perhaps even more tightly its other part, which lies between us and surrounding life. Sologub can feel and think in a pristine way only about himself and his internal experiences, but can neither see nor hear what is going on in the outside world.

To think; to subject to the incessant analysis of his consciousness every one of his emotional impulses, every one of *his*—but not others'—feelings; to place through the agency of his internally focused will these emotions at a certain distance from himself and, almost objectivizing them constantly to constrict the powerful flow of raging passions, the stormy, primeval instincts in his intense world; always to attempt to elevate the incidental to the general; to seek behind the anecdotal (or, as he expresses it, behind the drunk Aisa the reflection of the goddess Ananke's[4] Image)—in short, to perform a cold, impartial, almost scientific experiment upon his own soul—these aspects of his singular psychic make-up are what constitute Sologub's peculiarity as a writer. Indeed, he encases his internally raging world in a firm, thick shell, and the words and images which describe this world are extremely precise. As we have said, only an artist with a strong, internally focused will can create in this manner; it is this will which determines the character and degree of his consciousness.

As proof of this, we need only consider his style. I shall first speak in general terms. Are we not struck by its monotony, by its unusually severe finish, and by what I would say is its rather deliberate coldness? Do we not occasionally get the impression that life is not being depicted, but rather something is being proved or, more exactly, recorded, strictly logically? This is indeed the case. Take nearly any of his works—whether it be a novel, a story, a drama, or even a poem—and compare the content, which is so rich in powerful emotions, with the form in which it is embodied, and you will become immediately convinced of this. The author seems to be striving not so much to elicit reciprocal emotions in us (he must therefore be sure that they will be present), but to constrain them, to subdue our excitement and our feelings of anger or disappointment, of love or joy. He wants us to be calm, and to a certain degree he achieves his goal. His reader is always a bit restrained, as if the subject concerned, and yet didn't concern, him, as if it touched upon something very close to him, yet for some reason was also far removed from him. Of course, Sologub knows how to interest us in his people and events, and our attention is riveted to them, yet somehow we do

not participate in these events ourselves. This is not because his heroes live
a life which is alien to ours. No, in point of fact Sologub knows how to
make "the intimate become universal." The reason seems to lie in the
following: he wants the same thing from us as he wants from himself, he
wants us to follow his path, to practice—although to a lesser degree—his
method of objectification, to place ourselves at a certain distance from the
feelings he arouses in us—in short, he wants our reactions to be not so
much emotional as intellectual in nature. And we really do brood over his
work quite a bit. I am sorry to say that we think more than we feel, we
deliberate (and at times censure, although less than critics say we do) more
than we experience. In this sense, in the goals he sets himself and the reader,
and in his supreme awareness, Sologub has something of Tolstoy in him.
Like him, Sologub long nurtures one or another image or motif in his soul;
he, too, gives them time and opportunity to mature and cool before
presenting them to us always in a finished, polished form. This is the
general character of his style whose uniqueness is rooted in these two
distinctive features of his emotional make-up: his peculiar type of will,
internally directed (and externally *inactive*) and, tied to it, his *consciousness,* his rationalism, his unending and tireless urge to explain and, by the
power of reason, to illuminate that elemental and chaotic component
which reaches him from the sphere of his subconscious...

II.

Lyric poetry is an ardent confession. Though it may seem fleeting, it
contains the truest indicators of the poet's path. All its seemingly
momentary and fortuitous elements are merely multi-colored sparks from
one and the same fiery source, glowing links of one chain. Powerfully
affecting us with its images and its music, lyric poetry forces us to respond
with corresponding sounds, to be aroused by reciprocal emotions.

But Sologub's lyrics lack both fire and fiery brilliance. His burning
core, his *cor ardens,*[5] is too deeply concealed. And his melodiousness is
strangely morose. It is like a knell-tolling in a quiet valley at evening time,
monotone and doleful. Its tranquil tone and languid rhythm are designed
for the finest ear, the ear which can hear silence. There is precious little
movement, there are few traces of life and of man in his lyric poetry. It is but
feebly warmed by the light of day, rarely illumined by its fair rays. One sees
no supplely sculptured lines and figures here. In the gloom and haze one
barely distinguishes vague silhouettes of people and objects whose inward
gaze scarcely touches one. Bewitched by the quiet charms of the night or the
melancholy twilight, it loves continuity, it loves uniform valleys bathed in
the even, dead radiance of the long-dead moon.

The moon and sun, dream and reality, stasis and movement, silence
and sonorousness—these are Sologub's usual poles, and between them

there are no intermediate stages, no transitional modulations. This
opposition is also expressed by night and day, black light and "white
darkness," desirable death and evil, unnecessary life. To the first he devotes
all of his attention, all of his tenderness and love; about the second he
speaks much more rarely and always with near malice. Two antithetical
poles—two parts, far from equal either in quantity or quality. In one, the
larger, he appears whole, with his agitated soul, morbid pathos, sad
thoughts and tragic doubts; in the other, the smaller, he appears as if in
passing, merely to say why he is so gloomy and nocturnal, why he bears so
much malice toward our bright sun.

He hates the sun because *it* is the cause of life and movement on earth,
the cause of "evil, earthly languor and evil, earthly life." The sun "has
created the forever indissoluble barrier of deceiving white mist, has
concealed from our weak eyes what is dear and sweet to the heart"; it has
nurtured our earthly sensibility, "bringing down perfidious dreams and
deceptions to this mad and terrible earth." It is hateful to him, like our
whole evil and tormenting existence. Salvation is to be found only in the
"lifeless haze," in the quiet night with the cold glimmer of its consoling
stars, with its "young, beautiful, hopelessly ailing and impassive moon."
With touching affection, similar to the tender adoration of a quiet boy for
his permanently departed "white mother,"[6] Sologub loves the night, the
stars, and the moon. He loves them precisely for their serenity and quiet,
for their incapacity to live. To them and only them he entrusts his entire
soul—his joy as well as his sadness, his bold, absurd fantasies as well as his
pure, serene dreams. Only under their charm is his soul pacified, and he can
begin to create his legends of unearthly dreams and visions—his secret
world (so unlike our usual human one), to which he tirelessly and
irresistibly summons us. These calls are quiet and doleful, born of the
stillness, but our ear continually detects them because they are emitted
amidst silence.

Sologub's favorite state is quietude and silence, which can be
understood only by contrast, as the absence of all signs of life, of all sound
and motion. Silence and quietude, against a background of night or
twilight, are the predominant motifs of Sologub's poetry.

But let us leave the general setting of his lyrics and turn to his
descriptive methods and language. One can and should always trust the
latter, since it *directly* renders the nature of the artist's perceptions and
directly indicates the sphere from which his colors are primarily drawn.
And here one is struck first and foremost by Sologub's external perceptions—by their scantiness and ordinariness. It is difficult to find
another artist of Sologub's stature who so poorly, so inadequately
perceives colors,[7] hues, and shadings, the contours, lines, and shapes of
objects, and any kind of movement or posture in space; in whom concrete
signs, the external details and nuances which make every object so

perceptible, clear and, I would say, apparent, are lacking to such an extent. His favorite colors are black and white (much more frequently black); only rarely does he notice blues, and other colors even less. But what is almost totally missing in him are transitional or *merging* colors—those fine shades which are perceived only by gazing fixedly at something. Night and the nocturnal, darkness and the dark, haze and the hazy, gloom and the gloomy, dark places and dark dwellings, dark clothing, dark fabrics, dark days, dark skies, dark dreams, and so on and so forth—these are his favorite words, his favorite combinations.

The same is true regarding Sologub's spatial and motor perceptions. He very rarely places an object on a plane or on a surface, thus affixing it to a definite place. His characters and objects almost always appear out of some kind of vague distance, emerge barely outlined out of the darkness or mist. One catches a glimpse of *someone's* traces, *somebody* passing by, *someone* withdrawing, *something* slipping away, etc., etc. A dark or moonlit night (but definitely a night); silence all around; distant expanses; someone's hardly perceptible traces; someone's barely audible whisper— this is Sologub's favorite, most prevalent picture. In full or in part, you will invariably find it on almost any page of his lyrics, with the exception, of course, of those cases where he is speaking exclusively about himself and his "dark cell." But what most frequently recurs is *silence* and all of its synonyms and derivations. Silence, peacefulness, quietude, taciturnity, blessed silence, profound silence, a quiet friend, a quiet song, a quiet world, quiet stars, a quiet dream, and so on and so forth.

Perhaps this vagueness and indivisibility of perceptions and impressions from without, which, it seems to me, stem from his *organic* inability to communicate with the external, surrounding world, also explain his love of abstract concepts and rigid substances, his frequent use of these lifeless symbols of living objects without either defining them in concrete terms or supplementing them with any epithets.

A possibly related characteristic is the rather significant amount of so-called negative attributes in Sologub, such as *un*-earthly, *un*-clear, *in*-comprehensible, *im*-perceptible, *in*-accessible, *never*-ending, *un*-solved, and so on. Removing a certain quality from an object or concept is not equivalent to defining it.

But on the other hand, he makes quite extensive and free use of descriptive methods of a so-called psychological or, more accurately, subjective nature, methods which are taken from the realm of his personal experiences. Thus, one occasionally feels that he comes to know even the external world not according to our usual externally objectified perceptions, but rather according to the *responses* and *emotions* which this world arouses in him. And one involuntarily wonders whether this is not the basis of his philosophy of *self-will*. Does not Sologub thus subjectivize the surrounding world, deeming himself its exclusive creator, because his

personal reactions, his *personal* feelings concerning objects and phenomena of the external world screen from him the very objects that engender
those emotions? To continue—these subjective descriptive methods are the
very foundation of Sologub's style. By their means he expresses all of his
terrible loneliness, his detachment and estrangement from "the evil, cruel
world," his stubborn unacceptance of life with its ordinary, and to him
insignificant, values; through them he creates his strange, secret world and
his fantastic legends which contain so many wild dreams and sick fantasies.
Read practically any one of his poems and you will immediately be
convinced of this, you will feel the gloomy will embodied in his poetry, a
will turned in on itself and tirelessly gravitating toward a center, the poet's
"I," his occasionally monstrously cruel and sinfully voluptuous, occasionally quiet and tender, sick and tormented soul. To be sure, there is a
certain monotony here, too: Sologub has a whole series of favorite words—
evil, cruel, mad, lonely, sick—which he constantly repeats (especially evil
and sick). But this monotony, which is often oppressive, stems largely from
the constancy of his mood, from the uniform direction of his intense
spiritual activity.

III.

Let us move on to Sologub's prose and drama. Unfortunately here as
well we are necessarily limited to a cursory analysis of only a few of his
works, although admittedly they are his best. Let us take first and foremost
his novels. In all of them—*Bad Dreams, The Petty Demon, A Legend in
Creation*—there is a striking sluggishness of pace, an extremely low
intensity of action. The canvas is enormous, the backdrop is vast, and
Sologub deals with a large number of people. However, what we call "life"
is greatly lacking. All of his characters are depicted rather one-dimen-
sionally (Sologub always likes to observe unity of place); only one side of
them is captured, as it were, one which is remarkably constant and virtually
unchanging. The explanation lies in Sologub's predilection for treating
only one aspect, only one emotional state of his hero; granted it may be his
most important characteristic, yet it is still the only one treated. Sologub
prefers—if I may apply these terms to psychological phenomena—the
static to the dynamic. It is not surprising that we get the impression that his
characters are somehow removed from spatial and temporal dimensions,
removed from any ties with their past, from their "old" life, from the crucial
moment they are presently living through. In this regard, if one were to
paraphrase Tolstoy's words about Shakespeare[8] and apply them to
Sologub, one could say: "In Sologub it is always this way. Somewhere, in
some place, stands a house; in the house some person is languishing—
sullen, immobile, focused on some one thought or experience. That is all."
And that is indeed the way it is. Let us take, for example, Login in *Bad*

Dreams. Here is how the author himself describes him on the very first page: "His nearsighted eyes look about absentmindedly; he does not intently scrutinize either people or objects. His face appears weary. His movements are slack, his voice dull. At times he gives the impression of a man who is thinking of something which he will not tell to anyone." It is evident from all of this that Login lives a predominantly introverted life. Of what does it consist? From the very first chapter we are privy to all of it. His soul is an arena where two elements struggle: the light and the dark, "the angelic and the demonic" or—what amounts to the same—the living and the dead. (Here the living still retains its normal status of a positive principle.) The dark element is his oppressive past which hangs over him—a past full of castings about and strivings, ups and downs (mainly downs), sinful passions and dissipation. Login has no strength to struggle; he is perishing: the "dark" principle is overwhelming him. But from time to time there appear in his reveries the trusting, pure eyes and the radiant, caressing smile of Niuta Yermolina, she who will subsequently become one of Sologub's frozen symbols, his "eternal bride," his Dulcinea.[9] She symbolizes the positive, bright principle in life and she prevents Login's ultimate destruction; in her he will find his salvation. Login vacillates between these two principles, languishing in his sick dreams. Now and then he dreams about "the impossible," about "a miracle," but he himself is unable to find a way out of his situation; his *will* remains constantly passive. We know all of this, I repeat, from the very beginning. But that is really all there is to Login: later very little is added to his characterization. There will be the same waverings, the same "bad dreams" and anguished nightmares, the same struggle with them, the same smiles and quiet gaze of Niuta Yermolina, the same passivity and inaction on Login's part. Thus, throughout the entire novel we are presented with a single emotional state in a man who by virtue of his emotional make-up is torn from life *organically,* who has gone through a lot that has affected him painfully, but it has concerned only him and he has kept it all to himself. Is Login really weak-willed? Apparently, yes. In life he is undoubtedly so. But he thinks a lot: like the author, he analyzes his every emotional impulse, he *objectifies* his experiences and, on the basis of these experiences, *and only them,* he constructs entire theories. In a word, he rationalizes. Thus, we can say of Login, too, that his will is *centripetal*—directed not outward, toward and among others, but inward, toward his "I"—and it essentially reinforces the workings of his reason and increases its intensity. I do not think that I am mistaken in saying that Login is a self-portrait of Sologub; at least that is the way Sologub appears to us in his lyrical works.

The same can be said about the novel's heroines. They, too, are always in the same emotional state; they, too, make no headway; seething within, they remain outwardly inactive. This is true as much for Klavdia Kulchitskaya as for the above-mentioned Yermolina. The former is seemingly caught up in a real-life struggle (over Poltusov, whom she and her mother both love). But she is only "seemingly" so. In point of fact there is practically no struggle at all: any real one is replaced by evil visions, dreams, and nightmares growing out of an already accomplished fact and by sick hallucinations in which reality (in the form of a living person, her mother, who appears to her at night) loses its concreteness, is reduced to a shadow, turns into an embodied phantom. Yermolina also has visions and brooding thoughts, but she never realizes these thoughts, nor does she experience living life, which requires animation, action, and a constant change of condition. Like Login, these two heroines live their detached life, detached not only from people, but from nature; and one can aptly apply the author's verse to them, "it is their fate not to live or to act, but only to see"—themselves, their own souls, other people or the life that surrounds them. The verse definitely applies to Yermolina no matter how much the author assures us that she loves and understands nature and lives in harmony with it. For in her as well, one does not feel a oneness with the cosmos, nor has she reconciled within herself "the world of coarse muslin and fine linen," even though "she walked about barefoot, like a genuine peasant girl, and was dressed like a real young lady" (see Sologub's article, "The Demons of Poets"[10]). Perhaps it is because she is supposed to symbolize the reconciliation of two principles (one of which, "the world of coarse muslin," is alien to Sologub) that she is the weakest, one wants to say the most colorless, figure in the novel. If there are some successful touches in her characterization, then they occur only in those places where she, too, becomes absorbed in herself, retreats inward, dreams, and fantasizes. It is precisely because all of these characters live an internal, inwardly focused existence, with very faint outward manifestations that the novel is so lacking in the dramatic, that the threads which connect the main characters and the clashes between them are so weak—so much so that at times the reader has the impression that he is dealing not with a unified novel, but rather with a series of separate episodes, each of which is highly significant and interesting but has very little intrinsic connection with the others. Nor does the abundance of little snatches of life—the drinking bouts, the picnics, the balls, the evening get-togethers, and so on—dispel this impression: they do add variety and a certain animation to the novel, but hardly change its general character.

Already in this first novel of his, Sologub showed himself to be a great and exceptional talent. He was a mature, accomplished artist endowed with *innate* virtues and shortcomings. His analysis is extremely sharp and refined; but he is a writer of depth and not of breadth; he investigates internal rather than external life, rich in content, but not in action. He is privy to the world of passions and blind instincts, the realm of hoary chaos. But he depicts this world not in its external manifestation, as it is reflected in life and among people (except insofar as he can't get along without these externals), but rather in its internal cloistered seething. The inner rather than the outer world, the world of phantoms rather than of reality, the world of sick or inner-directed people who have withdrawn from life or who have never embraced it—this is his sphere, his element, his inspiration. For in all of them Sologub has depicted himself, himself alone, and all of his images are merely temporary objectifications of his one Persona in the process of formation.

Let us move on now to *The Petty Demon*. This novel is also extremely typical of Sologub. In it, in the figure of Peredonov, Sologub has once again objectified himself, presenting us with an analysis which, although it deals only with one side of his soul, is truthful to the highest degree; indeed it is almost merciless. As for the tempo here it is even more sluggish than in *Bad Dreams*. Whereas in the latter the other figures besides Login are connected to some extent with the basic plot, and the inserted episodes in that novel at least do not contradict the basic tone and in a sense even clarify the book's overall setting, in *The Petty Demon*, Sologub focuses almost exclusively on the central figure of Peredonov, being preoccupied chiefly with him, his fate, and his experiences. Here the simultaneously repulsive and tragic image of the "petty demon" looms over everything— the gray, terrifying Nedotykomka is constantly bustling about. Small wonder that the episode between the schoolboy Sasha and Liudmila Rutilova does not fit into the general framework of the novel, or that it contrasts with the main plot, standing out from it in bold relief as a kind of antithesis, or perhaps—as one critic believes[11]—a kind of escape from the world of Peredonovshchina. Of course, such focusing is a plus for the novel in terms of unity, but this results in even less life and movement and more of Sologub's specific kind of inward concentration. The latter is all the more curious in that Peredonov himself seems to be totally a part of our ordinary coarse reality and to be striving with all his might to affirm himself in it. But the point is that one senses *not his tie to* life, but rather his complete separation from it, his vague, unconscious terror of life in its entirety. His whole environment, not just people but all of nature, the entire world, is hostile to him and wants to destroy him. The gray *nedotykomka* is certainly not a symbol of philistinism; if it were, then why would Peredonov be so frightened of it? Or are we really supposed to see Peredonov as someone who does not accept our philistine life? No! The gray *nedotykomka*, the image which torments and persecutes Peredonov the most, is a symbol of the whole of life which so horrifies him, a delirious notion which embodies his *central* idea (actually a distorted form of Sologub's own idea) that everyone and everything is mocking and trying to ensnare him. Does this perception really differ radically from the attitude (but of course not the world view) of Sologub himself, and what we shall later find to be one of his most characteristic antitheses—the world and I? I think not. We need only imagine the same spiritual chaos, the same psychological make-up which we know of in Sologub from his lyrics and his first novel (minus, of course, his extreme awareness) and then picture them in a distorted form, in caricature—and we come up with the image of Peredonov.

He has an indifferent, somnolent face; he is indecisive, *passive,* silently morose, and his responses are lifeless and dull. This is the way Peredonov is characterized from the very beginning of the novel. We immediately learn about his fears, about his total estrangement from life and the world, about his desire to assert himself as strongly as possible because everyone and everything persecutes him. As in *Bad Dreams,* we have before us an emotional entity which is immediately defined, which neither moves nor changes, and, once presented, always manifests itself in the same manner. Should someone or something strike a certain chord of this perturbed soul, it will immediately give forth a corresponding sound; strike another chord—and the sound will be virtually the same. Once again, we are presented not with a *genuine* sequence of events, as occurs in our lives, but merely with a *formal* or forced one, insofar as we unavoidably place everything in spatial and temporal order. Peredonov's soul appears to us not as an *organic* chain whose links are all directly connected to one another—each flowing from another—but as a whole series of threads originating from the same knot, from one central idea, from one central feature.

A Legend in Creation is not much different in this regard, and I shall touch upon it only briefly, to the extent that it serves as proof of my basic idea. Two worlds are juxtaposed within it: Trirodov's invented world and our customary, human one. The former is created by the active will of man-the-creator, a man who knows only the commands of his "I." But the ways of this will are a mystery to us, they are the reverse of ours: it is not engulfed by its surroundings but, on the contrary, engulfs them. Like tentacles extending in all directions, it seizes as much living matter as possible, but it does so rather strangely, apparently not intending to create vital new forms from it. No kind of life exists in Trirodov's world of legend. In it there is only a strange silence, an unearthly calm, an almost absolute, sepulchral calm. A high, insurmountable wall separates it from man and the world; behind this wall are lifeless objects and creatures; deathly-peaceful lakes, tormenting and tormented plants, quiet children, ghostly paths. Over all this reigns Trirodov himself, about whom we know the following: he rarely and unwillingly deals with others, he prefers solitude and silence, melancholy is his customary state, he lives in dreams, in the past, in the dead. Is it necessary to explain that Trirodov is Sologub himself and that his world is a realm of phantoms and visions, created by the unhealthy imagination of a man *organically* estranged from life?

But even more curious in this respect is the second world, our ordinary one, which rages at the shores of Trirodov's ideal realm. Here, more clearly than ever, all of the peculiarities of Sologub's work manifest themselves—

the peculiarities of an author who by nature does not know, *does not feel* our reality. Take a moment of the utmost strain in this world of ours, the period of "Sturm und Drang" which we have recently experienced. The masses have been set into motion. And it seems that all of the turbulent, elemental events of this revolutionary time are here before us in Sologub's novel: gatherings, meetings, demonstrations, funerals, pogroms, and so on. But what evil fairy has killed the living life of these events? Where is all of our exhiliration which was replaced by such profound despair? Where are all of our ups and downs, our great joys and no lesser sorrows? Where is all of this? Some sorcerer has indeed performed a magic act—and everyone and everything has lost the liveliness of true impulses, all have been transformed into phantoms which move about smoothly and evenly. Some kind of magic shadow has descended from the heights of Trirodov's quiet lunar realm onto our tempestuous earth, hiding its sun-influenced agonies from us.

Sologub's dramas are infused with the same spirit, stamped with the single imprint of their creator—inwardly focused and innerly tense, outwardly calm, immobile, and almost cold. Where else, if not in drama, should there be movement and animation? Yet just the opposite is the case with Sologub. His plays are his stiffest and most lifeless works, as a reading of any one of them demonstrates. Consider them from the point of view of structure alone. In each there is usually no more than two high points, and only the second one is central: in it the drama's entire meaning and all the hero's psychological impulses—if they exist at all—are concentrated. Such a procedure would be quite in keeping with the fact that these high points never follow each other in a regular sequence, never flow directly from each other: they are invariably cut off from each other by a large interval, an unfilled void. In this sense Sologub almost reaches his ideal—a genuinely compressed drama in which the three unities of time, place, and action are maintained. (See his article "The Theater of One Will."[12]) But even more curious are the topics he treats and the ideas he introduces into the majority of his dramas: they fully conform to the compressed form and cause the extreme slowness of pace. In *The Gift of the Wise Bees* we are always in the realm of death or close to its shores: consequently we witness the very process of the killing of life—the destruction of those concrete characteristics, those events and phenomena so dear to us which give it all its rich colors, lines, and forms. In Lethe people abandon their entire past, they forget everything that has ever happened on earth, and appear in Hades as unembodied shades. The Greek gods and goddesses, kings, and queens, are all lifeless symbols of abstract ideas, outlines devoid of any concrete elements; they are essentially introduced to add a bit of color to the monotone background against which the play's leading heroine, Laodamia, is drawn—she is supposed to symbolize one of Sologub's favorite ideas: *love* is crowned only by *death*.

The same is true in *The Victory of Death*. The servant of Queen Berta, Algista, momentarily embodies the eternal Image of Dulcinea. She temporarily appears among us as a brief and radiant dream of eternal beauty and love and as proof of another of the author's favorite ideas: the sun and diurnal life "have hidden from us forever what is dear and sweet to the heart." Thus, she, too, is not a living being, nor is she portrayed in earthly colors; she is merely a frozen symbol, one of those fossils into which everyone is transformed at the last moment.

Or take his most recent drama, *The Hostages of Life*. At first glance it might appear that this play contradicts our argument, that at least in the first acts there are genuine ups and downs, taken straight from life with all its fluctuations, joys, and woes. But it only seems this way. In point of fact, there is very little movement or action in these acts either, as is borne out by the unusually long stage directions, in which the instructions to the actors are lost among the detailed descriptions of the cast of characters; these thorough descriptions would be superfluous if the action spoke for itself. Moreover, these acts in general must be taken with a grain of salt: they are too unlike Sologub in spirit and form; there is too little of the specifically Sologubian in them (this is probably why they are so banal). Who knows, perhaps this is no more than a gift or even a tribute to the Alexandrinsky[13] theater. But aside from this, we again have two contrasting high points which embody Sologub's customary antitheses: night and day, fantasy and actuality, dream and reality; and he who knows Sologub will immediately agree that no matter how much he has tried (intentionally?) to conceal his personal attitude toward these two elements, he is totally on the side of the first. The victory belongs not to Katya, the earthly daughter of our diurnal existence, but to the legendary Lilith, the incarnation of the lunar dream: not a concrete dream which we ourselves create, not an active, creative force in life, but an eternal, peaceful, incorporeal, impassive dream. She has done her deed, she has "left her indelible traces: joy is pervaded with sadness."

Thus, I believe that in Sologub's dramas as well there is no living life, there is no genuinely life-like action, that here, too, he does not recognize—for he is organically unable to do so—the surrounding world, in its individual concrete and transient aspect: he himself does not participate in it and always speaks of himself and himself alone. This is most likely why he does not really care where his subject matter comes from. Whether it is the ancient or medieval world, Russia or a foreign realm, he is at home everywhere but belongs nowhere; he always speaks for himself and about himself but never about anyone else. His historical plays are not at all historical, his national figures are not Russian, his children resemble adults and his adults often resemble children. His characters are not tied to an epoch, to a country, to a particular age: they all bear the stamp of the author's single persona, they are all symbolic, they all appear in the universal, inevitable forms of Ananke.

The necessity of Ananke and the irrelevance of drunken Aisa, the constancy of the Image and the fortuitousness of its changing guises and temporary masks—these are also Sologubian antitheses, in utter conformity with the previous ones of night and day, fantasy and actuality, and dream and reality. It is clear that here as well he is fully on the side of the first terms. Neither the concrete nor the incidental are important—they merely get in the way (and in any event, he does not see or know them well, for reasons which are already clear to us); only the essence is significant, that which lies behind the transient and momentary. Consequently, it is completely natural that Vanka the Steward duplicates exactly the story of the page Jean,[14] that Queen Ortruda dreams about the life of Elisaveta Rameyeva,[15] that Login senses another self, and that the author himself resurrects all of the guises which his Image assumes in the course of its long, periodically recurring life on earth. From this perspective, he is fully correct when he asserts: "All that was, was many times and once again will surely be." We repeat, he must think this way, if he *organically* does not see all that is concrete and individual, i.e., that which exists only once and is never repeated.

It stands to reason that if our sketch is essentially correct, if it truly outlines the basic features of Sologub's peculiar psychology, then it should define his world view and metaphysics as well.

It is to these that we now turn.

IV.

We are all descended from Dostoevsky. Many of our serious contemporary writers could, in fact should, say this of themselves. But they are not only fully descended from him; to this day they have not emerged from him. His ideas are far from exhausted, and the problems he raises have not yet been solved, have not yet grown obsolete.

Dostoevsky is broad and all-encompassing, and each takes from him what is most kindred to his own soul, what conforms most to his personal needs. Of the three antitheses which he disclosed so powerfully and passionately—I vs. society, I vs. the world, I vs. God—and which correspond to the three spheres from which mankind has heretofore derived its highest and most life-affirming values—ethics, science, and religion—each writer feels essentially only one, no matter how closely bound he is to the other two. Thus, for example, Remizov is totally consumed by Dostoevsky's ethics, by those issues which are most painfully raised by Raskolnikov or Ivan Karamazov, and if he does search for the meaning of life, it is primarily the meaning of our own human life that he seeks, the justification for that evil which *we humans* feel most keenly. Remizov may feel the suffering of every creature on earth, he may agonize not only over Verochka or Marakulin, but over an innocent dog or the cat

Murka breathing its last—in short, he may feel primordial evil in the entire world—yet one has the sense that this universality is merely a backdrop which even more acutely throws into relief his endless grief over the torments of his fellows, over the sufferings of humans at *human* hands.[16] To repeat, it is in ethical problems, in the exposure of our unjustified torments, in the search for the meaning of life for *everyone,* not just *himself,* that Remizov's spiritual disquiet finds an outlet and the moving spirit of his work resides.

Does Sologub know such anxiety? Does he also agonize over mankind, over his fellow man? Such notes do occur in his work. He, too, sometimes reacts to human suffering as a man of our world, with all of our pain and anguish. But such responses are extremely rare, and these are not the motifs which create the unique charm of his sad music. Estranged and *organically* detached from life, he seeks its meaning only for himself, he tries to answer only those questions which he poses in conjunction with his *personal* "I," which remains outside of society and other people.

That the first antithesis—I vs. society—and all of the problems which ensue from it are completely alien to Sologub is evidenced by his attitude toward those "norms" or more accurately their violation, which so troubled Dostoevsky. I will not dwell on the reflection of this attitude in the design and composition of his works. Recall *Crime and Punishment.* There the crime is executed almost at the very beginning: the whole structure of the novel is built on this crime, on the retribution—the internal retribution—for it, on the great emotional torments which result from it. The book's significance lies in these torments. In Sologub the criminal act always occurs at the end: he is interested not in the hell which breaks loose in the soul of a man who has violated the "norm," but rather in *how* the crime is prepared for, how those dark and unknown areas which lie hidden in the lowest regions of one's psyche gradually creep to the surface of awareness, how "that ancient demon.... who is present in all destruction" is resurrected. But I will not dwell on this indirect reflection. Rather, I will take the facts as they are. In all of Sologub's three novels the heroes are criminals. Login, Peredonov, and Trirodov commit murder—the latter several murders. Most typical here is Sologub's attitude toward Login. Peredonov kills Volodin in a fit of madness. Trirodov's past is very obscure, and the author intentionally hides it from us. But Login, a deep, sensitive, and complex person, kills Motovilov and not only fails to be agonized by the act, but actually feels something akin to joy and to expiation for all his oppressive emotional ailments. True, he has killed the kind of viper about whom even Yermolina, the incarnation of purity and justice, had said: "Here is someone who has no right to exist." But still, this viper is not much worse than Raskolnikov's louse, the old hag; moreover, Login's radiant bride (Sologub's "eternal bride") not only fails to advise him, as Sonya advises Raskolnikov, to bear his cross and suffer, but actually kisses his bloody hands and insists that he hide the traces of the crime as carefully as possible.

Or take the relationship between the sexes. In *The Petty Demon* the pure and life-loving pagan, Liudmila Rutilova, is contrasted, like a kind of ideal, to Peredonov and his cohabitant, Varvara. Like Grushina, Varvara is a symbol of "defiled bodily beauty." Both of them are "dirty, brazen, wicked, lewd, and vulgar females," their manners are coarse and their words are unbearably vulgar." Not so Liudmila. She has a pure, rapturous, almost innocent love for the human body. For her beauty is not the object of barter, but a cult of life, which alone justifies it and gives it meaning. In her semi-forbidden encounters with the schoolboy Sasha there is vibrant joy, cheerful merriment, "divine ecstasy." But what is the upshot? It makes no difference to this beautiful pagan which body she enjoys, whose gazes she captures with her charms. At the very beginning of the novel we learn that even she is not against satisfying "the vile lusts" of Peredonov's limited and filthy imagination; all that stops her is Peredonov himself.

Katya in *The Hostages of Life* is the same, with her decision to "lose (her) innocence" but "to acquire a tidy sum" in the process by fleeing to the vulgar Sukhov, a man she does not love, for eight years, while her beloved Mikhail realizes his dreams to become a genuine artist. Given our point of view and our "ordinary" values we cannot excuse her just because a dark force has welled up inside of her, or because "a wave once foamed up inside her and came crashing down" and her heart "cannot live by treason; there is no treason—only love." For Sologub these are merely facts which he notes calmly and indifferently, the results of ancient chaos, whose voice he hears so clearly in his estranged soul. He notes them with a dispassionateness that is so unusual to us that we feel he is mocking us and intentionally provoking our morality. Yet we must acknowledge that there is only sincerity here, only, if you will, a supreme dispassionateness in laying bare one's inner world. In his soul the layers which separate "the dark and unknown" from the conscious sphere are all too fine, and this higher sphere of his consciousness contains too few of those necessary and useful features which result from human intercourse and which become established as absolute "norms" and unshakeable ethical values.

Is this feature a cause or an effect? Psychology alone can provide the answer but undoubtedly this phenomenon completely conforms to those separate aspects of his soul which we have already elucidated, to the fact that he knows only his private experiences and personal emotions, and that he not only consciously keeps aloof from life, but has been estranged from it *from the start* by nature, insofar as his peculiar *will,* so unlike our usual one, so "ineffective" as it were, is not directed outward toward surrounding reality, but inward, toward the center, toward his "I." Such a person *organically* reacts feebly to our human moral problems, is *organically* alien to those very values which by their nature are called upon to regulate and

sanctify interpersonal relations *in life* and society. These values are too
necessary and sacred to us; we are too accustomed to approaching almost
every phenomenon from an ethical point of view: we can sooner forgive the
negation of morality than the complete indifference to it. Behind the
impassioned "No" we always sense a great longing, an intense craving for
the joyous "Yes"; behind the dispassionateness of the "observer" gapes
absolute emptiness, a total absence of what we who live a social life perhaps
need most of all. In this sense, indifference toward morality sometimes
offends us more than the most awful blasphemy.

Sologub, I repeat, is precisely indifferent; morality simply doesn't
affect him.

But to make up for it, he agonizes over the other antitheses all the more
painfully: I vs. God and I vs. the world, or, more accurately, only the latter.
Lonely, melancholy, turned in upon *himself alone,* he lacks even those
feeble illusions with which all of us still blind ourselves, exaggerating the
value and significance of our everyday work; he is ignorant of that all-
powerful fetish which we all worship: society, humanity. Therefore one
should not seek a world-view analogous to his in the philosophy of
Raskolnikov or Ivan Karamazov, but rather in the ideas of Kirillov (from
The Possessed) and Ippolit (from *The Idiot*), who oppose themselves not to
man or society, but to the whole world, to the cosmos, who search for the
meaning of their individual life (or death), and who (particularly Ippolit)
passionately protest against the cruel and inexorable "mechanicalness" to
which everything and everyone is subject.

Neither Ippolit nor Kirillov accepts the world; both reject its edifice—
but not because "the Principal Architect has committed an error": the tears
of a tortured child do not affect them in the least. All of "life consists in our
uninterrupted devouring of one another," and we must merely take care
somehow to vouchsafe for ourselves "a place at the table" so that we
ourselves can devour. The trouble lies in something entirely different. It lies
specifically in nature's inexorable mechanicalness, in the mercilessness of
its laws. "How can one overcome them," moans the tubercular Ippolit, who
is doomed to death, "how can one overcome these laws if. . . . it (nature) has
senselessly seized, has blindly, unfeelingly crushed and devoured the great
and invaluable Being, a Being which alone was worth all of nature and its
laws, all of the earth that was created perhaps solely for the appearance of
this Being?" There is and can be no salvation from this ugly machine called
nature, for there is, has been, and can be no miracle on earth. For Ippolit,
doomed as he is, such an awareness is unbearable; he lacks the strength to
look the oncoming horror straight in the face, and he decides to exercise his
pitiful "self-will"—he will die before the affixed time.

What in Ippolit is an act of despair becomes for Kirillov the basis of a
thoroughly calculated system. Yes, death is the most horrible thing. It is the
reason for God's existence; people save themselves from it in the bosom of

the Great Being, which was invented by man himself. Therefore the fear of death must be destroyed. One must exercise *self-will*, not partially, but to its full extent. No one thus far has dared to kill himself without any extrinsic cause. "But I will dare to," reasons Kirillov, "and thereby destroy the fear of death and along with it, God: for God is the fear of death." And a monumental upheaval will come to pass: man will take the place of God, he will become a man-God, for, having ceased to fear death, he will begin to be regenerated physically, and he will, therefore, overcome the mechanical-ness of nature. However preposterous these thoughts may be in themselves, one thing is clear: in order to save oneself from Ippolit's torments one must replace God's will, or rather the will of the entire cosmos, with *self-will*. Either/or: either nature has power over me and then the illusion of God is necessary as the only salvation from death, or I and my will, creatively free, stand alone. Ippolit expresses the first line of thought, but since he does not believe in God, he adds: I am ruined, I am insignificant, I am a zero. Kirillov attempts to present the second argument. But if one really places self-will over everything, then can one fail to take the following step: I am I and all nature is my creation, and there is no one and nothing besides me and my free play. Sologub takes this step, continuing Kirillov's thoughts and making them concrete; he takes it, despite all of its apparent absurdity, because he has a certain *psychological*, if I may so put it, right to.

Herein lies the essence of Sologub's world view: the body of ideas around which he continually revolves is to be found in Ippolit's inquiries and Kirillov's answers.

V.

Ippolit hates the world and all those who surround him. How stupid, obtuse, callous, evil, and, most importantly, insensitive these normal and healthy people are! What right have they to be happy, to make merry, to devour one another, when *he* is perishing unceasingly and irrevocably, when the fatal, inexorable end is approaching closer and closer every moment? And there is no salvation, nor can there be, if there was no miracle, even then, if even He suffered like everyone else, and a beaten, tortured, mutilated corpse was all that remained even of Him. Yes, nature is implacable; the all-devouring maw of the "terrible, dumb, mercilessly cruel beast" already gapes open before him, and he will soon be swallowed up by it. He has only two weeks left to live, but he will not accept this pitiful, contemptuous gift; he himself will withdraw, he will not wait for the forced breaking of the string—he will go off early, at dawn, just when the sun is beginning to rise and hateful life, which arouses such burning envy in him, awakens with all its strength and passion.

Do we not see the same thing in Sologub? As we know, he too does not participate in life, he too is estranged from it forcibly, *organically, by his nature,* and he too, in his own way, is "deprived a place at the table," and therefore cannot rejoice and grieve together with and among us. Life is outside of him and he is outside of life. It is a process which someone incessantly sets in motion and in which he does not participate in the slightest. How tormenting, how unbearable this is! Such a world, which is even more screened off from him than from us, can inspire only terror. And here again one recalls Peredonov, who represents one of the courses which Sologub has conceived but never carried out. Surely he himself has experienced similar dismay and helplessness before his surroundings. True, he is accorded substantial possibilities for overcoming this terror; he has his other world where he feels himself the ruler and sovereign God, where, in short, Kirillov's self-will is realized in full. But here, among us, on earth, in our life, he must be totally in the grip of this terror and dismay. It is not for nothing that Sologub says of Peredonov that "he too was vaguely searching for truth in life and was perishing because he could not find it." However, he should not have sought it among people, he should not have demanded it from them, but rather from all of nature, from life in its entirety: it is life in its entirety which has always lain in wait for him and pressured him from all sides like a frightening, implacable enemy which has sent fears and nightmares down upon him—in the repulsive form of the evil, omnipresent Nedotykomka.

> The gray Nedotykomka
> Keeps whirling and spinning around me...
> The gray Nedotykomka's
> Insidious smile has exhausted me—
> Its shaky squat-dance has exhausted me
> O help me, mysterious friend.

This is the plea of Sologub himself, who is haunted by the same fear of life.

But the similarity with Ippolit goes still further. The sun and life are almost synonymous. Or rather: the sun is the mother who gives birth, it is the cause; life is the effect, the offspring, which responds to its mother with countless smiles, dispersed into billions of the most diverse fragments—the acts of man and all earthly creatures. Therefore the sun is the main cause of Ippolit's torments and the object of his intense hatred. As we know, it is against the sun that Sologub wages his most tireless battle, against this evil, golden, monstrous serpent which has eternally created the indestructable barrier of white deceptive mist; it is the sun which more than anything else he refuses to accept. "I am weak and small," he says of himself—weak and small and therefore "spiteful." And therefore, in those rare instances when he speaks about life and its evil machinations, both the small amount which, like every man, he is vouchsafed to see in the surrounding world and the excessively large amount that he knows from his own world are combined equally in his sharp and biased attacks against our life and its agonizing diurnal commands.

We know that there is salvation in Sologub, a salvation which is not contrived or fabricated, but completely natural to him because it corresponds to his entire emotional make-up. This salvation is to be found in the night, in the darkness which is so dear and sweet to him. Here, by himself, he can create his own world through his own personal will. Here he does not feel any evil mechanicalness or terror before his surroundings; for no other life besides his own exists here, there is nothing around except the progeny of his fantasy which he himself generates and over which, of course, he has full control.

> It is I who dispense the pain and the darkness,
> Who extinguish the day and summon the night.

However, Sologub summons the night not to find peace or rest but rather to avoid the intolerable day through its charms, to create his new world which is subordinate to him alone.

> But alarm imbues my night,
> And my garden dark is rustling.
> Lo, my road is all ablaze,
> And my little brooks are thundering.

But if during the brief night which replaces the long, wearisome day, one sometimes senses the quiet, elusive traces of a hidden mystery, if one feels this mystery in the darkness, in the silence, and within oneself, within one's own world, and not in external life, then perhaps when the time comes for one's last rest this secret will be revealed in all its beauty, becoming clear and accessible. Might it be that death, in the guise of night's wonderful darkness, is the true salvation from day's frightening disorder?

Yes, death is an endlessly long night, even more beautiful and comforting than night itself.

> Why be pained by this, our mortal life?
> Why strive for its ephemeral delights?
> One bliss alone exists: oblivion in dreamless sleep,
> Eternal death...
>> For only in death do we find
>> The blessed secret, the longed-for news
>> Of perpetual creation.

This is a leitmotif which resonates quite frequently in Sologub's night songs. Obviously it represents a complete and, in relation to Sologub's psychology, totally natural resolution of the problems posed by Ippolit. What do I care about the inexorable mechanicalness of nature if I can withdraw into my own world in which I exist to the exclusion of all others, and which I create by my own will in my own image and likeness? I do not know the fear of death, the only reason—according to Kirillov—for the existence of God. I not only do not fear it—I await and desire it as peace and tranquility, as longed-for news of eternal and true creation.

Yet for all this, what is to be done about the mechanicalness of nature? One can withdraw from it and hide in one's own self-willed world, but nature does not cease to exist as a result. The external world still exists as an indisputable fact which somehow needs to be explained, especially if one wants "the intimate to become the universal." Furthermore, such a resolution of the problem of death is too unreliable, too lyrical, I would say. Here is where Sologub tries to create his own philosophy, to rationalize somewhat the sober mysticism of Kirillov's self-will. (He devotes the entire fifth volume of his Collected Works to this.[17]) Certainly more than anyone else, Sologub is predisposed to this cult of self-will; as we know, it is rooted in his entire psychological make-up—*in his centripetal will, in his estrangement,* which is reflected in his primary means of salvation: my inner world, my inner designs and inventions are more real for me than the everyday world of solar torment.

The external world, he now tells us, is also one of my dreams which this same will of mine has made real. And if previously I spurned it as something alien to me, I now accept it; instead of a lyrical "No" I will address it as an "ironic Yes," for it is mine, summoned by me to life. I know myself and only myself—and both the external and internal world fuse into one: they are both my creations, and I am their sole creator:

> I am in everything and there is no Other,
> In me is the spring of the living day...
>
> And is it not I who fill
> The sky, the water, earth, and fire,
> Creating them with my soul?
> Joys and torments...
> I alone perpetrate them all.
> I conjure up all the elements,
> All the wheels of fortune are subject to my will.

Sologub's fifth volume is filled with such haughty declarations, particularly the second half. His "I" is magnified and becomes God, the creator, something greater than Kirillov's man-God.

Yet even if one considers this philosophy to be more than a momentary consolation, even if one takes it seriously and allows that Sologub at least believes in it, the question still remains: how does one explain the autonomous existence of the objective world, which is independent of him, the creator? How does one explain the fact that his creation so often rises up against the creator himself and threatens him like an antithesis, like some independent existence which remains indifferent to all of his haughty declarations? That very mechanicalness, the goddess Ananke, wields too much power in nature, and "wheels of fortune" which were not established by his "I" make themselves felt all too clearly. To be sure, one can attribute all of this to the "great error of existence," of which he himself is guilty, "having once desired to separate himself from his other self." One can temporarily console oneself with the self-deception that in creating earthly life "in the great delusion of my creative play, in my craving to manifest my 'I' in the outside world" "I willfully fettered myself with the unbreakable chain of time and space and became like a tombstone."

But still, how is it that the creator bound himself so firmly that he is now unable to break free from his shackles? Now that he is "bored with the empty, vain, doomed game, the magic of creation has disappeared and the time has again come to join himself to his other self," why can he, the creator, not *himself* accomplish this great deed, appropriate "the freedom to create"? Kirillov, of course, would have been more consistent here. He would have manifested his self-will in its entirety, since he is God and his "I" is the sole creative principle in the world. In the infinite repetition of time, he might have said, he always reached a point where the charm of the "false dream" ended and always manifested his self-will. But Sologub does not want to act in this manner—it would be "insolence" to him. Rather he prefers at this greatest of moments, when "the time has come again for miracles...and the great task lies in store of creating the bright world anew," to sit idly by and submissively await his deliverer, to call upon an alien, external power, upon the highest manifestation of mechanicalness— death, which is the most terrifying of them all:

> O death, my friend, do not delay,
> Destroy this vicious nature
> And give me back again
> My freedom to create...

However, this signals the complete failure of his haughty system of "self-will"; his entire edifice collapses and the "legend in creation" perishes. What kind of God, what kind of creator is he if his will is so bound that he cannot free himself from the fetters of necessity, if, like one of the meek of this world, he needs outside assistance and takes his freedom from someone else's hands? Here his circle runs its full course and he is again at the beginning. In his nightly kingdom he can find only a temporary haven and only partial tranquility, but nothing which approaches a solution to all of Ippolit's and Kirillov's problems. I do not know whether Sologub himself ever totally believed in his own philosophy, but in any case, he now acknowledges that he is not God the creator and that his "I" is as small and helpless as ours. The objective world exists and he is estranged from it. And precisely because he is so estranged from it, this world frightens him with its strangeness and fills him with Peredonov-like fears. Blind, like us, and also like us a humble slave, he will henceforth howl and suffer with the rest of us on the threshold of hermetically sealed doors; or at best, as before, he will vacillate between two principles: between repudiation of the diurnal world and craving for salvation in the kingdom of darkness, in the dead glow of a long-dead moon. If one considers the chronological scheme which Sologub has assigned to his work, then his ninth tome is one of the last volumes of his verse, and it could be called the book of Sologub's great anguish.[18]

In the first poem of this volume, which echoes previous motifs, Sologub still speaks about his will, but without his former power and previous boundless pride.

> And among the silent expanses
> Where hoary chaos reigns
> It is I, through my will,
> Who have raised life to consciousness.

He has only raised life to consciousness—not created it; before him there already existed "chaos, silent expanses." In the poem that follows this one his spirit is totally fallen. He is not "a sickly slave" whose fate is "to become exhausted by needless toil." "Once again bitterness is aroused" in his soul, and "where is patience, where is love?" Life and death are the "devil's swings." "Death roams about the world," and not only does he no longer await it as "longed-for news of eternal creation," but he suffocates, grows numb and freezes before it. Horrified, he "feels the outflow of (his) waning powers and the age-old anguish of the "merciless graves," for there "beyond the grave is dark nothingness and terrifying, gloomy night." No one has free will: "Only one's lot is chosen—this one or that one in one's mind—but the unbending will is blind." And so on and so forth.

Sologub seeks other forms of consolation. He turns to religion, wanting to "get to the bottom of prayer-offerings and lamentations, before saving icons," to "believe in a creating God, in the divine injunctions of the heavens." He even attempts to draw closer to life, to "bless" the earth for its beauty, for its "greatest miracle—children"—but all of this is only fleeting.

Thus do the various roads of Sologub, the most estranged of our writers, come to their end in a full "circle of fire"; thus do his insulated and inwardly focused soul and his peculiar will manifest themselves—a will which alienates him from life, from us and our values, and determines his course inward, toward his center, his "I," thus placing before him in its most acute form one of Dostoevsky's three antitheses: "I vs. the world."

I am aware that my analysis of Sologub's work is extremely incomplete. Given the limitations of a scholarly article, I could only note the *basic* motifs of Sologub's work—his *tendencies,* so to speak—and explain his work according to them. I should add that I have attempted to be entirely objective and to avoid as carefully as possible my personal attitude toward the content of the author's ideas. Merely to abuse or praise is not very difficult, and besides, it is a matter of "secondary importance." First and foremost one needs to *understand*. And in any case, Sologub is such a great and original artist that he fully deserves calm, impartial analysis, even from those who in essence do not accept him.

Notes

1. Belinsky, Vissarion Grigorievich (1811-1848). Extremely influential critic, philosopher, and social thinker of the 1830s and 1840s. He called for a national and naturalist (by which he meant "progressive" and realistic) literature, one which championed the "small man." The assertion "We have no literature" comes from his *Literary Reveries* (*Literaturnye mechtaniia*, Dec., 1834).

2. The theme of transformation and changing "guises and masks" is an important one in Sologub's writing. One collection of his short stories is entitled *The Book of Transformations* (*Kniga Prevrashchenii*, 1913), another—*Decaying Masks* (*Istlevaiushchie lichiny*, 1907).

3. These are Sologub's words from the Preface to his collection of poetry *Circle of Fire* (*Plamennyi krug*, 1908).

4. Aisa and Ananke are Greek deities. Aisa is the third goddess of Fate. Ananke is often considered to be the mother of the Fates and symbolizes dreadful necessity. Sologub frequently uses these names in his theoretical writings.

5. *Cor Ardens* is also a collection of verse (1911) by the symbolist poet Vyacheslav Ivanov.

6. The reference here is to any number of Sologub's literary children (e.g., Trirodov's son in *A Legend in Creation*), who pine for a past existence of innocence and harmony, symbolized by the "white mother." Kornei Chukovsky was the first to treat this theme seriously in his excellent article "The Phantom Charms of the *Petty Demon*" ("Nav'i chary 'melkogo besa'") originally published in *Russian Thought* (*Russkaia mysl'*, II, 1910). For a fuller discussion of this theme in Sologub's work, see Stanley J. Rabinowitz, *Sologub's Literary Children: Keys to a Symbolist's Prose* (Columbus, 1980).

7. The rather paltry variety of colors in Sologub is especially surprising since the symbolists introduced and used in their writing a greater spectrum of hues than had ever appeared in literature. For an informative article on this phenomenon, see Katherine T. O'Connor. "Theme and Color in Blok's 'Stikhi o prekrasnoi dame'," in *Studies Presented to Professor Roman Jakobson by his Students,* ed. Charles Gribble, (Columbus, 1968), pp. 233-245.

8. Tolstoy's derogatory remarks about Shakespeare are to be found in his essay "On Shakespeare and the Drama" ("O Shekspire i o drame," 1904).

9. Dulcinea (and her antipode Aldonsa) are two characters from Cervantes' *Don Quixote*. The impact of this novel on Sologub's thinking was enormous, and the theme of dream's transcendence over reality is primarily embodied for Sologub in Cervantes'

contrasting women. The contrast is epitomized in *A Legend in Creation* in Trirodov's first and second wives, Lilith (Dulcinea) and Elisaveta (an Aldonsa who will be transformed into a Dulcinea), and is discussed theoretically in Sologub's article "Don Quixote's Dream ("Mechta Don Kikhota"), written for the American dancer Isadora Duncan, whom Sologub believed to be Dulcinea incarnate.

10. This is one of Sologub's most important articles in which he develops his theory of the writer's two guises ("liki"), representing the two poles of poetic expression. One is the lyrical which says "yes" to life, the other is the ironic which says "no" to it.

11. Dolinin has in mind Blok's piece on *The Petty Demon,* published in *Zolotoe runo,* 1907, No. 5, pp. 125-127.

12. "The Theater of One Will" ("Teatr odnoi voli," 1908) is Sologub's longest and, perhaps, most important article. Sologub's theories interested the innovative director Vsevolod Meyerhold, who produced several of Sologub's lyric dramas and believed his *Gift of the Wise Bees (Dar mudrykh pchel,* 1907) to be one of the most beautiful modern plays. For a brief discussion of this article and of Sologub's theory of drama, see Andrew Field, "The Theatre of Two Wills: Sologub's Plays," in *The Slavonic and East European Review,* (Dec. 1962), pp. 80-88.

13. The Alexandrinsky Theater was the oldest Russian theater, originating with a small troupe of Petersburg actors in 1756. The theater was called the Alexandrinsky from 1832 to 1920, when it assumed its current name—the Pushkin Theater. Meyerhold became the director of the Alexandrinsky in 1908 and in 1912 presented Sologub's play *The Hostages of Life (Zalozhniki zhizni,* 1912).

14. These are the two main characters in what may be Sologub's best play *Vanka the Steward and the Page Jean (Van'ka-kliuchnik i pazh Zhan,* 1909).

15. These dreams occur in the second volume of *A Legend in Creation, Queen Ortruda.*

16. Dolinin is referring to Remizov's novel *Sisters of the Cross,* which is discussed in Ivanov-Razumnik's article in this collection.

17. Volume Five of Sologub's *Collected Works* (issued in twenty volumes in 1913-1914 by the publishing house Sirin) is called *Ascents (Voskhozhdenia).*

18. Dolinin is correct in stressing the importance which Sologub placed on the chronology of his writing in the *Collected Works* of 1913-1914. However, Sologub's later work is much more optimistic than Dolinin allows for here, as the title of Volume Thirteen (published shortly after Dolinin wrote his article) suggests: *Pearly Lights (Zhemchuzhnye svetila).*

7

Between "Holy Russia" and "a Monkey": The Work of Alexei Remizov

R. Ivanov-Razumnik (1878-1946)*

Trained at the University of St. Petersburg as a mathematician, and beginning his career as a literary critic and intellectual historian in 1904, Ivanov-Razumnik (pseudonym of Razumnik Vasilievich Ivanov) had an early and long record of anti-governmental political activity—both in pre- and post-Revolutionary Russia. He was arrested in 1901 and exiled from Petersburg in 1902 for organizing a mass student demonstration; he was jailed several times and exiled once between 1933 and 1941, and was on the verge of being seized again by the Soviet police, but was captured by Russia's German invaders (and released in 1943). A bitter, disillusioned anti-Bolshevik, he died in exile, leaving a gripping record of his life, entitled Tiurmy i ssylki *(published posthumously in 1953 and translated into English in 1965 as* The Memoirs of Ivanov-Razumnik).*

Ivanov-Razumnik is generally remembered for his extremely popular two-volume History of Russian Social Thought (Istoriya russkoi ob- shchestvennoi mysli, *1906)—a study which draws upon biography, history, sociology, and literary criticism to produce a work that reproduces an historical era by recreating the individual persona of the author and the collective life of a single class—the intelligentsia. Such a unique and certainly non-Marxist approach prevents the book from being republished in the Soviet Union. Another major work is* On the Meaning of Life (O smysle zhizni, *1910)—a collection of three long essays on Sologub, Andreyev, and the philosopher Leo Shestov, all centering around the theme of Ivan's tormenting questions in Dostoevsky's* Brothers Karama- zov, *which Ivanov-Razumnik discusses in his book's elaborate intro- duction. Also significant is the 150-page monograph* Blok and Bely *(1919), both of whom, incidentally, were profoundly influenced by Ivanov-*

---

* Besides Ivanov-Razumnik's own memoirs, a most informative piece on him is Linda Gerstein's "Ivanov-Razumnik: The Remembrance of Things Past," in *Canadian-American Slavic Studies*, VIII, no. 4 (Winter, 1974), pp. 532-538.

*Razumnik in their poems "The Twelve" and "The Scythians" (Blok) and "Christ Has Risen" (Bely): in 1917-1918 Ivanov-Razumnik developed his theories on Scythianism, depicting revolutionary Russia as a resurrected country, with its people as martyred Christ-figures who would ultimately triumph. His initial enthusiasm for the Revolution faded quickly, yet not before it led to a falling out with the very same Remizov whose work he so enthusiastically greeted in 1910 (for which, see the following article), but whom, in 1918, he accused of anti-Bolshevik sympathies. Ivanov-Razumnik's life was one of both internal and external wandering and exile, parallelling somewhat the experiences of another of his literary subjects, Alexander Herzen, about whom he wrote a monograph in 1920 and after whose memoirs—*Byloe i dumy (My Past and Thoughts)—*he in part modelled his own.*

Between "Holy Russia" and "a Monkey"*

I. *Burkov's House*

Alexei Remizov's "Sisters of the Cross" (1910) has at last directed the reading public's attention to one of the greatest and most original writers of modern Russian literature. The story is actually quite beautiful, and in many ways it is the most important piece of Remizov's *oeuvre,* the key to his work. After finishing "Sisters of the Cross" you inevitably return to the beginning in order to re-read it, with an oppressive kind of joy. The painful impression made by the tale's contents bears down heavily on you, nonetheless you rejoice in the knowledge that you are confronting a genuinely outstanding work by a major writer.

What a strange fate Remizov has had! After a few insignificant performances he made a smashing literary debut with the large novel *The Pond* (1905) and immediately "frightened" large segments of the reading public with it: Remizov was firmly established as the most extreme "Modernist," the most excessive "decadent." The most insightful critics detected the influence of Przybyszewski[1] in this novel, although Remizov has absolutely nothing in common with him. *The Pond* is a difficult piece of writing and the reader finds it rough going: as you read it you sink more and more deeply and hopelessly into the sticky slime of the pond which to the writer represents all of life. Since I shall have more to say about this novel later, I would do better merely to note here the general impression which has stuck with most readers: *The Pond* is an extreme example of "modernism," a broad but unclear, impressionist canvas.

But then, at practically the same time, Remizov's book of fairy tales, *Sunways,* appeared: bright, simple, crystal clear, and childlike. It would seem difficult to repudiate this lyrical book in which fairy-tale motifs, children's games, and superstitions are reworked with such seeming simplicity. However, people did not take to *Sunways,* and to this day it remains a book for "the select"; in the minds of most Remizov is firmly established as the author of *The Pond.* Nonetheless, these two strains run side by side in Remizov's work; it cannot be understood if you ignore either one of them. He writes *The Pond* but follows it immediately with *Sunways;* he writes the frightening piece *The Clock* and alongside it the naive story "The Wrinkle" and the apocryphal narrative "Limonar," in which he quite remarkably penetrates the sphere of popular religious culture and even humor. ("What is Tobacco?" is an apocryphal tale which unfortunately is inaccessible to the reading public since it was published "copyrighted" in an edition of twenty-five signed copies.) Remizov alternates between stories

*"Mezhdu 'Svyatoi Rusyu' i 'Obezyanoi' (Tvorchestvo Alekseya Remizova)," published in *Rech,* 1910, No. 279, October 11.

which, like *The Pond,* are oppressive, gloomy, and nightmarish and his highly successful, tender, subtle tales from children's life ("Maka," "The Baby Elephant"). But both of these are for the "select few," for even in his realistic stories Remizov always maintains his own peculiar form of writing, his own method of depiction. Yet despite this—and at first glance this is what is most remarkable—Remizov is regarded just as coldly in Russian "modernist" circles as he is among the broad masses of the reading public. Of course, he is acknowledged, but *The Scales* hardly considers him as one of its own and he is not printed in *Apollo,* the organ of Russia's contemporary aesthetes. Our "God-seekers"[2] also shun him. What is going on here? The fact of the matter is that Remizov does not see God on earth, nor does he limit himself to pure aestheticism. His nightmarish stories, *The Clock* and *The Pond,* and others, constitute one continuous, tormenting groan, one single question about the truth and value of life. Remizov seeks God, he seeks man, and at the same time he seeks universal truth here on earth; he seeks but he does not find. This is why he is too unpleasant for our "God-seekers," too complicated for our aesthetes, and, like a "decadent," too alien to broad circles of readers. Truly this is a tragic fate.

And now we have his "Sisters of the Cross." It is as weighty and oppressive a piece as *The Pond* or *The Clock,* but it is newer, clearer, and simpler in form. Remizov has long been working up to this deceptive simplicity and he has come especially close to it in his latest works ("The Polovtsian Camp"). But "Sisters of the Cross" is a big step forward in this regard. To be sure, even from the very start, Remizov never reached the point where refinement and pretentiousness of style were carried to excess and turned into the kind of horrible, coarse tastelessness which, for example, spoils Andrey Bely's remarkable novel *The Silver Dove.*[3] But now Remizov is seemingly convinced that simplicity of exposition can actually serve to strengthen the shattering impression of painful subject matter. This simplicity, I repeat, is deceptive and only apparent: behind it is concealed hard and painstaking work—not for nothing has Remizov passed through "modernism." Most everyone nowadays would likely agree upon at least the stylistic significance of modernism and "decadence," and great strides have truly been made in language and style. Remizov uses these to the limit in his work. In short, still the same Remizov as before, he has appeared in a new guise, and this is true not only in regard to the form of his work. The content and substance as well of "Sisters of the Cross" completely harmonize with this formal brilliance, and I hardly err when I say that "Sisters of the Cross" represents a giant step forward, the full blossoming of Remizov's talent.

The content of "Sisters of the Cross" is impossible to convey; it is a piece which you have to read yourself. But for our purposes we need to outline the basic contours of this work, which is central to Remizov's entire opus.

The bank official Marakulin is fired from his job; he undergoes hardships and is forced to give up his apartment and move into some poor furnished rooms in Petersburg. These rooms are located in the house of General Burkov, and it is "Burkov's house" which becomes the scene of the tale's entire action. Who doesn't Marakulin see and what doesn't he come to learn in this house! There is the old man who rents a corner "for a ruble and a half in cucumbers"; there is the Johannite Gorbachev, who combines praying and singing with coarse language, and hates children; there are the students who collect alms for their poor comrades and turn out to be "the most downright scoundrels"; there is the landlady of the furnished rooms, Alonya Ivoilovna, a flabby, devout merchant's wife who every summer makes the rounds of the monasteries; there is the master of the house himself, General Burkov, a "self-destroyer"; there are the two "artist" brothers—Vasily Alexandrovich, "the clown," and Sergei Alexandrovich, "the ballet dancer," who is captivated by the idea of importing Russian art to Paris; there is the German doctor, Wittenstaube, who cures every illness with x-rays; there is the general's wife Kholmogorova, who has rooms in front—she goes for walks with a folding chair and is healthy, well-fed, and "immortal"—she eats, drinks, digests it all, and "toughens herself up." The entire "Burkov house" soon becomes intimately known to Marakulin and he is literally crushed by the burden of that inescapable, senseless, and terrible human grief which is revealed before his eyes. Just before his move to the furnished rooms in Burkov's house, Marakulin looks out of the window at the suffering of Murka the cat, whom someone has fed broken glass "just for the fun of it"—and tormenting questions plague his poor mind. In the past, when his life was carefree, Marakulin did not know how to think and ask questions; now the questions come of themselves. What is it all for? Who will answer for this suffering, who will give out the rewards and who will keep the balance sheet at the very least with regard to the torments of the poor cat Murka?

At first Marakulin tries to avoid these questions: he does not seek retribution in the future but allows for some original sin of Murka's in the past. But his soul cannot bear this Old-Testament justice of punishing seven generations for an original sin—especially when Marakulin comes into tormenting contact with perpetual human grief. In an adjoining room lives Verochka, who dreams of becoming a "great actress" so that the man who has shamed and abandoned her (and whom she madly loves to this very day) will see whom he has lost and return to her. In another room lives Vera Ivanovna, a stubborn, tireless worker who dreams of completing her secondary education so that she can go to medical school: she will eventually die, Marakulin thinks, behind one of her physics textbooks. In the one case there is a broken love and a shattered life; in the other, hopeless labor which destroys life. And in both instances the grief is inescapable. There is also the maid, the good, old, semi-fanatic "divine Akumovna," who, when still a girl, was burdened by her dead father with the curse to wander about the world her whole life. Marakulin learns about Aku- movna's hard life and his heart is gripped with even greater coldness. Nor does the old woman's favorite adage help: "No one is to blame." Let there be no guilty ones, let there be no original sin; nevertheless, hopeless, oppressive sadness and grievous suffering still exist, so is life any easier? There are no guilty ones, but right next door there lives the well-fed, healthy, "immortal" general's wife, "the louse," as she is nicknamed in Burkov's house; she eats, drinks, digests it all, and toughens herself up, sleeping peacefully at night. All of Marakulin's agonizing hatred of "Someone" descends upon this "immortal louse." She grows into a symbol, a nightmare for him, and he transfers onto her his hatred for all the suffering, all the horror of human life. There are times when he desperately wants to live the blissful, serene, thoughtless life of the general's wife, even for only a day, to become, if only for a little while, such a human "louse"; but he immediately feels that an entire life of sadness and horror is better than one hour of this woman's placid existence, and he hates this "immortal louse" even more. Once, during the night, when he hears Verochka silently beating her head against the iron grating of her bed in a fit of deep anguish, and remembers that the general's wife is now sleeping calmly after her daily dosage of walking and toughening up, he is seized with such hatred and spite that he throws open the window and screams out into the dark and silent courtyard like a madman: "Christians, help! The louse is sleeping!"

As the story continues to unfold further, new characters appear: there are two incidental figures, teachers from a provincial school and the abandoned wife of one of them, who has lost faith in everyone and goes about crushed, grief-stricken and deceived by everyone; there is Aku- movna's helper, the girl Verusha, who has been rudely outraged by beastly people. Marakulin sees and painfully grasps all of this. His former neighbor, Verochka, who has dreamt of becoming a great actress, quickly and irrevocably degenerates: initially the kept woman of a wealthy dignitary, she quickly becomes a street walker. Marakulin loves her, himself not even aware of it; he is tied to her by her suffering, which has become his suffering. Marakulin is hopelessly caught in the noose of human grief; to continue living in this way is impossible, and one gets the sense that just another step, another drop, and he will no longer bear it, he will condemn himself to death. But suddenly fate gives him a small respite: he is called to Moscow, to the house of his schoolfriend, the rich merchant Plotnikov, who himself expects Marakulin to save him, exclaiming, "Petrushka, I believe in you as I do in God!" This merchant is sitting drinking in his study, *on the wall of which hangs Nestor's "Holy Russia" and on the other, a cage full of monkeys.* This is an amazing picture "of everyday life" and, as we shall see, it is the key to all of Remizov's work. Plotnikov mouths drunken nonsense and Marakulin becomes increasingly tangled in his ponderous questions; he cannot make sense out of this man, caught between the monkeys and "Holy Russia." On the Petersburg-Moscow train he had recalled his childhood, his mother Eugenia, and one more drop of bitter reminiscence was added to his cup of grief. The meek, gentle, weak young Zhenya, who was had by anyone who wanted her, including her own brother, and who blamed only herself for everything and craved atonement for her sin, this Zhenya further increases in Marakulin's mind the number of "sisters of the cross" who share this grief, suffering, torment, and violence. Marakulin returns to Petersburg and again finds himself in an atmosphere of hopelessness, despair, and awareness of life's horror and senselessness. For a moment a wild hope flares up that salvation exists somewhere outside of himself, that he must immediately leave Burkov's house and escape, perhaps to Paris, where his neighbor the "ballet dancer" is going, totally content in bringing Russian art to France in his person. Just as Chekhov's sisters cry "To Moscow! To Moscow!" and seek salvation in it, so Marakulin momentarily wants to hope that some unknown, distant "Paris" will save him. He thinks that his rich friend Plotnikov, who believes in him "as in God," will send him a thousand rubles, but he sends only twenty-five, and the hope by which he had tried to deceive himself fades in his heart. There is nothing left to hope for, nothing left with which to deceive himself; it is no use living any more—the horror of human grief frees his heart. A scene which Marakulin once again sees in the yard of Burkov's house from his window is the final drop that fills his cup: a little legless beggar girl called Masha, singing as she wanders from yard to yard. This is the last straw! Marakulin need no longer deceive himself with answers about "Murka's original sin"; this is a pitiful answer before the body's sufferings and the soul's torments. Too much human sorrow has permeated Marakulin's heart, and deep down he has already condemned himself to death. When, tormented by life and hounded by his own and others' agony, Marakulin dreams that in two days, on Saturday, death will come for him, he fearfully waits to see whether or not this prediction will come true. Saturday arrives and like a hunted beast Marakulin rushes tirelessly about all of Petersburg in a totally desperate and hopeless state of mind: he is fleeing from his own death. This day is a nightmare so vividly described that the boundary between reality and unreality disappears. But Marakulin has already lost the feeling of reality and nothing can surprise him; even when he witnesses Kholmogorova's accidental death on the street he can only dully repeat: "There's your immortality for you! There's your immortal one for you!" But he no longer feels his former hatred for this "immortal louse," he knows that "no one is to blame!" And if anyone is to blame then maybe it is that Bronze Horseman, "by whose fatal will this city was founded," to whom Marakulin turns with the mad and poignantly desperate phrase: "Peter Alexeyevich, Your Imperial Highness! The Russian nation drinks a potion of horse manure and wins Europe's heart for a ruble and a half of cucumbers. I have nothing more to say." There are no guilty ones, but this does not ease Marakulin's pain over human suffering; and though he still desperately tries to escape death he nevertheless knows that he is deceiving himself and that death will not pass him by, that he himself will go after it. On Saturday night he returns home and when the clock strikes twelve he feels released from his obsession and from the death which has been pursuing him. But he has already condemned himself to death, and it is not accidental that five minutes later he leaps out of the fifth floor window onto the pavement of Burkov's yard. He who lacks strength to accept and endure human grief cannot live and must depart from life. So Marakulin departs; he has drunk the bitter cup—the cup of universal human bitterness—to its last dregs.

This is Remizov's "Sisters of the Cross." Perhaps even this sketch will convince the reader of the story's depth and power, so realistic and "everyday" in form and so symbolically profound in content. Everything is real in this story—from "Burkov's house" on Kazachi Lane, located between the bathhouse and the Belgian electric works, to Marakulin himself... Yet Burkov's house is not merely one Petersburg residence, it is the entire world. The sisters of the cross are not only Verochka, Vera and Verusha, Akumovna, Zhenya, and Mashka-Murka; they are all those who are taxed beyond their strength, tormented, and destroyed. "The insulted and the injured" is how Dostoevsky called them at one point, and his influence is surely felt in terms of the story's literary aspect. But Dostoevsky's novel is not free of a certain sentimental, idealizing tendency: the insulted and injured take pride in knowing that they are right, even though they are vanquished. Subsequently, the same Dostoevsky showed how such people live not by their arrogant awareness of their rightness but rather by their humiliation, suffering, and perpetual questioning—we need only recall Raskolnikov or the father of the dying "Ilushechka." Remizov's brothers and sisters of the cross are similar: they are perpetually crucified by life and are always asking bitterly: "Father, Father, why hast Thou forsaken me?" They question God while simultaneously believing in Him; they question life while simultaneously believing in it. And if indeed there is a question or a howling query, then it comes only from the mouths of the "sisters of the cross"... Only those who have lived life to the last, to the hilt, can pose the question of the meaning of life as a major question of their existence. There is no answer—and Marakulin leaps out of his fifth-floor window onto the pavement of Burkov's yard.

One inevitably recalls the concluding lines of *The Pond*, which Remizov just as easily could have used as the conclusion of "Sisters of the Cross."

"The Devil was distressed in his kingdom, and terror cried out from the human eyes, gummed together and weighed down by sleep. And piercing through the red waves, the densely packed stars stared fixedly. And there, beyond the stars, in the heavens, fixing her gaze at the Throne, her eyes full of tears, the Mother of God grieved and asked her Son: 'Forgive them!' And there, in the heavens, there was a great darkness. 'Forgive them!' And there, in the heavens, as He had once been at that ninth, forsaken hour, He hung, crucified, with His drooping head in a crown of thorns...'Forgive them!'"

Forgive them, the crucifiers: is this an answer to the crucified's vital question? Is this the kind of prayer you can address to that Bronze Horseman who, seeing, does not see and hearing, does not hear? And what is to be done if one cannot clearly distinguish between the crucifiers and the crucified, the bloodthirsty "monkeys" and the suffering righteous people of "Holy Russia"? What is to be done if these two camps are mixed up, confused and shuffled, if it is impossible in life to discern where "Holy Russia" ends and the monkey cages begin? What if the crucified themselves crucify others, and the crucifiers, in their turn, are crucified?

No one is to blame. One can only accept or reject the tormented and the tormentors, the righteous and the monkeys. We arrive at this conclusion having passed through "Burkov's house" and we shall come to the same conclusion when we have studied all of Remizov's work. The key to his work, as I have said, is "Sisters of the Cross," and the key to this tale is the "genre painting" we see in the merchant Plotnikov's study.

II. Between "Holy Russia" and a Monkey

"The study was divided into two halves, two sections. On one side there were copies of Nestor's pictures and on the other there were two monkey cages.... Marakulin stood between 'Holy Russia' and the monkey and could understand nothing at all."

But we readers understand. This is not the merchant Plotnikov's study but that of Remizov himself; this study is a clue, a key to all the writer's work. Moreover, Remizov stands between "Holy Russia" and the monkey not only in his study but in life itself. These are the two poles of his life and work between which he vacillates, like a little ball caught between two opposite electrical charges...

All of this would be rather uncomplicated if Marakulin-Remizov were correct in his simple description of the study, precisely divided into two halves, two sections...If Remizov's work were so perfectly rectilinear then it would hardly be worth speaking or writing about. But that is the point: the complexity of Remizov lies in the fact that in life as he sees, feels, and portrays it, everything is mixed up, confused, and intertwined. The righteous martyrs wander out of Nestor's "Holy Russia," they intermix with the crowd of monkeys, and abandon themselves to an orgy of beastly cruelty and all kinds of indecency: only their radiant, "lost" eyes betray their inner horror and torment. All is fused together: good and evil, truth and falsehood, the monkey and the righteous. And amidst this jumbled, frightening crowd, amidst this nightmarish life which he depicts, stands Remizov himself, like Marakulin in Plotnikov's study.

Sometimes, when you read all of Remizov's works one after the other, you simply suffocate in that frightening mist which envelops every human life in his stories and novels. The slimy, viscous filth of *The Pond,* Remizov's first novel, sucks you in like mire...Everywhere we find the ultimate degradation of human personality, violated human souls. A depraved, kind-hearted, and foolish monk, Father Gabriel, greedily devours all kinds of leftovers and other slop; a student, committing suicide, slits his throat "with a penknife in a latrine"; a lackey with the arrogant nickname of "Prometheus" performs "a foul and burdensome task with the elephants during mating" in the zoo *(The Pond);* the exterminator Pavel Fyodorovich, "a mangy dog," kills women during his fits of animal lust ("The Little Devil"); the postal clerk Volkov lives with his wife and "her faithful little dog" and in the end he kills them both; the clockmaker Semyon Mitrofanych forces a submissive little boy first to cross himself and kiss his foot and later to drink from "a dish in the corner" *(The Clock);* the cheerful scoffer and clown Borodin is a corpse among the living ("The Victim"). And so it is literally in every story, on every page: an unmitigated nightmare. And this is life. As if this were not enough, whoever they are—monkeys or suffering people—Remizov's heroes are unable to escape life's tormenting horror, either awake or in their dreams. This is a fact worth focusing upon since no writer endows his heroes with as many dreams as Remizov. These characters do not *sleep* as much as they *dream,* and all of their dreams are one uninterrupted, tormenting nightmare. Nor is this surprising. What exists in life is to be found in dreams as well. It is not for nothing that Remizov's own dreams, which he describes with such subtlety (e.g., "A Dangerous Lot"), are also one unending, agonizing nightmare. Read these "dreams" and you will understand how Remizov conceives human existence. One of them, entitled "The Monkeys," tells how the author imagined himself as the "leader of the chimpanzees," who are so cruelly punished "on the Field of Mars,"[4] that the whole earth "is swollen with the shed blood of monkeys." This dream gives us a clue to the meaning of all these "monkeys" in Remizov's life and work: they themselves are clearly *victims* of something or Someone else. The murderers, torturers, and human beasts who spill blood and tears all over the earth—all of them are themselves victims, for whom one must demand the same answer as one does for their victims...Remizov gives no answer—but he tirelessly and ceaselessly asks the question. He turns away from "the monkeys" and seeks purity, sanctity, innocence, and love as justification for the world. Where is one to seek and find all of this? Of course, among those about whom Christ said: if ye be not as children, ye shall not enter the Kingdom of Heaven. Remizov does turn to children; he hopes to find among them a "Holy Russia" as yet unsoiled by cruelty and blood, unencumbered by the torment of life's heavy cross...

Only a few Russian writers have been able to portray children as Remizov does, to peer into their soul with his love and tenderness. Four year-old, pot-bellied Bebka with the protruding lips ("Devil's Gulley"); the schoolboy who dreams of making off with a toy from his teacher's closet ("The Baby Elephant"); the youngsters who flee "to America" with the cook's Feklusha's passport and three rubles ("Tsarevna Mymra"); the tiny "queen" Sasha with the nose "that has a tweak" and the extremely crafty blue eyes ("Maka"); the fantastic yet so real "Zaika," the merry prankster— all of them, I repeat, are described tenderly and lovingly by a great artist who is close to the child's soul, close to children themselves, "those singularly dear and pure forget-me-nots." So let us see what Remizov does with these children, what life does to them.

Pure and unconscious first childhood elapses. Eight-year-old Kolya *(The Pond)* is already beginning to recall "something good that existed at one point when he was three." Something shameful, secret, and illicit is commencing, blue circles are forming around his eyes. Accompanying this is something beastly, "monkey-like," and cruel. A shaved rat is "stealthily scalded with boiling water, *aimed right at the eyes*"; the rat, convulsively washing itself with its paw, screams like a human. "Fat, white worms are dug out of manure, scooped up in large handfulls and squashed along the paths." Frogs are caught and gleefully tormented: "Their legs are torn off, their eyes poked out, their bellies ripped open so that their insides can be examined." And at the same time these children merrily joke and fidget "like little monkeys." And indeed, the grimace of a cruel, dirty "monkey" does begin to peer out of their saintly faces. "There was no face, no object in the world upon which their eyes could rest. Even children, those singularly dear and pure forget-me-nots.... The children's faces seemed to be encased in beastly steel muzzles. And their sharp, silky teeth were bared behind the grating" *(The Pond)*. And these are the ones about whom it is said: if ye be not like them, ye shall not enter the Kingdom of Heaven! Where are the purity, innocence, and love; where are the child angels? They no longer exist! Children grow—and cruel, mangled thoughts grow with them; the child's soul becomes embittered and soiled. Life takes its toll. The schoolboy Atya, who has fled unsuccessfully to America, loves his "Tsarina," his "one and only" Klavdiya Guryanevna, with a pure, childlike love. One day, escaping punishment, he hides under his "Tsarina's" bed precisely when her lover arrives. Life takes its toll, and Atya leaves a different person, with a heavy heart and an empty soul. His love has been mocked and defiled, life has shown him its "monkey" face ("Tsarevna Mymra"). These children no longer dream children's dreams: their dreams are visions of filth, blood, and grimaces.

And often, although their soul still contains that spark which makes their "lost" eyes the radiant eyes of homeless "Holy Russia," they nevertheless fully accept and display the beastliness and cruelty which exist in man. Now no dividing line can be drawn between "Holy Russia" and the monkey: everything is confused, mixed up, intertwined . . . And then at one and the same time "a look of angelic tenderness and purity melts over their faces and the trumpets of justice and indignation blare, but in their hearts parasites swarm foully, ruling in their domain with absolute authority" *(The Pond)*. And again it becomes clear that both the crucified and the crucifiers are all *victims,* and the *horror before life,* which this aspect of Remizov's work epitomizes, resonates loudly.

Here is where the *sisters and the brothers of the cross* come onto the scene. Willingly or not, they all bear the burden of the cross, they are all violated spiritually, they all know life's horror and are crucified by it. They are the heroes of Remizov's works and this is why his magnificent tale "Sisters of the Cross" occupies such a central position in his *oeuvre.* The sisters and brothers of the cross are not saints or righteous people; at times on their faces as well there is "a look of angelic tenderness and purity," while in their hearts "parasites swarm foully, ruling in their domain with absolute authority." If such a combination seems improbable to anyone, let him turn to Dostoevsky and recall, for example, Liza in *The Brothers Karamazov.* Much is said there about the indissoluble bond between the holy and the "monkey-like," between the pure, suffering soul and perverted thoughts and acts. The brothers and sisters of the cross are not holy; at times they reach the bottom limits in their "monkey-like" decline. But still, if "Holy Russia" does exist then it is only in these people—tortured, crucified individuals who carry the heavy cross of inescapable suffering. And when you see and feel the true weight of this burdensome cross you no longer divide people into crucified and crucifiers, you understand that they are all *victims* of Someone and that an answer must be provided for them. All are victims of the *One-eyed Evil* that reigns over the world and life.

"Life itself is incomprehensible," says Remizov's Judas, Prince Iscariot, who hopes for Christ. "People live and suffer not knowing why . . . Life has no justification. You have your truth, I have mine; truth is everywhere but is to be found nowhere. *He* will give life its justification and will bring a new law." And *He* does come, He comes and goes. And again there is no truth or justification for life in the world. He did not rise from the dead, He did not conquer evil—instead, crucified and abandoned by everyone, He became the prey of Satanail (so Remizov writes in the apocryphal tale, "On the Lord's Passion"). Satanail takes Christ's dead body, throws it to the devils to be defiled, and then dresses it in fine princely rainment, whereupon he raises it to a throne of glory on top of the highest mountain. "And there, at the summit, by the foot of the throne, Satanail rose up and, showing the sublunary peoples, past and future, the horrible corpse in princely clothes, proclaimed in a loud voice: 'This is your King!' And from the throne, the huge, dull eyes of the inanimate, decomposing body looked at the surging waves of heads and outstretched arms" ("Limonar"). God is crucified, and eternally so. Satanail rules the world forever and jeers, grimacing at mankind. People suffer, perish, and are crucified—and high above them "in the window opening of the highest tier of the cathedral belfry, leaning his bony palms on the stone ledge and stretching out his long neck like a goose, Someone was laughing, screwing up his gray, tear-filled eyes, guffawing on that starry night"(*The Clock*, last page). "Holy Russia" is crucified and "the Monkey" chortles. One inevitably recalls Pushkin's phrase about Fate in his letter to Vyazemsky:[5] "Imagine it as an enormous Monkey, which is allowed total freedom ...Who will chain it up? Neither you, nor I, nor anyone."

The monkey rules the world. It is no accident that in one of Remizov's works there appears on stage to the accompaniment of a "monkey's march" "His Majesty, the Monkey Tsar, Monkey the Great, Valakhtantarararach-tarandarauf Asyka the First," with a large retinue of monkeys (*The Tragedy of Judas, Prince Iscariot*). Here again, as in all of Remizov's works, monkeys merge with people, blood flows once again—both monkey and human. People are decorated not with orders but with "monkey badges" and phalli. Monkeys torment people. But are people any less savage than monkeys? "It's simply a scream what they did to that cross-eyed monkey! This one guy—as quiet and meek as could be—stroked and stroked her, and then all of a sudden stabbed her, and the blood came spurting out." This entire episode with the monkeys, from *The Tragedy of Judas,* can be extended to all of Remizov's work. And we inevitably identify the "Monkey Tsar" with Pushkin's "Monkey Fate," with the Bronze Horseman. Pitted against them, what is man? Prayers and curses are powerless.

And yet people go on living. But how can they live and on what can they sustain themselves? They need an iron will or stony indifference. "If people would look and take note of each other, if everyone were given eyes, only the person with a *heart of iron* could endure life's horror and enigma" ("Sisters of the Cross"). The brothers and sisters of the cross are "given eyes"—and many of them cannot endure the spectacle of ceaseless human torment. Marakulin cannot bear it and without realizing it, he unwittingly condemns himself to death. He is like another of Remizov's heroes, who "all his life took life's smallest details to heart, down to the last blade of grass— and never met a creature whose heart did not ache even just once" ("In Secret"). True, at times people try to deceive themselves with any old answer, if only to go on living, to convince themselves of their right to live; they try to justify both their own torment and others' suffering... As we have seen, Marakulin, too, tries to soothe his tortured soul by finding an explanation for world suffering: someone has fed the cat Murka broken glass—and she is suffering in Burkov's yard. But Marakulin wants to see in this "some higher justice, a punishment for some original sin of Murka's—unexpiated and uneffaced." Andreyev has written a clever and biting story on this topic—"My Notes": should one so desire, everything can be rationally explained and justified. Marakulin and the brothers and sisters of the cross do not reason about human suffering, but painfully endure it. This is why they are ultimately unable to content themselves with cruel, Old Testament justification for suffering; their human heart cannot bear the inhuman truth. No, better that an oppressive, unjust law rule over the world: *there is suffering, but there is no justification for it.* He who can, may endure this burdensome truth; he who cannot, will escape it for ever. Marakulin does not endure it and flees. Remizov continues to live. What of it? Does he have an "iron" heart? Or maybe not only an iron heart but an ordinary human one can endure this burdensome truth?

Life itself answers this question: yes, the human heart is capable of accomplishing this tormenting truth. Look around at all the brothers and sisters of the cross. And only a few of them end up as Marakulin does. Humanity finds in itself the strength to live. To be sure, a sizeable portion of this humanity consists of people with *wooden* hearts, tightly insulated from the next man's grief and suffering. These are the various Kholmogorovas ("Sisters of the Cross")—the well-fed, healthy, and self-satisfied "chosen vessels" who have an "imperial right" to life. Kholmogorova, "the immortal louse," is a terrible symbol, for all of her realness; she represents an endless number of people—"their name is legion..." And if Marakulin-Remizov can feel hatred toward anyone, it is not toward the murderers, oppressors and physical and spiritual crucifiers, who themselves live, suffer, and reach the final limit, but rather toward the worst of the "monkeys," who wear the mask of contentment and sinlessness, to the Kholmogorovas. For Marakulin-Remizov the sinlessness and carefree life of these "immortal lice" is more repulsive and horrible than the most tormenting, the most "crucified" life. Nor does he deceive himself in any way: he thinks that if all humanity were offered the louse's content and tranquil existence everyone would rush forth in a huge crowd to this new Zion, this Crystal Palace, to use Dostoevsky's expression. But he himself will not head for this new Zion, nor will the brothers and sisters of the cross. He who has once understood and felt human suffering will sooner languish and suffer sleeplessness than bring himself to don a cow bell and, without a care in the world, eat, digest it all, and toughen himself up. And he who has endured this difficult ordeal, who has earned through it his *right to life,* will live, suffering his own and others' torment, imbibing his own and others' joy, resonating, like an echo, to all of life's sounds. Marakulin does not endure this trial, but Remizov has survived it. Remizov cannot *understand* life, but he can *accept* it. This constitutes the second aspect of Remizov's work; he combines horror over life with a tender and affectionate attitude toward it in all its manifestations.

III. Holy Russia

Just as Remizov relates it in his apocryphal tale "Nikolka and the Saint," so he himself blesses that which he damns, accepts that which he does not understand. He sees man's bitter, hungry, reckless, terrible life all around him—and with the insight of an artist he accepts it in its lucidity, with all of its pain and suffering. Suffering exists and there is no justification for it, but there are no guilty ones: "No one is to blame." One must accept all of life— "to the last blade of grass." One must love all of it and soak it all up. Human existence is enveloped on all sides by an ocean of natural life—and Remizov sensitively and lovingly communicates to us in his work its most tender, finest, and most mysterious manifestations. Human life, with its ceaseless suffering, weighs down upon him like a nightmare, and at times he is ready to exonerate it and blame himself alone. "You think you're struggling with the world" he exclaims, "but no, you're struggling with yourself: you yourself have created this world, you have endowed it with your lusts, you have made it loathsome, vile, and soiled with your impurities" *(The Pond)*. And when in a dream (again a dream!) he wants to see all the earth's beauty and to float through the clouds in a boat, he hears a voice: "You vile parasite, no more than your own ears shall you see— neither the clouds nor what is behind them; first cleanse your eyes, which see only filth in everything, and then be our guest" ("An Unlucky Fate"). This is how Remizov views life: without abandoning the heavy burden of his cross, he greedily imbibes life, taking "life's smallest details to heart, down to the last blade of grass." And only when he has accepted all of life in his heart does he see God in heaven: "and I want such a life" his heart shouted, "yes, life, its depths, and you, God!" It is at this point that a tender and delicate poet is born in him, who "soaks up every living thing that swells with life around him, down to the blade of grass which breathes and the small reed which grows; he soaks up everything with a sort of greed and infectious happiness." Then he experiences (see "Sisters of the Cross") an inexplicable "extraordinary joy," which would seemingly suffice for the entire world (in philosophy this is known under the coarse name of the "universal effect"), and which fills his heart with a "quiet radiance and warmth." It is then that he writes his tender, poetic *Sunways* which has heretofore been so underestimated; it is then that he writes "Maka," "The Wrinkle," "Kotofei Kotofeyevich," and all of his poetic scenes and fairy tales; it is then that he occasionally escapes to the fantastic "Holy Russia," which is still alive for him and which he can create with such profound poetry.

It is wrong to suppose that Remizov escapes to his "Holy Russia" as if withdrawing to some romantic kingdom in order to seek refuge from the nightmares of surrounding reality. There are no fewer nightmares in "Holy Russia"—there may even be more of them. The serpent Skarapeya slinks past with his twelve heads—"bloated, queasy, vomity, nauseating, bubble-blistered"; devils dance, jeering at human torment ("The Devil's Act"); and a "black rooster" is burned *(Sunways);* vampire-corpses drink the blood of a living man; the witch's assistant Kolovertysh laments his bitter fate, and an owl laughs maliciously ("To the Ocean-Sea"). And how can we speak of Remizov's "Holy Russia" as being carefree and romantic when such scenes as the massacre of fourteen thousand babies (in the apocryphal story "Christmas") occur in it? Just read this one scene . . . But we now know that although he does not comprehend life, he "accepts" it. Otherwise he would not be able to go *"Sunways"* to meet "beautiful spring (and) lovely summer," to see off "warm autumn" and to await "fierce winter," or to travel the difficult and joyous road "to the Ocean-Sea." The weighty burden of the cross is consequently combined with a greedy immersion in all of life "down to the last blade of grass." While undergoing the ordeal of unjustified suffering, one can—and must—remain alive, one must experience all states of soul, the entire fullness of being.

I repeat once again: in retiring to his "Holy Russia," Remizov in no way hides from the horrors of life in a "created legend."[6] There is nowhere to escape from life and when he withdraws into the fantastic, Remizov is in no way evading life. His entire work shows that the kingdom of "Holy Russia" is truly within us, at least within those of us who are capable of feeling all the poetic charm of popular "mythmaking," all the profound, childlike wisdom of folk beliefs, concepts, and ideas.

Extinct rituals, games which have lost their meaning, and primitive wooden toys are resurrected before our eyes—all of them are genuinely brought back to life in Remizov's work. This is because he allows himself to be imbued with "childlike" wisdom and he is able to look at life and the world with "childlike" eyes, without forgetting for a moment either the serpent Skarapeya or the fourteen thousand massacred babies.

"Children's eyes are weak-sighted but attentive," Remizov says in his comments to *Sunways,* and what he says about children applies to himself as well. "For them, it appears, there is no nook in the world which is empty, everything swarms with life. . . . Not distinguishing dream from wakefulness children confuse day and night when they are in the care of Dream and not of their mothers or nurses. Every night Dream comes to their beds and takes them out for a walk in its fields to meet its friends. At night the familiar faces of games and toys live a full-bodied life and this affects children's relationships to the objects of diurnal life."

All of this is part of Remizov's work. Life regarded as acceptable—isn't this life as children perceive it? How bright everything is, how clear, airy, desirable, simple, and sweet! There is nothing terrible, nothing incomprehensible; there are no tears or drama, and if there are, they are only simple and innocent tragi-comedies. "Games, ritual, and toys are seen through childlike eyes as living things which function autonomously" (commentary to *Sunways*); the cat plays with mice in the happy, harmless game of "cat and mouse"; "the geese and swans" practically nip the gray wolf at the bottom of the hill so that the wolf is barely able to get away, saying "just don't rip off my tail!"; "there the ploughed fields are radiantly green; there in the blue forest God's beasts come out of their burrows and lairs and run along the black, pounded-down tracks, along the worn-through paths.... there a song weaves and flutters from the flowers to the grass like a multicolored ribbon." Where, now, is that "Someone" with the tear-filled eyes and the long goose-neck, the malicious and mournful Devil who mocks mankind? Instead of him we find the good-natured "horned Devil—Sparker"—honking and poking at the earth, counting the little birds; the little devils hop out and "raise such a racket...fencing and sparring with their horns, turning somersaults, squeaking, butting one another, dancing—well it's just too much to describe..."

Perhaps nothing better and more graphically explains Remizov's internal "acceptance" of life and the world than an analysis of the external form of his "Holy Russian" works—*Sunways,* "Limonar," "To the Ocean-Sea," and the spectacles. Such an analysis remains for the future when Remizov's work will be treated with the attention it has long deserved and people realize that Remizov is one of the most remarkable Russian stylists.

Take, for example, *Sunways*. What virtuosity it shows, what love, not only of life but of the word, not only of reality but of style! This is not the cold virtuosity which we find, for example, in Merezhkovsky's[7] artistic work. In Remizov's writing we do not find lifeless virtuosity but truly vital, artistic creativity. Before our eyes the artist creates a miracle: he rummages in "miraculous books, written in a semi-uncial hand," and in the codices of the eighteenth century, he retells "tales, parables, stories, and legends"; he lovingly collects words and appends them with extensive commentaries; he matches words like colors and strings them onto the thread of his story like beads—and as a result we have before us a vividly poetic, vital and truly artistic work. This constitutes the miracle of creation, the mystery of art.

This is a difficult road and it is accessible only to a genuine artist. It is fraught with two dangers. Believing only in words, one can weave not a vital artistic fabric but a lifeless verbal network—Merezhkovsky's virtuosity exemplifies this. Or one can get carried away by words, overstep all measure and limits, and forget the boundary between the essential and the secondary, i.e., not distinguish the work from its words—as so often occurs in Leskov.[8] There is much of Leskov in Remizov but, genuine artist that he is, Remizov masters his words and not vice-versa, for he does not proceed to life from words but rather arrives at words from life.

Remizov's love and acceptance of words clearly demonstrates his acceptance and love of life. Read *Sunways* and see what transparent tenderness exists there. And how simply, so it seems, it is attained. Look particularly at "Kostroma"—it is built entirely on diminutives. But try resorting to this device if you are not an artist and it will become repulsive lisping! Or read the apocryphal story "The Anger of Ilya the Prophet" in "Limonar"—for sheer power and imaginativeness there is hardly anything comparable in all of Russian literature. Follow the author of "To the Ocean-Sea" and you will see how genuine life overflows and sparkles in everything Remizov touches upon. Take, lastly, the "spectacles" and you will find in them not the sort of stylization which everyone has come to detest, but a genuine artistic revivial unique in Russian literature. And after all of this, switch to "Sisters of the Cross" or *The Pond,* where the author penetrates the depths of modern man's soul with the same finely wrought style.

It is not without significance that Remizov has passed through "decadence." He has retained all of its achievements and in many areas he has paved the way for future developments. But he has been able to overcome everything which ultimately reduced decadence to degeneracy and impoverishment. Only imitators of decadence are now writing in the style and manner of *The Pond;* a typical example is Ivan Rukavishnikov's[9] novel *The Accursed Race* (1911). The cheap effects which were new ten years ago, the deliberate refinement, the affectedness of feeling and style— all of this has now become accessible to the countless imitators of decadence. And precisely at this time the profound and sophisticated Remizov is consciously moving to a greater and incomparably more difficult simplicity of line and form. It is interesting to compare the 1911 edition of his *Collected Works* with the original text of those same works: the undertaking provides most valuable material for the study of the psychology and evolution of creativity. Compare the first edition of *The Clock* or *The Pond* (1905 and 1907) with the texts of these novels in the *Collected Works*—practically no sentence has escaped change, and some pages are totally unrecognizable. Literary history will one day return to study all of this.

But what is even now clear is the basic character of this artist who so lovingly seeks old and new words, who so bitterly resents life and the world but who so heartily blesses them with his mighty benediction. Without understanding them, he accepts life and the world; but he who accepts understands—if not by reason, then by intuition. The crucifiers and the crucified, the monkeys and "Holy Russia," all of life "to the last blade of grass" and the heavy burden of the cross are combined in Remizov's work into one whole, for this is how they are combined in life itself.

This is difficult to accept and understand, and therefore Remizov's work remains for many an eternally sealed book. But those who feel both the tormenting depth and the artistic charm of his work will, now and in the future, highly esteem this truly great writer.

Notes

1. Przybyszewski, Stanislaw (1868-1927). Polish writer whose modernist/decadent fiction enjoyed considerable success in Russia between 1900 and 1910. He is believed to have influenced particularly Konstantin Balmont and Valery Bryusov, two of the leading poets of the first phase of Russian symbolism.

2. The "God-seekers" were a group composed largely of writers and philosophers such as Gippius (see note 2 in Zhirmunsky), Merezhkovsky (see note 6 in Nevedomsky), and Filosofov. They were occasionally called the "Evangelists of Decadence." Petersburg based, they founded the Religious-Philosophical Society and published for a short while the journal *New Path (Novyi put').* Criticizing contemporary bourgeois values, the God-seekers strove to found a Christian-utopist society.

3. For a discussion of Bely's *Silver Dove,* see Berdyaev's article in this collection.

4. The Field of Mars is a large square in the center of Petersburg (now Leningrad), containing some of the city's most beautiful buildings erected in the late eighteenth and early nineteenth centuries.

5. Vyazemsky, Pyotr Andreevich (1792-1878). Poet, critic, and close friend of Pushkin.

6. This is probably an allusion to Sologub's novel-trilogy *The Created Legend* (more accurately translated as *A Legend in Creation*) which began to appear in 1907 and which was completed in 1914. For a brief discussion of Sologub's novel-trilogy, see Dolinin's article in this collection.

7. See note 6 in Nevedomsky.

8. Leskov, Nikolai Semyonovich (1831-1895). A major short story writer and novelist of mid-late nineteenth-century Russia. Leskov's works, like Remizov's, are distinguished by a profound interest in, and knowledge of, old Russian culture and lore, as well as enormous linguistic virtuosity, especially in the use of exotic, vernacular, occasionally archaic words gleaned from Russia's many linguistic dialects. Both writers create a style which can be described as elaborate and fantastic.

9. Rukavishnikov, Ivan Sergeevich (1877-1930). A writer whose early works fell under the influence of decadence and symbolism. *The Accursed Race* was Rukavishnikov's most popular work, and one of the book's ardent supporters, A. V. Lunacharsky, the Soviet Minister of Education and Culture under Lenin, argued that it was "of significant artistic, historical, and social value."

8

The Farsighted Ones: Bryusov's *Fiery Angel* and Kuzmin's *First Book of Stories*

Lyubov Yakovlevna Gurevich (1866-1940)

Short story writer, novelist, critic, and theater historian, Lyubov Gurevich is probably best remembered today as an influential journalist of the 1890s who forwarded the cause of the then highly controversial symbolist art. As publisher of the Petersburg monthly The Northern Herald (Severnyi vestnik) *from 1891 until 1899, Gurevich (along with the editor, A. Volynsky) opened the journal to fledgling writers such as Gippius, Lokhvitskaya, Balmont, and Sologub. This early organ of the "new" literature provided a crucial forum for the discussion, propagation, and dissemination of modernist literature and literary theory and allowed the young artists-idealists the exposure they so badly needed. Gurevich went on to describe this exciting period of Russian literary history in a long article in Professor S. Vengerov's* Russian Literature of the Twentieth Century (Russkaya literatura XX veka, *1914), entitled "The History of the* Northern Herald" *("Istoriya* Severnogo vestnika").*

*Not very successful as a writer of fiction, Gurevich was well known in the decade before the Revolution as a literary and drama critic, and in the latter capacity she wrote for two widely circulated publications—*Speech (Rech') *and* Russian Thought (Russkaya mysl'). *So influential were her views that Leonid Andreyev confessed about his play* Samson Enchained *(*Samson v okovakh, *1915): "I am altering* Samson *for the third time; I want to please Lyubov Gurevich." Her major collection of articles, from which the following piece is taken, appeared in 1912 under the title* Literature and Aesthetics (Literatura i èstetika). *Introducing the volume, she writes: "Having lived through the twenty-year period in Russian literature which in the future will probably be called symbolism and decadence and in which elements of artistic renewal and distortion were uniquely combined, I have tried more precisely to discern those laws of artistic creation and perception without whose observance—whether instinctually or consciously—the writer, like all participants in art, cannot create anything integral, vital, and truly significant." Yet for all of Gurevich's support for symbolism and the* *"new" art, she had her limitations and prejudices when it came to artistic "laws"—especially when she deemed literature to be "decadent" or to betray signs of "aestheticism." Already in 1896 Sologub observed such narrowness when Gurevich forced him to make some significant cuts in his first novel* Bad Dreams (Tyazhelye sny), *which* The Northern Herald *published serially. For this Sologub accused Gurevich of "aesthetic conservatism," traces of which are found in her article on Bryusov and Kuzmin.*

Like so many critics who remained in Russia after the Revolution, Gurevich moved away from literary criticism as such into the safer area of literary history and scholarship. A good friend of the director Konstantin Stanislavsky and an early supporter of his experimental Moscow Art Theater, Gurevich was the first editor of his theoretical writings, as well as of his autobiography My Life in Art (Moya zhizn' v iskusstve, *1926). In the twenties and thirties Gurevich devoted her energies primarily to her long-time and ardent interest in the theater, producing two books*—The Actor's Art (Tvorchestvo aktera, *1927) and* The History of Russian Theatrical Life (Istoriya russkogo teatral'nogo byta, *1939).*

The Farsighted Ones*

I.

Not long ago I reread Bryusov's *Fiery Angel* and Kuzmin's *First Book of Short Stories*. These books are not the newest things around. Bryusov's tale was printed in *The Scales*[1] in 1907, and some of Kuzmin's pieces included in his new anthology date as far back as 1906. But only now, it seems, on the eve of a new period in literature,[2] when the originators of the defunct decadent period themselves show a clear need to surpass themselves, and new slogans issue from their own lips—only now do Bryusov's and Kuzmin's works appear in proper perspective. Only now do their literary merits and shortcomings seem particularly characteristic.

It is no mere coincidence that both of these books, so different in style and aesthetic approach, are marked by exoticism. Bryusov's tale takes us to sixteenth-century Germany; Kuzmin's stories either concern past ages, both in content and in local color, or reflect the exotic tendencies of the author. All of contemporary art, in Russia as well as in Europe, every aesthetic trend of the last decade of the nineteenth century and the first decade of the twentieth, not only in the field of literature but also in the sphere of painting, is colored by this love for the exotic, for the distant, for the pristine and the colorful—enticing in its vivid originality and primitiveness or in its stylistic beauty and perfection, and alluring in its inaccessibility.[3] All contemporary aestheticism is colored by this attraction to the exotic, and through the veneer of modern fashion we can feel in everything with which we like to surround ourselves and beautify our lives this same love for the variegated beauty of the distantly picturesque and the antique. "How he loved this spacious green room filled with the sounds of Rameau and Debussy.... this study lined with books from floor to ceiling, where they read Marlowe and Swinburne; this bedroom with the wash-stand where dark-red fauns danced in a circle against a bright-green background; this dining room all in red copper; these stories of Italy, Egypt, India; these raptures over *any piquantly beautiful thing from whatever country or age* ..." So says Kuzmin of the young hero of his modern tale *Wings*. In fact, this page expresses something quite typical of certain strata in our modern age. "It is amusing," says the author in another part of the story, "to what extent we see what we want to see and understand what we are seeking. Take the way the Romans and Romance nations of the seventeenth century saw only the three unities in Greek writings, while the eighteenth century focused on the thundering tirades and libertarian ideas, and the Romantics on the feats of lofty heroism,

---

* "Dal'nozorkie"—published in *Russkaya mysl'*, 1910, No. 3, pp. 143-155.

whereas our own age has seized upon a sharp note of primitiveness and the Klinger-like luminescence of distant horizons."

I will not enumerate here the names of European and Russian writers, poets, and painters who are entirely under the grip of these exotic tendencies, nor will I talk about the sources of this movement and about what positive things it has brought about. I would like to emphasize something else. Our modern art, while it does not reject the name "modernism," loves the phenomenon of modernity least of all; it is able least of all to draw inspiration from living motifs and peculiar shapes and forms of the present, to see what is beautiful and eternal in them. All the sensitivity, all the curiosity of the typically modern poet and artist are directed beyond the bounds of his surroundings. He will stop at nothing to pierce the thick mass of life's appearances which mean nothing to his soul. Yellowed folios[4] with their agitating odor, works of art and handicrafts of past ages, and, in extreme cases, blind daydreams, are supposed to save the modern artist from confronting reality, which for him is as oppressive, dead, and tiresome as a prison cell. He simply cannot see reality's most characteristic patterns, the colorful nuances and delicate artistic quality that beg to be described.

This is indeed the crux of the matter. There are nearsighted people who cannot distinguish anything in the distance, and farsighted ones who have to make a special effort to discern things right in front of them. Old age is always farsighted, as are people who have lost their childlike and generally human spontaneity, people whose great and enduring feelings have been destroyed by the acuity of their deliberately cultivated sensations, people who have renounced the vitality of an active life and have transferred their soul's entire creative energy to the sphere of the intellect. The modern generation of artists and poets—certainly the most significant and "genuine" of them—is distinguished by a particular keenness of sensation, a particular development of awareness, a broad artistic and historical field of vision, as well as the farsightedness of old age, with everything it entails.

I am speaking here precisely about the farsightedness of old age. What great poet of any epoch did not surge into the distance, did not traipse all over the world in his fantasy, was not carried by his creative imagination beyond the borders of his country and his age, did not tremble with delight before the artistic debris of a past and unfamiliar life? But this is something different from what I have in mind, a plenitude of vital and spiritual energies which no reality can ever satisfy, the happy keensightedness of a soul expanding the narrow horizons of our concrete existence. Shakespeare, Goethe, Pushkin—each wanted to see everything, the near and the far, and each was able to see the distant as well as the near. They recorded not only their own lyrical "I" with its exotic daydreams, but also their age with its colors and forms—the specific features of its beauty—and with its anxieties, passions, worries, and joys—the specific features of its rhythms. They were not only *poets,* grasping and interpreting the subtle music of their own souls and creating beautiful shifting mirages from the various elements of their knowledge and fantasy. They were also *artists,* greedily imbibing all the characteristic forms of their surroundings and responding fully to the characteristic motifs of their day. Feeling the full range of simple and complex, intensely heated and subtly transparent human passions, they could, to use a term from contemporary aesthetics, "intuit" the phenomena of quickly fleeting life and extract from it priceless literary themes and vivid details. And their artistic instinct, welling up in a soul that had not lost its human spontaneity, suggested methods of writing which aroused a sense of creativity in the reader himself and, through magical allusions alone, evoked in his fantasy images which are both aflutter with life and clear in their spiritual meaning and content.

Among the fairly substantial pleiad of writers who tend toward everything exotic there are many with obvious talent, many versatile and genuine poets. Yet there is not one artist among them who delights us with the vibrant beauty of integral and finished epic creations. Unable to "intuit" people, they lack the gift of reincarnation without which no literary creation, with the exception of certain kinds of lyric poetry, is possible. Furthermore, the instinct which unconsciously governs the artist in the construction of his literary works has largely dried up in them along with the spontaneity of organic and emotional life...

I do not, nonetheless, mean to claim that such literary works of our time as Bryusov's *Fiery Angel* or Kuzmin's short stories are without interest. Not at all. For those who love art and who enjoy examining the life of a literature which is perhaps already imperceptibly revealing signs of the future, the creations of these two talented authors will prove to be absorbing, interesting, and instructive. One writer, through stubborn and unceasing work, is attempting to break through the walls of his own individuality and peculiarly contemporary limitations; the other, by giving free rein to his fantasy, loosens the artistic fabric of his works, which is sometimes held together merely by an anti-literary tendency.

II.

Bryusov's *Fiery Angel* impresses us first of all by the sheer wealth of historical knowledge which informs the story. One cannot approach this gigantic and enterprising endeavor, so permeated with scholarly and literary inquisitiveness, without a certain amount of respect. The writer's mind absorbed hundreds of books imprinted with the spirit of a former life; his gaze greedily devoured many hundreds of documents, museum treasures, and artistic works of the past. He has captured and resurrected the life of nearly four centuries ago; he *sees* this Germany of the sixteenth century in which emerging rationalism is struggling to overcome the specter of medieval prejudices. And if we ask ourselves what provoked Bryusov to create such a book, we have to say that it was most likely the sheer need to render a cultural-historical picture of all that he gleaned from his scholarly labors. This same stimulus motivates the works of every talented scholar and historian, but not works of art. Bryusov, however, clearly intended to create a work of art.

Bryusov chose an exceptionally clever form to accomplish his goal. His tale—for he chose not to give his work the banal name of historical novel, which evokes so many unpleasant associations in literature[5]—is told by the hero in the form of notes about his recent experiences. A subtle calculation! Bryusov knows the limits of his literary talent. It is with good reason that when he published his fictional prose in *The Earth's Axis*,[6] he completely discarded thirteen of the twenty stories which had been printed earlier, and that in the foreword he asks the reader to note that of the two kinds of short stories—"stories of character" and "stories of situation"— his pieces belong to the second category, and "therefore it would be unfair to blame the author for a depiction of characters insufficiently complete." One can, of course, ignore the author's division, or at least formulate it quite differently and arrive at other conclusions, but it is impossible not to perceive Bryusov's distinctively acute self-awareness and self-criticalness in these lines.

Thus, *The Fiery Angel* represents the hero's notes on *recent* experience. I am reminded of one of Chekhov's letters in which he says that he never writes about what he has recently seen and lived through, since memory must first filter out all that is truly characteristic, i.e., artistically valid about it. Bryusov's hero has not succeeded in distilling the truly characteristic and artistic elements from the variegated impressions of his recent experiences. By the first person device Bryusov divests himself of responsibility for the artistic blunders of this sixteenth-century man who, furthermore, as is noted in the foreword to the second edition of the tale, "is evidently showing off his knowledge." Yes, he is unquestionably showing off. In other words, the author himself feels the irresistible urge to spread out before the reader's wondering gaze these gems of cultural and historical details—probably tracked down one by one in various sources and then lovingly strung into endless chains and necklaces. "The ladies play lutes, zithers, and flutes, and dance the alegarde, the passionaise, the mauritanian and other modern dances"; "... at first an argument sprang up among us about the merits of various sorts of wines: Italian Rheinfall and Spanish Canor, Speier Gensfüsser and Wurtemburg Eilfinger," etc.; "then the count showed me various scientific instruments, of which he had many: terrestrial and celestial globes, astrolabes, armillary spheres, torquettes, and some other unheard-of ones..." I will refrain from providing other similar excerpts, for example, the lists of various dishes of the time which twice appear in the text, and the full-page enumerations of contemporary scientific and magic books, or of the names, types, and forms of all possible demons as described in the works of practitioners of black magic. Or that picture of a witches' sabbath which is supposed to convey the fantastic and nightmarish dreams of the hero brought on by special drugs, but which is presented with such bookish precision and sobriety that our imagination refuses to follow the hero. Finally, there are those descriptions of houses, rooms, furniture, and costumes... Everything is presented here with the thoroughness and precision of a museum catalogue composed by a true lover of antiquities, who, however, is not guided by the laws of aesthetic perception. In fact, the more the author provides us with names and businesslike descriptions of unfamiliar objects which neither speak to our imagination nor evoke any living associations, the more impotent our creative contribution as readers becomes. Yet the secret of every living art lies in the mutual creation of both reader and writer, and a writer is an artist only when he can—albeit momentarily—awaken the artist in the soul of his reader.

Up to now I have been talking about Bryusov's work as though it were not a novel at all. But it really is a novel. Human passions are depicted in it with all of their fateful laws and deadly caprices, as well as the torments of human souls in pursuit of divine shadows. The fiery angel descends to the unhappy Renata in her sickly visions and summons her to the delights of otherworldly perfection and bliss. An insane longing gnaws at her inflamed soul while she is in the embraces of earthly lovers, and demons of voluptuousness torment her in times of solitude. Her chaste prayers to the Savior alternate with criminal—to her mind—invocations of dark powers, and the horror of sin drives her to the monastery. But no sooner is she rapt in the ecstasies of her repentance than she is crushed by a kind of curse from within the very bowels of her human nature: while some nuns consider her a saint, many others are overcome by "strange temptations." The storm of the Inquisition gathers over her, and a gloomy trial takes place in a dungeon, attended by her recent beloved; there are tortures; Renata, thrown into prison and seeking only death, dies operatically in her friend's arms just when he has come to release her. How much movement and, it would seem, internal drama there is in this plot; how fiery and colorful is the book's basic motif! Add to this the external peripeteia of the novel, full of adventures and journeys through sixteenth-century Germany, acquaintances with the famous scientist of the time, Agrippa of Nöttesheim, and his pupils, meetings with Dr. Faust and Mephistopheles as they appear in documents which have preserved the legend, and to some extent as they are presented poetically in Goethe's profound conception. What a combination of fantasy with psychological and everyday realism!

But this is the point: it is not creative fantasy, but a sober, clear mind cultivated by science that prevails in Bryusov—an uncommonly sober and cold mind which, like an anatomist's, disassembles even the human soul into its composite parts. Bryusov does not trace the course of passion as any artist would. Rather he expresses it in rational terms, always explaining everything completely, revealing the causal dependence of every emotional state on events preceding or accompanying it, and almost always seeking out some kind of analogy for inner experience from the external world. "I do not know whether the art of my words prevailed or whether there was at that time so much fire in me that it could not help but be transferred to Renata's being and ignite her, or, finally, whether it was a case of the forces of passion, which had been forcibly confined by the thick walls of reason, finally erupting in Renata herself, such that the goddess of love triumphed that evening." Or, "my feeling for Renata, which suddenly revived under the influence of her vision, began to die away again, like a ball someone kicks accidentally, but which even so cannot roll freely down a rocky road." This is the nature of Bryusov's psychological portrayal and this is the style of his story, which belaboredly abounds in similes, but which lacks the vitality and scope that an artist needs in order to evoke bright and colorful visions. The image of Renata, in spite of the fact that she is continually discussed, is definitely unsuccessful. She does not live; with all her emotional complexity, she still fails to intrigue us. The blame may first of all be placed on a personal blunder of the author which is as striking as it is characteristic. From the very first moment of our acquaintance with the heroine, Bryusov unequivocally gives us to understand that we are dealing with a clinical subject: before our eyes Renata suffers a typical attack of so-called *grand hystérie,* as it is described in any textbook of psychopathology. This treatment suffices to put our fantasy to sleep and to call into action our memory and our reason. But it is not enough for Bryusov: his insurmountable fondness for what is called positive science prompts him to provide even his hero with appropriate explanations on this score, to the extent that they were available at that time. Through the mouth of one of his episodic characters, Bryusov gives his hero a whole little lecture about the fact that "there is a certain disease which cannot be called insanity but which is near to it," that "these women truly believe in their stories and truly suffer from phantom ills," etc., etc.

Just what is this notorious hysteria whose symptoms are so well studied by doctors? Do we, in fact, really know? And do we, in life, lose interest in a person with a deep and outstanding soul when we learn that he suffers from hysteria? Dostoevsky's Nastasya Filippovna[7] is also an unquestionably hysterical woman; however, we are gripped by the violent outbursts and perturbations of her sick soul. She lives before us as an individual, whose hysteria only strengthens and reveals that which lies stored in her human nature and which she can have in common with other, healthy people. The secrets of a truly deep soul are equally unfathomable in a healthy and in a sick person, and only shallow minds seizing on medical terms think that the word "hysteria" expresses everything. Bryusov, of course, understands this and therefore is not afraid of making a hysterical woman the central figure of his novel. But to attach this label to the heroine and to emphasize, through the terminology of medical science, this hysteria in her means consciously to disregard the laws of art. Associations, associations! Clinical prose accompanies Renata from her very first appearance. And what is more important, throughout the whole novel nothing compels us to *feel* the human and universal tragedy of her soul, which is kindled with evil earthly passions by the fire of its higher ecstasies and is always tormented by aversion for its real being.

While the contents of the tale might be spellbinding, it cannot be read without considerable effort even by those who find it interesting to skim through the author's copious and purely scholarly notes appended to the second edition of the book.

But I should stress that we do not derive only cultural and historical data from Bryusov's story. The novel is written by an intelligent and perceptive man, by a great lyric poet who, through both the music and subtly thought-out words of his verses, has related to us quite a few sad and bitter truths about the soul of contemporary man. The hero of the story, just barely disguised as a man of the sixteenth century, reveals to us in his memoirs a soul which is fascinating in its almost boundless awareness and which, for all its constant analyzing and rationalizing, is nevertheless full of indefatiguable energy. This is a soul that has mastered the high art of self-control and sobriety, which helps the hero escape unscathed from all the ordeals of life in order to proceed further with the one goal before him: to experience and learn. Subject to stormy passions, this man, at bottom, is not capable of really loving and believing. Shut off in his conscious "I," he is deaf both to the disturbing noises of life and to those mysterious voices which sound from the depths of our own unconscious spirit; and no matter what happens to him and around him, his mind works as though it were confined to the peace and quiet of a study. What an appropriate emotional apparatus for dauntless and merciless observations! And this hero's notes are truly full of the subtlest remarks and self-observations concerning both the perfidies of the human psyche, the play of human passions which know nothing immutable or sacred, and reactions such as take place in our immediate life as a result of the intervention and influence of firm and clear reason. A barely audible hint of melancholic irony sounds in these psychological analyses of Bryusov's, which in themselves are of serious interest. And there are cleverly devised and magnificently recounted individual episodes, such as, for example, the first acquaintance with Agrippa of Nöttesheim and his pupils. And, finally, Bryusov the lyric poet makes himself felt in certain places here—in the beauty of sudden turns of phrases, in the charming poetic similes, in the unexpectedly bright and resonant words which convey the moods and feelings of nature.

Yet upon closing the book, one involuntarily mutters: "Well, so what?" So much is described, told, and narrated here, but something important—very important—is lacking: a conception which cannot be conveyed through words of reason and which lies, so to say, not on the plane of depicted realities but deeper, under it, and makes up the invisible soul of each work, its invisible center toward which all of its parts, all of its details, gravitate.

Such works, however, are created not by positive minds but by people of a completely different emotional make-up, and neither mathematical clarity of thought nor a wealth of scientific knowledge can help create them.

III.

Kuzmin, outstandingly gifted by nature, although hardly Bryusov's equal, represents the latter's complete opposite in several respects. Bryusov is not a painter. This is the weakest side of his art. Kuzmin, of all the writers of his literary generation, is the most vivid word painter. His ability to evoke visions in the soul of the reader is so great that in connection with him one inevitably recalls Pliny's words about Timanthes,[8] words that apply only to true artists, namely that "in his pictures we always see far more than is actually expressed." All of Kuzmin's descriptions, in verse as well as prose, are carried out in a few strokes; whether he takes us to eighteenth-century France or to ancient Alexandria or to the apartment of a contemporary aesthete, we are given the illusion of space illuminated by the sun or by flickering lights, and of air suffused with fragrance. Almost everywhere we feel movement and hear life's sound in Kuzmin's writing. We see before us the muddy street of an old French town; down it, his coat fluttering in the cold wind, rides Aimé Leboeuf, for the sake of adventure and travel leaving forever the haberdasher's family which had taken him in. We can hear his heart beating when, led by a secret passage to Louise de Tombelle's chamber, he stops after brushing against a chair in a dark room where the squeaks of mice and muffled music, as of a distinct harpsichord, sound ... The external world, the sensual world in the philosophical sense of the word, comes to life before us in his descriptions. Our imagination joyously runs to meet his fluent and colorful words.

Does this mean, however, that Kuzmin is a real artist? No, it is not that simple. Much is needed—not only native talent—to become a real artist.

But perhaps before we look more intently into Kuzmin's literary physiognomy, we should discard the widespread prejudice about him among members of the public who know him only by hearsay or who, even if they have read him, are given to confusing concepts. Kuzmin is called a "pornographic" writer. This is absolutely untrue: he never displays "seductive" images before us, he never uses his gift of expression to present the external details of erotic life. His reputation as a pornographer is based on the fact that he openly treats a motif which is considered to be psychologically aberrant.[9] But his very manner of treating this motif is such that if some nasty youth were to rummage through his books hoping to find some kind of explicit instructions, he would leave disappointed. Any contemporary writer treats the themes of normal erotica much more realistically. Pierre Louÿs[10] in *Aphrodite* and "The Songs of Bilitis"—those clever imitations of corresponding ancient works—goes incomparably farther than Kuzmin in presenting the erotic realistically, yet nonetheless serious readers do not judge his works to be "pornography." One might even go further and respond to accusations that Kuzmin almost maniacally, obsessively returns to the same theme by saying that many writers and artists of whatever kind essentially repeat the same motif all their lives. But the point is that this never happens with great or major writers; excessive specialization is always a sign of some kind of mental and spiritual limitation, or of some internal defect in the artist.

As I reread Kuzmin's stories, once again won over from the very first pages by his soft, tender, and rich descriptive talent, I want to see him as an artist. But I do not see him as such. The excellently initiated, finely styled, quick-paced story about the adventures of this scoundrel Aimé Leboeuf soon takes on the character of fragmentary sketches, increasingly fleeting, disorderly, and diffuse. There are wild improbabilities. There exist in Kuzmin—the beautiful stylist—humorously careless errors of language, such as "they gave me *to drink* hot chocolate, then *dinner.*" Next to living characters who are drawn clearly and distinctly flash others who are hardly sketched at all, and finally there are some vague patches which say nothing whatsoever. In a word, the story is written, by and large, exactly in the manner which Kuzmin now rejects in his critique "On Beautiful Clarity," published in the first issue of *Apollo.*[11] Yet this is one of the most important stories of the book under consideration. "The Letters of Clara Valmont" is an insignificant sketch. "Flor and the Robber" has an interesting plot, reminiscent of Edgar Allan Poe,[12] but it is only a vague outline. "The Shadow of Phillida" is a rather pale piece from the psychological point of view. "Anna Meyer's Decision" is a story based on an anecdotal match-up of initials, with an unsuccessful psychological ploy at the end: when would enamored Estonian governesses, or whoever it may be, thank their deceivers, moreover the minute after the deceit is discovered, for the sweet illusion they have created and then ask permission to go on, consciously now, with their game of sending love letters? "Aunt Sonya's Couch" is well-written but meaningless nonsense. Finally, there is *Wings.*

This rather large piece, which is also written in fragments and patches—not in vague but colorful ones—merits serious attention. Here, as in some of Kuzmin's poems, we find the key to understanding his literary personality. Here stands revealed his entire ideology, so characteristic of the whole group of "exotic writers." And we not only feel and divine this ideology to be the hidden skeleton of the work, we simply cannot fail to see in it Kuzmin's predilection, expressed in precise, clear "cerebral" words. The same thought is expressed here in many ways—in the beginning, the middle, and the end—by different characters, as if to make sure that no one might think it merely the subjective view of any one of them. Here is this idea as it is expressed in the words of the main hero of the story, Stroop: "And people saw that all beauty, all love is from the gods, and they became free and brave spirits and grew wings." This idea of the wingedness of *all* love, of the ugliness of *every* form of self-limitation is repeated by the schismatic Marya Dmitrievna on the Volga and by the "red-haired, ugly, and charming Mme. Monier in Florence." "Man should develop *all* the capacities of his spirit and body as far as possible," says one of the secondary heroes of the story, and the arguments of another character, the wise "Hellenist" teacher who justifies the animal love of an intelligent being for a beautiful, impudent bath attendant as a "function" "not at all degrading" for man, reveal in full the author's world view. The statement "a man should be like a river or a mirror, accepting all that is reflected in him," develops the same idea further, to its ultimate logical conclusion. This doctrine rings with the pathos of real conviction in the story, as does the summons to unbridle all human passions, biases, and inclinations, and to justify everything in which even passing pleasure can be found. "We are Hellenes, lovers of the beautiful, the bacchantes of the coming day ...Thither, over the sea, through mist and darkness, we will sail, my Argonauts!"

This seemingly daring enthusiasm with which Kuzmin expresses thoughts that are so quickly snapped up on the streets, so hopelessly vulgarized by third-rate writers and which turn out to be so cheap, sounds remarkably funny in this story from several years back. The philosophical arguments to the effect that "there is neither finality nor good and evil" and that "it is not fact and bare reality that are important, but one's relationship to them," and the references to the Hellenes all seem terribly unserious here. In Plato's *Symposium* Pausanius also proceeds from the reasoning that "every act committed is in itself neither beautiful nor shameful," but he does not therefore conclude that *every* love is winged, he does not call for the anarchy of human passions. Rather he sets up a distinction between heavenly Eros and "popular" Eros, i.e., between exalted love and vulgar love, and advocates loving a beautiful soul more than a beautiful body. In the words of Socrates, love is presented as an ascent up a ladder to the ever more beautiful, subtle, spiritual, and divine.

It is understandable why Kuzmin's story made me recall Plato's immortal dialogue: the theme of the arguments is the same in both. But what do the proclivities of the contemporary poet and the wisdom of the Hellenes have in common? And why does Kuzmin refer to the Hellenes when his views constitute merely a decadent individualism which does not extol the idea of a personality integral and noble as it strives to realize its higher, ideal "I," but rather which praises a specific human being, pluralistic, variegated, and fragmented in the contradiction of its inclinations? It was to this specific human "I" and to each of its contradictory elements that the decadents wanted to give free expression. One recalls Ibsen's splendid fable *Peer Gynt:* the madhouse in Cairo where each man "appears himself only because he is *beside himself,*" and the scene with the Buttonmaker who is to smelt in his ladle the ill-starred "individualist" Peer Gynt, who has not understood what the *real* human "I" is ...

The idea which inspires Kuzmin is a poor and unoriginal one, and yet it is all that holds his artistic edifice together. Where it is lacking, the creations of his fantasy unravel and crumble like a fine, motley-colored fabric touched with rot. And if in Kuzmin's verse, for all the monotony of its motifs, I see primarily an enthralling artistic talent, then, reading his prose, I say to myself "No, he is not an artist." He is so talented in everything, yet at bottom his work is neither beautiful, nor serious, nor deep. Neither do I feel here a creative spirit or a wealth of psychological content. Kuzmin has a rare gift of grasping characteristic pictorial features. I see in his work not only landscapes, but the figures of his characters, their faces. Yet on looking deeper, I realize that these are just artistically constructed masks: they have empty eyes; behind them there is no real human soul with all the endless variety of its experience, sufferings, strivings, and interests. Life passes Kuzmin by: he is farsighted, like an old man; he does not see what is happening around him in our languishing and raving contemporary world. He dreams of Alexandria, the green sea, the sounds of distant flutes, the dance of a dark-skinned dancer, or manicured avenues along which walk slender men in light satin vests, or his own ancestors—"sailors of ancient families in love with distant horizons who drink wine in dark ports and embrace gay foreign girls." Sensitive and frivolous, sophisticated and sometimes trivially ribald, he seems spiritually immobile, as though hypnotized. And there is something disconcerting in the gaze that stares out at us from his artistic works and which, as in some of his heroes, represents "a combination of fixed concentration and absentmindedness, of acute vision and blindness."

Notes

1. *The Scales (Vesy)*. A Moscow-based literary journal, published between 1904 and 1909. Although not officially the editor, Bryusov was very much in charge of this important symbolist organ which published works by the leading modernist writers.

2. By 1910, when Gurevich published her article, symbolism was beginning its decline as the dominant aesthetic movement. This year saw a major challenge to literary symbolism on the part of a new group, the acmeists, a discussion of whom is found in Zhirmunsky's article in this collection.

3. Primitivism and an interest in folklore, myth, and legend were an integral part of the modernist movement, giving rise to some of the period's most original works of music, literature, and painting. One thinks of Stravinsky's three ballets (*The Firebird,* 1910; *Petrushka,* 1911; *The Rite of Spring,* 1913), of Remizov's charming folktales and legends (discussed briefly in Ivanov-Razumnik's article in this collection), and the canvases of Nikolai Roerich.

4. Into this category of "yellowed folios" also fits Merezhkovsky's trilogy of historical novels *Christ and Antichrist* (*Khristos i Antikhrist,* 1896-1905), which Gurevich surely must have in mind here as well. But not all modernist novels were directed beyond the bounds of the writer's surroundings (e.g., Sologub's *Bad Dreams,* 1896 and *The Petty Demon,* 1905), and beginning precisely in 1910, when Gurevich wrote this article, there begins to appear a whole series of major prose fiction devoted to contemporary problems—from Remizov's *Sisters of the Cross* and Bely's *Silver Dove* to Sologub's *A Legend in Creation* and Bely's *Petersburg,* both completed at the end of the symbolist period, in 1914.

5. Gurevich most likely has in mind here the crude historical novels of Mikhail Zagoskin (1789-1859) and the didactic historical fiction of Faddei Bulgarin (1789-1859).

6. Bryusov's first collection of stories *The Earth's Axis* (*Zemnaya os',* 1907) displays that same penchant for exotic adventures as is found in *The Fiery Angel* and in his later and less successful novel of fourth-century Rome, *Victory's Altar* (*Altar' pobedy,* 1911-1912).

7. The heroine in Dostoevsky's novel *The Idiot* (1869).

8. Timanthes was an ancient Greek painter, chiefly known for one of the greatest pictures of antiquity "The Sacrifice of Iphigenia." Gurevich is referring to Pliny the Younger (ca. 62-113A. D.), whose *Letters* deal with a wide variety of issues, including Greek painting.

9. Gurevich is referring here to homosexuality; Kuzmin was an avowed homosexual.

10. Pierre Louÿs (1870-1925). French novelist and poet. His novel *Aphrodite* (1896), upon which his reputation in France was largely built, recounts courtesan life in ancient Alexandria. His "Songs of Bilitis" ("Chansons de Bilitis," 1894) are allegedly translations of a contemporary of the poetess Sappho; in fact they are highly successful literary hoaxes.

11. *Apollo (Apollon)*. This lavish Petersburg journal, published between 1909 and 1917, dealt with all aspects of artistic and cultural life. The poet Nikolai Gumilyov had a regular column, "Letters on Russian Poetry," as did Kuzmin, who surveyed contemporary Russian fiction in his "Notes on Russian Belles-Lettres."

12. A perceptive observation. In his youthful letters to his good friend —future Soviet Foreign Minister, Georgy Vasilievich Chicherin (1872-1936)—Kuzmin expresses deep affection for Poe, as well as for the German romantics.

9

Russia's Temptation: On Bely's *Silver Dove*

Nikolai Alexandrovich Berdyaev (1874-1948)*

*Berdyaev is one of the leading religious thinkers and Christian philoso-
phers of the twentieth century, and no biographical sketch can possibly
come close to capturing the profundity of his world view or the
sophistication, range, and depth of his thinking. The author of almost
thirty books and dozens of essays, his writing touches upon such areas as
ethics, metaphysics, Christian existentialism, aesthetics, history, sociology,
literature, and autobiography. Berdyaev was at the center of, and was one
of the leading participants in, the Russian cultural renaissance which
occurred during the two decades preceding the Russian Revolution; he was
acquainted with virtually all the leading literary, cultural, and intellectual
giants in the Russia of his day.*

*Descended from a long and distinguished line of Russian gentry,
Berdyaev was born on the family's estate near Kiev in 1878. His first
publication (on the philosopher Lange) appeared in Germany in 1899,
while he was waiting to be sentenced for participating in a student uprising
in Kiev in 1897. Arrested in 1898 and exiled to Vologda for three years in
1900, the undaunted Berdyaev wrote his first book (on the critic-
philosopher N. K. Mikhailovsky) and put together a collection of his essays*
(Problems of Idealism) *while serving his sentence. He lived in Petersburg
between 1904 and 1908, where he attended Vyacheslav Ivanov's famous
"Tower" (the weekly Wednesday meetings which brought together the
major figures of the Russian cultural renaissance), and where he became
particularly close to Zinaida Gippius and Dmitry Merezhkovsky. In 1907
his interest in Christianity fully developed, and this was to determine the
course of his thinking and writing for the rest of his life.*

In 1908 Berdyaev moved to Moscow, where he began his friendship

---

* Although several studies on Berdyaev's life and work exist in English, the most accessible
and useful to the general reader is Donald Lowrie's *Rebellious Prophet: A Life of Nikolai
Berdyaev* (New York, 1960).

with Andrei Bely which would last for fifteen years and undergo periodic ups and downs. It was at this time that Berdyaev began to study (and ultimately reject) the popular mystical philosophy of Rudolph Steiner's anthroposophy, as is reflected in the review of Bely's Silver Dove *which follows. The years between 1910 and 1917 saw the production of four major books and several essays; in 1918 he published* The Fate of Russia (Sud'ba Rossii) *and* The Crisis of Art (Krizis iskusstva), *the latter being a collection of three essays, including the piece on Bely's* Petersburg *which follows. In that same year he wrote his "Philosophy of Inequality" ("Filosofiya neravenstva," published in Berlin in 1922), where he states his firm opposition to the Bolshevik Revolution.*

Forced to emigrate along with other Russian dissidents in 1922, Berdyaev spent two years in Berlin (where he met up again with Bely, although briefly, since Bely returned to Russia in 1923) and finally settled near Paris for the rest of his life. Although not a literary critic by training or profession, Berdyaev showed a life-long interest in literature and wrote major works on several figures who were directly or indirectly connected to it: on the religious philosopher, Slavophile, and poet Alexei Khomyakov (1912); on Dostoevsky (1922); and on the nineteenth-century philosopher, critic, and prose writer Konstantin Leontyev (1926). Berdyaev's autobiography Self-Knowledge: An Essay in Philosophical Autobiography (Samopoznanie: opyt filosofskoi avtobiografii, *1947) is available in English under the title* Dream and Reality.

Russia's Temptation *

Andrei Bely's astonishing and unexpected novel *The Silver Dove* gives
cause to return once again to the eternal Russian theme of the intelligentsia's relationship to the people. In Bely, however, this theme is tinged
with Russian mysticism; it is thus made more profound and transferred to
an entirely different plane. Bely's novel is one of incredible scope,
penetrating the breadth of national life and sounding the Russian soul. The
force of his creative talent enables Bely to transcend subjectivism and
fathom the objective elementalism of Russia. We can unhesitatingly say
that modern Russian art has produced nothing more significant. One feels
in Bely's novel a return to the traditions of classical Russian literature, yet
we are still quite firmly grounded in the new aesthetic. *The Silver Dove*
combines symbolism and realism in a highly original manner. Bely belongs
to the Gogol school and he is a genuine successor to the Gogolian tradition.
But my goal here is not to evaluate the literary and aesthetic merits of *The
Silver Dove*. Literary critics are sure to praise the novel highly, although
they will find some uneven spots in it, some places which verge on
caricature, some parts which are formally muddled and which present the
reader with certain obstacles. The image of Katya, for example, is totally
unrealistic; it is interpolated into a faithful depiction of life like a beautiful
painting. Consequently, Daryalsky's affair with her remains far removed
from life, and all of Gugelovo seems but an inserted drawing. But there are
moments of enormous artistic power in the novel. One of these is the scene
in which Daryalsky loses his way in the forest on the road from Tselibeyev
to Gugelovo. How remarkable is the correspondence between what is
taking place in Daryalsky's soul and what is occurring in nature. In a
physical sense, Daryalsky has gone astray in the forest just as, internally,
his spirit has lost its bearings. Everywhere in Bely the world of nature fuses
with the life of the spirit. Everything is refracted in Daryalsky's soul, but the
cosmicality of natural and national life remains intact. Bely's novel is
striking in its artistic truth, in its profound feeling for Russia, and in its
deep penetration of national life. It contains neither false idealization of the
people nor populist sugariness. Bely has felt something new in Russia's
elemental life; in the life of the people he has sensed a kind of terrifying
passion which has been missing from Russian populist literature. This
terrible passion, this voluptuousness of the languishing soul lurks not only
in Russian mystical sectarianism but in Russian popular life as well. For
indeed the hero of *The Silver Dove* is Russia itself, its mystical elements, its
nature, its soul. Matryona is the Russian land. True, elemental Russia is
refracted in the soul of the cultured intellectual Daryalsky, but there is no

* "Russkii soblazn—Po povodu 'Serebryannogo golubya' A. Belogo"—published in
Russkaya mysl', 1910, No. 11, pp. 9-20.

impressionistic individualism and subjectivism in this. The hero is not
Daryalsky but Russia. All that is morbid and decadent in Bely is expressed
in Daryalsky; all that is deep and meaningful, in his feeling for Russia.
Daryalsky has a sense that life is illusory. And this feeling of illusoriness
cannot help but exist in one whose attitude toward life is passive. Only an
active relationship to life gives one a feeling of life's realness. Volition
presupposes a differentiation between the real and the unreal. Daryalsky
lives as if he were under the power of a hallucination, in an atmosphere of
magic and sorcery. There are two sides to *The Silver Dove:* the morbid,
decadent passivity and limpness of Daryalsky and the novel's powerful
insight into the popular element, into Russian nature. A breathtaking
greatness, an immeasurable breadth and profundity emanate from the
novel.

The theme of *The Silver Dove* is the encounter of a cultivated Russian
intellectual who has experienced all the latest fads from Marxism to
occultism, with the Russian mystical sect of the Doves, who are spiritually
akin to the flagellant Khlysts.[1] Bely has coped quite remarkably with the
formidable task of fathoming the spirit of Russian mystical sectarianism
and, through this sectarianism, the spirit of the Russian land in general.
Daryalsky's encounter with the Doves is really the confrontation of
cultured mysticism and popular mysticism. Daryalsky's union with
Matryona is the union of the intelligentsia with the people, from which the
new Russia is to be born. But Daryalsky goes to the people empty-handed,
yielding passively to them, and contributing nothing to their life. With
regard to the popular element he is neither a bearer of light nor is he in any
way luminous or steadfast; he does not bring order to elemental chaos,
Logos to life's matter. Daryalsky's destruction is an inevitable result of his
passivity and willessness. Daryalsky is seduced—by Matryona, by the
feminine element, by elemental Russia, by the elemental being of the
people. There is not a trace of will, free choice, manly self-possessiveness,
or steadfastness mastering and informing Daryalsky. It is as if he lived in an
enchanted kingdom, passively submitting to the elements; he is a medium
through whom magic forces pass, pushing him in different directions. He is
enveloped in a nightmarish phantasmagoria which both lures and repels
him. The mystical inclinations of this cultured intellectual—first a Marxist,
then a decadent, then a bit of an occultist—are passive, "mediumistic,"
willess. His mysticism is weak and womanish. The powerful popular
elements stand opposed to him and attract him. But popular mysticism,
the mysticism of Kudeyarova and Matryona, is dark, elemental, demonic,
and terrifying. Bely relays the horror of this mysticism with unusual force.
There is in Russian mystical sectarianism a terrible lack of lucidity, an
absence of Logos, an obscure self-affirmation, and a plunge into the abyss.
Bely has sensed this and has relayed it to us. *The Silver Dove* is a somber,
discomforting book. In their mystical elementalism the people are

powerful but they are also benighted, almost demonic. The cultured intelligentsia is willess, sick, and passive. Bely himself lives under the spell of elemental Russia, of the Russian fields, of the Russian pock-marked peasant woman. But no escape is in sight. What Bely's novel does is lead us squarely to the problem of mystical populism.

The spirit of populism is ineradicably inherent in Russians. There is no country which has such a strong cult of "the people," such fond hopes of securing the truth from the people, such a great craving to merge with the people. And nowhere is there such lawlessness and splinteredness. Populism has appeared in Russia in various garbs, constantly changing: first in the form of Slavophilism, then in the form of "populism" in the true sense of the word, then in that of Tolstoyism,[2] and has even crept into Marxism. It has currently assumed the guise of mysticism. Mystical populism constitutes the deepest impulse of the Russian national spirit; it is deeply ingrained in the nature of the Russian will or, perhaps, in the Russian lack of will. Beneath Russian populism, even the positivist kind, there lurks an original and unrecognized mysticism. Ours is a time when mysticism has been brought out into the open, and so even populism has assumed an overtly mystical slant. The intellectuals of the new mystical bent are not looking for anything genuinely revolutionary in the people, rather they are seeking something genuinely mystical. They hope to secure from the people not social truth but religious illumination. Yet their psychological relationship with the people remains the same as it was before: there is the same desire to submit to and be enlightened by the people, the same worship for it, the same inability to provide steadfast illumination, to master the elements and impart order and meaning to them. The Russian intelligentsia has always been essentially feminine; its members have been able to perform heroic deeds, to make sacrifices, and to give up their life; but they have never been capable of strong and steadfast activism, they have never had an internal anchor. They have yielded to the elements; they have not been the bearer of Logos. This may be connected to the fact that chivalry never existed in Russia. There are some similarities which link the Russian revolutionary and populist of the old order to the Russian decadent and mystic of the new one. Both are under the spell of the feminine popular element and both are powerless to bring to it the informing principle of Logos. Each is ready to bow before the people—one in the name of revolution, the other in the name of mysticism; both are isolated from the people; both are detached from the living popular organism; both go to the people empty-handed and want to get from it what they cannot obtain from the fountainhead whence the people itself draws its strength. Russia's most remarkable writers have tried to believe in the way the people believe, in what the people believe, and for this sake have agreed to adopt a "simple life." But they have failed to see that this was a terrible lie and falsification from the point of view of the people's beliefs.

The people believe because they see in their faith the light of truth. They place faith and the truth which this faith reveals higher than themselves. For the Russian mystical populists, the people were higher than faith and truth; and what the people believed in was the truth. The Slavophiles, Dostoevsky, and many others were not completely free of this false worship of the people and their faith. Such worship of the popular element manifested itself in our Old Believerism[3] and also in our nationalization of the Orthodox Church, which weakened the feeling of ecumenicalism in Russians. It is also the basis of Tolstoyism, which is quite characteristic of Russians. These same national peculiarities, in another form, have manifested themselves in the atheistic populists who also seek truth among the people and place the people higher than truth. Populism is a chronic Russian sickness which hinders Russia's creative rebirth. Vanquished and banished in one form, populism quickly revives in another. The latest form of populism is mystical populism. It is a lie from the point of view of religion, and it is a danger to Russia from a cultural and social point of view. The next historical task of Russian consciousness is to conquer all forms of populism, i.e., to change radically our attitude toward the popular element. The new national self-consciousness, full of messianic hopes, will be masculinely active, radiant, illuminating, the bearer of Logos, which will organize and master the elements. But this masculine principle of Logos is preserved in the Church and not in sectarianism, which is always elementally feminine. Non-ecclesiastical mystical populism does not contain Logos, but rather a false effeminateness, a passive submission to the elements. Only the church is masculine and only in church-conscious-ness is there an activist relationship to the elements, i.e., a proper correlation of masculine and feminine. Both the non-religious Russian populists and the non-ecclesiastical Russian mystics are always ready to submit to the power of the popular element, but they are unable to bring anything to it.

The desire to dissolve, to give oneself up totally is a purely Russian trait. The glance of the pock-marked peasant woman, Matryona, consti-tutes an eternal temptation; it perpetually lures us toward the pagan element in our national life. The penchant for deifying the national Russian element exists in Russian mystical sectarianism, in Khlystovism, in Old Believerism, and also in historical Orthodoxy insofar as the church became excessively nationalized and, consequently, lacking in ecumenical spirit. Russia is perpetually threatened by the danger of an elemental pagan nationalism, which is reactionary both from a religious and from a social point of view. This reactionary element manifested itself even in the Russian revolution of 1905. And this penchant is always felt in Russian mysticism. Only universal Logos opposes every form of elemental reactionism; only the truth of an ecumenical church can be opposed to all the different kinds of Russian reactionism; reactionary populism, reactionary paganism, reactionary effeminate mysticism. That Russian element which one senses in Matryona's glance is not destroyed by universal Logos, it is merely clarified and informed by it. Matryona is waiting for a husband and for too long has not found one. Why, even our militant anti-revolutionary element is lured by Matryona's glance just as, perhaps, our elementally chaotic revolutionariness is enticed by it. But the danger of an elemental pagan reaction is present in both, since reactionism is everywhere that Logos is not, it exists where masculinity, illumination, and enlighten-ment are lacking. Matryona, the artistically brilliant symbol of the Russian popular element, should not seduce and weaken; a husband should take possession of her. Only then will universal truth conquer our reactionism.

Bely connects the mystical sect of the Doves, who are spiritually close to the Khlysts, with the revolution. He brings together mystical and revolutionary elements. But the Russian Khlysts are more reactionary than revolutionary. They represent a reaction of the pagan popular element against universal Logos. The Khlysts are revolutionary in relation to the Church, and this is precisely why they are reactionary. Everything is reactionary that defies ecclesiastical Logos and universal meaning in the name of the primordial element which precedes any light of consciousness, any awareness of self. Kudeyarov, the head of the Doves, is the most intense mystical reactionary; he is permeated with the element that is hostile to earth-possessing Logos. Kudeyarov lacks a relationship to the Visage of Christ, lacks the awareness of self and the affirmation of self in God which can be associated only with Christ. Sectarianism is devoid both of the Visage of Christ and of personality; it contains only the Spirit—the Spirit within man. And the kingdom of the Spirit is a faceless kingdom, preceding Christ and smaller, not larger than Christianity. Kudeyarov and Matryona are not mystical Christianity, they are mystical paganism, the element that comes before Christ, before Logos, before personality. The element of mystical sectarianism is reactionary in relation to culture as well, since culture is inseparably bound up with universal Logos, with the victory of the light-bearing man over the feminine element. All that is genuinely progressive and liberating is connected with the mysticism of Logos and not to the mysticism of the elemental kind. And Logos lives in the Church. The failure of every sort of sectarianism, including mystical Russian sectarianism, indeed the failure of every sort of reactionism, lies in its desertion of the Church, in its self-affirmation. A false relationship to the Church and to ecumenical ecclesiastical consciousness gives birth to all sectarian tendencies. And the Khlysts more than anyone are guilty of defection from the Church, of affirmation of self against the Universal Church. From this stems the power of the pagan element over the Khlysts, the power of Nature, which is taken for grace; from this stems their demonism.

Bely penetrates deeply into the popular mystical element. But he overlooks that aspect of popular life which connects the Russian people to the Church. There is much paganism in Russian Orthodox church life, there is much of what Bely shows in the typical and clichéd figure of priest Vakula. But there is also genuine contact with the universal truth of Christ's Church. There is a little niche in the Russian people's soul where genuinely ecclesiastical Christian truth lives and radiates. Bely does not feel this, does not link anything to it. And yet only ecclesiastical mysticism is enlightened, it alone is connected to world culture. Non-ecclesiastical mysticism, seductive and terrible, lacks illumination and manliness. If there were no niche in the Russian people's soul pervaded by ecclesiastical Logos, there would be no hope of a great future in store for the Russian nation. For surely one cannot associate such a future with Kudeyarov or Daryalsky: there is only darkness and passivity in them. Bely has revealed this through his artistic intuition. He senses artistically the lie of mystical populism although he himself is not entirely free of it. He reveals the darkness of non-ecclesiastical popular mysticism and the willessness of cultural mysticism. In reading *The Silver Dove* one becomes ever more firmly convinced that one cannot depend upon the people, the intelligentsia, the authorities, the clergy, or any other human or natural element; one must only rely upon the Church as a mystical, ecumenical body. The light of ecclesiastical consciousness and the power of ecclesiastical will must be brought into the life of the people and the intelligentsia. Worship of the people, like worship of any natural element, is a lie and a sin. One can only worship God and submit to His Church alone.

Personality does not find or assert itself in elemental mysticism. Personality is formed and attains unshakable self-awareness only in the Church of Christ. Elemental mysticism exists entirely in Nature and does not extend beyond Nature's sphere. Yet personality can be established only by overcoming Nature, in a state of freedom. Without exception, the rites of the Khlysts immediately abide in Nature and there is consequently no transcendence to the blessed state of freedom. Thus personality is lost. There is no personality in the mystical ecstasy of the Doves, which Bely describes so remarkably. There is no personality and there is no freedom. Freedom transcends Nature and its elements. The Khlysts' and the Doves' expectation of the Holy Ghost's descent essentially amounts to naturalistic pantheism, in which personality and freedom are always lost. Until Logos illuminates Nature, until it uncovers the path of emergence from Nature, personality and freedom do not exist. The attraction of the refined and excessively cultured strata to the Khlysts and to mystical popular sectarianism indicates their weakness, feminine pliancy, and loss of personality and freedom. Enormous mystical craving and energy are latent in our mystical sectarianism. But he who submits effeminately to this energy perishes. One must master this energy actively, masculinely, and satisfy this craving with a higher meaning. And only ecumenical, ecclesiastical Logos makes it possible manfully to master this mystical energy and actively satisfy one's mystical craving. The false correlation of the masculine and feminine is a great sin and a terrible mistake. We are too guilty of this, and the ground beneath us has been crumbling for a long time. Daryalsky's destruction is profoundly symbolic. It stems not only from the false relationship between cultivated mysticism and popular mysticism. The Russian revolutionary intellectuals also perished this way because of their false relationship to the popular element. Our cultured, intellectual society is dying from enfeeblement, from lack of manhood, from its break with Logos and its loss of the general meaning of life. Even the more masculine and active intellectuals submit to Matryona, the popular element; and, having lost God, they deify the people; the more feminine and passive ones are completely seduced by Matryona—lustfully they strive toward the mystical element and perish. Mystical populism is a terrible lie and an awful temptation. Falsehood and danger lurk in the very formulation of the problem of the intelligentsia and the people, of culture and elementalism. Only the problem of the correlation of masculine and feminine, of Logos and the earthly elements, has a religious meaning. In the Church there exists not only the masculine Logos but also the eternal feminine. Through the Virgin Mary, Logos entered the world, and a cult of the eternal feminine which opposes the false power of femininity is characteristic of genuine manliness. Only an ecclesiastical consciousness eliminates the false problem and solves the genuine one. Bely brilliantly perceives the elemental force of Russia, of the Russian people, of Russian nature, of the Russian fields and ravines, of the Russian peasant woman. It is the feminine element of the land. But he is unaware of the Logos in the Russian national consciousness and therefore he does not sense the masculinity of our world mission. Only in the Church does one find the masculine principle of Logos, but Bely has overlooked the ecclesiastical side of our national life.

Bely himself is unable to master the mystical element of Russia through the masculine principle of Logos; he is in the power of the feminine popular element, he is enticed by it and submits to it. One feels this throughout his work, which is pervaded by his ever-present sense of life's illusoriness and nightmarish bewitchment. The mysticism reflected in Bely's work is primarily feminine and it often turns into mediumism. Bely is an elemental populist, an elemental nationalist, who constantly wants to dissolve in Russian elementalism. But the less Logos—the less masculine, ecclesiastical consciousness there is in him—the more he wants to replace Logos with surrogates—with critical gnosiology, with Rickert[4] and with the methodology of Western culture. It is there that he seeks the masculine discipline which will give form to the chaos of the Russian mystical element and avert collapse and disaster. The more Matryona lures him, and the more he is drawn to dissolution in the mystical element of Russia with its dark and horrible chaos, the more he worships gnosiology, methodology, scientism, criticism, and so forth. The cult of Matryona and the cult of methodology are two sides of the same rupture and disconnection of earth and Logos, of the elements of consciousness. There is as little Logos in critical methodology and gnosiology as there is in Matryona and Kudeyarov. And there is certainly none of the methodology by which Matryona might be mastered. Only the masculine Logos of the Church, and not methodology, gnosiology, or Rickterism, can control the stormy, chaotic, and dark popular element. The Russian land, full of mystical desire, is striving after the great Reason of the Church and not the small reason of gnosiology. There is as little Reason-Logos in critical methodology as there is in mystical sectarianism, and in neither does one find masculine will.

Bely's remarkable book *Symbolism* has appeared along with *The Silver Dove*. In it we find another extremely talented side of Bely, a side which is lacking in his poetry, in his *Symphonies*,[5] and in *The Silver Dove*. Here we have a Bely, who is philosophical, gnosiological, methodological, discriminating, and cultured. Bely's elemental nature is purely Russian, national, popular, Eastern; it is a feminine element—passive, enveloped by nightmares and forebodings, close to madness. Russian fields and pock-marked peasant women, ravines and taverns are close and native to this Bely. He displays a considerable amount of the unquiet, stormy, catastrophic Slavophilism associated with Gogol and Dostoevsky (and not with Khomyakov,[6] whose masculine Logos was too powerful). But as a philosopher Bely is a Westernizer and culturemonger *par excellence*. He doesn't like Russian philosophy, and the Slavophile consciousness is alien to him; his consciousness is exclusively Western. To *this* Bely, Rickert is closer than Vladimir Solovyov,[7] Nietzsche is closer than Dostoevsky, Jakob Böhme[8] is closer than St. Seraphim,[9] discriminating methodological philosophy is closer than synthetic religious philosophy. Through a methodologically strict, almost scientific method, he is prepared to inculcate Russians with the Western mysticism of Eckhart[10] and Böhme, so unlike the mysticism of Kudeyarov and the Doves. But are Bely's Eastern, Russian elemental mysticism and his Western European conscious philosophy so antithetical? In Bely's elemental mysticisms there is a sense of life's nightmarishness and illusiveness. And this same sense exists in his philosophical thinking as well. In *Symbolism* there is an amazing and, in parts, brilliant chapter, "The Emblematics of Meaning," in which Bely develops an original philosophical system, close to Fichteanism, but more artistic than scientific. In this original Fichteanism one feels a detachment from life and a fear of it. Bely deifies only his own creative act. There is no God as Being, only the creative act is divine; God is created. He is something that should exist, not something that is. And in the process of creation there is no end; there is no completion in absolute existence. The creative process unfolds under the nightmarish sway of a vile infinity and a nasty plurality. In Bely and his kindred spirits the Son is born without the Father, Logos has no patronymic, and thus the word of man exists, but not the word of God. And man has no origin. Bely ascends the ladder and destroys each rung beneath him, he hangs over an empty abyss, and he will never arrive anywhere in this nightmarish clambering upward since there is no end, there is no Person to whom he is going, there is only an eternal ascent, an eternal dawn, endless creation out of nothing and for the sake of nothing. His is a philosophy of illusoriness, of phantasmagoria, and of nightmare beauty. Even Rickert—a rung on which Bely so firmly tries to stand—is ungratefully destroyed and mocked brilliantly and wittily. Only the pure creative act remains, but without a basis, without substance, without essence. Bely is caught in that truly horrible delusion that one can *reach* the Absolute, true being, freedom. But one can only proceed from the Absolute, from true being, from freedom. There are no roads to the Absolute which do not begin at the Absolute; at the first rung one must be with God in order to ascend to the following stages, and cognition is impossible without a primordial tie to the Absolute, without the presence of Logos in cognition. One cannot reach God without the help of God, one cannot perceive the truth without Logos, which is born of the Father; one cannot arrive at the Absolute when one proceeds from the relative. There are no roads to being which pass through empty abysses, one must abide in being from the very beginning in order to move in it. To be in God and with God is not an end of movement but rather its true beginning. Synthetic wholeness must also be present in the beginning, at the first stage, and not only at the end, at the summit, since without synthetic wholeness it is impossible to take a step, to move—one's equilibrium is lost. God exists; He is not something that should exist, His being does not depend on our creative act. But the world depends on it because we participate in its creative enlightenment and transformation, in its reunification with the Creator.

Bely is no less cut off from Logos in his philosophical consciousness than in his mystical consciousness. In both spheres of awareness life is illusory to him and there is a blending of value and nightmare without any ontological foundation. Here lie the roots of Bely's attraction to that Western occultist discipline which creeps into his works. Bely is constantly seeking discipline, consciousness, and orderliness from without instead of procuring them from within. But discipline of will and consciousness cannot be obtained from without by the methods of critical philosophy or occultism; rather they are to be found in the depths of a spirit in unison with ecclesiastical Logos. I see in Bely a false combination of Slavophilism and Westernism, an erroneous junction of East and West. But Bely poses the problem extremely pointedly and painfully; he is too much a Slavophile, too much a Westernizer. He is drawn to both the Eastern mystical element and to the ineffable mysticism of the Western type. But the latter rejects the

basic religious truth that mysticism is expressed in the Word—in Logos.
Mysticism which is not expressed in the Word is anti-clerical and anti-
religious. As an artist Bely manages to overcome individualism and
subjectivism, but only as an artist. As a philosopher Bely remains cut off
from universal Logos. This severance plunges him into hopeless pessimism;
his work provides as little hope as Gogol's. Bely does not believe that one
can find the light of Logos in the depths of the spirit. He vainly seeks
illumination first in the Eastern popular element, then in Western
consciousness. He lives in the dense and troubled atmosphere of the
Apocalypse; his sensibilities are apocalyptic and catastrophic. And this is
where his significance lies. In Bely everything is strained to its extreme
limit, everything moves inexorably to its end. But one senses in him an
apocalyptic femininity, a special mystical impressionability; apocalyptic
currents pass through him. Along with this one feels an ethical, truth-
loving nature in Bely. And the danger of sharing Gogol's fate constantly
threatens him.

When you investigate the mysticism of our day you are particularly
aware of the truth of the great importance of mystical temperateness. This
mystical temperateness constitutes masculinity of the spirit, it represents
tireless opposition to any mediumism or debilitating pliancy characteristic
of the feminine element. The greatest model of mystical manliness is given
to us in the image of St. Seraphim of Sarovsk. The Khlysts lack this or any
other kind of manliness. Nor does this manliness exist in contemporary
cultural mysticism. Precisely the manliness of St. Seraphim must be
brought to bear on the popular element.

The Silver Dove is the first part of a trilogy called *East and West*.[11] The
novel raises in a new way the eternal problem of East and West. I do not
know how Bely will deal further with his subject, but part one of the trilogy
reveals an enormous, exceptional talent. One feels in Bely a great discord
between elemental instinct and consciousness, but there is an artistic truth
in *The Silver Dove* which rises far above any kind of disunity. Bely has
discovered much in Russia which even the greatest Russian writers had not
seen. The problem of East and West is a purely Russian problem. Russia
stands centrally between East and West, it is the nexus of world history and
only through it can the age-old feud be resolved synthetically. It is no
accident that throughout the nineteenth century Russian consciousness
was permeated by the feud between the Slavophiles and Westernizers. This
feud reappears in continually newer and newer forms, but the time will
come when we finally have to overcome both Slavophilism and Westernism. Both currents suffer from narrow-mindedness; in neither is there
genuine universalism. Universal reason and world-wide truth must be
imagined in the very flesh and blood of the Russian nation. Our national
religious calling can be understood only as that of an intermediary between
East and West, a link between Eastern and Western truth, a bridge

converting the two types of Christian religious experience and two types of culture into the life-experience of a single humanity. Therefore our national religious mission is directly antithetical to any reactionary nationalism. Our new, creative national self-awareness cannot be either Slavophile or Western, it cannot be servile either to Eastern elementalism or Western consciousness. Our overcoming of Slavophilism and Westernism will be a sign that we have reached national maturity and self-awareness. Slavophilism and Westernism indicate youthful immaturity; they are the growing pains of self-awareness. Currently Russia's historical task, in all its spheres, must be the achievement of the mature, masculine self-awareness connected with universal religious consciousness. All that is true in the Slavophiles' and Westernizers' thinking will become a part of this national self-awareness and their false and provincial aspects will be overcome. For indeed Westernism is narrow-minded as well. There are no Westernizers in the West; they are a provincial Russian phenomenon. The worship of Western consciousness, scientism, and cultivation is heathenism. Consciousness can only be universal and not Western nor can science and culture be the exclusive property of West European provincialism.

Praise be the artist who draws us anew to the problem of East and West and who turns our literature toward much larger concerns. Bely is first rate among our contemporary writers. His thematics are always profound and important, serious and pulsating. Everything in Bely is symbolic, everything evokes uneasiness. He is a more forceful and extreme expression of something characteristic of many "Russian boys."* His talent is so great that fear for him turns into fear for many Russians. May the beneficial power of masculine Logos be granted to him and all "Russian boys."[12]

---

* Dostoevsky's words in *The Brothers Karamazov* (author's note).

Notes

1. The Khlysts were a mystical sect of flagellants dating back to the mid-seventeenth century. In addition to self-flagellation (whence their name, derived from the verb khlystat' or khlestat', to whip, flagellate), the sect believed in the pre-existence and transmigration of souls.

2. Tolstoy's religious, social, and moral beliefs attracted the attention of people throughout the world, some of whom formed themselves into groups or circles which preached his doctrines, known as Tolstoyism.

3. Old Believerism is a religious movement dating to the mid-seventeenth century and consisting of schismatics who doubted the accuracy of the reforms in church text and ritual made by the Russian Orthodox Patriarch Nikon. Its most famous adherent was the Archpriest Avvakum, who has left a colorful and entertaining *Life* (1672-75), and who was burned at the stake as a heretic in 1682.

4. Rickert, Heinrich (1863-1936). German philosopher. He was a neo-Kantian who advanced the Kantian critique of knowledge theory. Rickert's fear of the influence of modern science—and particularly his opposition to the doctrine that the naturalism and positivism of science furnished an accurate assessment of human existence—found favor with Bely. During the years immediately preceding the writing of *The Silver Dove*, Bely had turned to studying Kant and the German neo-Kantians, particularly Rickert.

5. Bely's four *Symphonies* constitute a synthesis of prose and poetry and are written in a quasi-musical form.

6. Khomyakov, Alexei Stepanovich (1804-1860), poet, philosopher, and religious thinker. He was one of the leaders of Russian Slavophilism, an extremely important school of thought which argues that Russia's destiny lies in its Slavonic roots (as opposed to its Western heritage) and that its spiritual mission is to redeem the West from its individualism and materialism. Berdyaev himself came under Khomyakov's influence as has, in our own time, Alexander Solzhenitsyn.

7. See Gurev, note 5.

8. Böhme, Jakob (1575-1624). German philosopher and mystic who profoundly influenced idealism and romanticism.

9. St. Seraphim (1759-1833). A monk and mystic who was one of the most famous spiritual teachers of the Russian Orthodox church. His asceticism and spiritual counselling are traits which can be found among the monks in Dostoevsky's *Brothers Karamazov*, namely Father Ferapont and Father Zosima.

10. Eckhart (Eckhart von Hochheim, ca. 1260-1328). German speculative mystic whose writings have, like Böhme's, influenced idealism and romanticism.

11. Bely's projected volume of the trilogy grew into the independent novel *Petersburg* (1913), which departs in many ways from the original scheme. A third volume was never undertaken.

12. In his famous conversation with Alyosha which precedes his reading of "The Grand Inquisitor," Ivan states that masses of Russian boys do nothing but discuss the eternal questions of God's existence and immortality.

10

An Astral Novel: Some Thoughts on Andrei Bely's *Petersburg**

Nikolai Alexandrovich Berdyaev (1874-1948)

Petersburg no longer exists. The life of this city was primarily bureaucratic and its end was also bureaucratic. An unfamiliar and still strange-sounding city has arisen named Petrograd. Not only has an old world ended, with a new one taking its place, but an entire historical period has come to a close, and we are entering into a new, unfamiliar one. There was something strange, something eerie in the origin of Petersburg, in its fate, in its relationship to the enormity of Russia, and in its isolation from Russia's popular life; something which was at once imperiously enthralling and spectral. Petersburg arose out of nothing, out of the marshy fog, by the magic of Peter's will. Pushkin gave us a feeling for the life of this Petersburg in "The Bronze Horseman."[1] Dostoevsky the Slavophile and champion of the Russian soil was strangely tied to Petersburg, much more than to Moscow, and he exposed its mad Russian element. Dostoevsky's heroes are largely Petersburg types, tied to Petersburg's slush and fog. He has some truly astounding pages about Petersburg and its spectral quality. Raskolnikov wanders near Sadovaya Street and the Haymarket, contemplating his crime. Rogozhin commits his crime on Gorkhovaya Street. Dostoevsky the lover of the soil adored soilless heroes who could exist only in the atmosphere of Petersburg. In contrast to Moscow, Petersburg is a catastrophic city, and Gogol's Petersburg stories, in which the city's spectral terror is to be found, are also characteristic. To Moscow Slavophiles, Petersburg seemed an alien, foreign city, and they feared it. And not without reason, for Petersburg perpetually threatened the Moscow Slavophiles' equanimity. But the fact that Petersburg seemed a totally un-Russian city to the Slavophiles was due to provincial delusion and narrowmindedness on their part. Dostoevsky disproved this error of theirs.

The ephemerality of Petersburg is purely Russian; it is a specter created by the Russian imagination. Peter the Great was Russian to the

---

* "Astralnyi roman: Razmyshleniya o romane A. Belogo 'Peterburg' "—published in *Krizis iskusstva* (St. Petersburg: 1918), pp. 36-47.

core. And the very Petersburg bureaucratic style is the unique handiwork of Russian history. The German graft onto the Petersburg bureaucracy created the specifically Russian bureaucratic style. This is no less true than that the distinctive form of French used by the Russian nobility constitutes a Russian national style, which is as Russian as is the Russian empire style in furniture. "Petersburg" Russia is our other national image alongside that of Muscovite Russia.

Only a writer with a totally unique feeling for life's cosmic aspect, and for its transitoriness, could write a novel about Petersburg. We have such a writer and he has written *Petersburg*. He wrote it just before the end of Petersburg and the Petersburg period of Russian history, as if he were summing up our strange capital and its equally strange history. In *Petersburg*, which is quite likely the most remarkable Russian novel since the time of Tolstoy and Dostoevsky, we do not find an entire picture; the whole of Petersburg does not occupy its pages; all of it is not accessible to the author. Yet something characteristically Petersburgian has truly been recognized and reproduced in this amazing novel. The book is an artistic creation of a Gogolian cast (and thus may give cause for charges of libel against Russia), of an exclusive perception of the distorted and the ugly, for it is hard to find in it one who is made in God's image. Andrei Bely is the most important and the most original writer of the current literary epoch, for he has created a completely new form of artistic prose fiction, an entirely new rhythm. But to our great shame he is still insufficiently acknowledged as such, although I have little doubt that in time his genius will be recognized. This is a sick genius which is unable to produce perfect creations, but which strikes the reader with its new feel for life and its previously unencountered musical form. When this is recognized, Bely will be ranked with the greatest Russian writers, as a true successor of Gogol and Dostoevsky. His novel *The Silver Dove*[2] secured this place for him. Bely possesses an inner rhythm which is peculiar to him, and it corresponds to the new cosmic rhythm which he feels. His artistic innovations found expression in his *Symphonies*, a form which, prior to Bely, did not exist in literature. His advent in literature can be compared only to the phenomenon of Scriabin[3] in music. And it is no accident that both artists are attracted to theosophy and occultism. This attraction is connected to their sense of the dawning of a new cosmic era.

Bely has his own unique artistic sense of the cosmic division, scattering, and decrystallization of all things in the world, the destruction and disappearance of all firmly fixed boundaries that exist between objects. Human images themselves decrystallize and disperse in Bely; the solid borders which separate one person from another, and from the objects of the surrounding world, are lost. The firmness, the organicity, the crystallized quality of our corporeal world collapse. One person turns into another, one object becomes another object, the physical shifts to the astral, the cerebral is transformed into the existential. A displacement and merging of different planes occurs. The hero of *Petersburg*, Nikolai Apollonovich, the son of an important bureaucrat, a follower of Cohen[4] and a revolutionary, locks himself up in his study; then it begins to seem to him that he and the room and the objects in it are instantaneously transformed from objects of the real world into intellectual symbols of purely logical constructs. The room's space mingles with his desensitized body in a general existential chaos, which he calls "the universe"; Nikolai Apollonovich's consciousness, separating itself from his body, spontaneously merges with his electric desk-lamp, which he calls "the sun of consciousness." Thinking over the tenets of his system, which is gradually being elevated to perfect unity, he feels his body spilling into the "universe," i.e., into the room; "the head of this body mingled with the glass head of the electric lamp under the coquettish lampshade." Here we have a description of Nikolai Apollonovich's meditations, by dint of which his own being is splintered. Behind them lie Bely's own artistic reflections, in the process of which his own nature and the nature of the entire world are shattered. The boundaries that separate the ephemeral world from the existential are destroyed. Everything in *Petersburg* amounts to a cerebral game between the important bureaucrat-father, the senator, department head and privy counsellor Apollon Apollonovich Ableukhov and his hardly differentiable son, the revolutionary Nikolai Apollonovich, who is a bureaucrat turned inside-out. It is hard to determine where the father ends and the son begins. These enemies, who represent the contrary principles of bureaucracy and revolution, are blended into a kind of uncrystallized, unformed whole. This likeness, blending, and destruction of boundaries symbolize the fact that our revolution is the close kin of the bureaucracy and that, therefore, the seed of decay and death lies within it.

Everything becomes everything else, everything intermingles and crumbles. Life's contours are abolished. It is characteristic of Bely, as a writer and an artist, that words and assonances begin to spin in a whirlwind of combinations, wherein reality disperses and all boundaries are swept away. Bely's style ultimately turns into a frenzied circular movement; there is something of the religious flagellant in it. Bely sensed this vortical movement in cosmic life, and found its proper expression in a whirl of word-combinations. Bely's language is not a translation of his cosmic life-experiences into another, foreign tongue, as are the colorfully feeble paintings of Churlionis.[5] Rather, Bely's style is a spontaneous expression of cosmic whirlwinds in words. One can only reproach him for his style's lack of consistency; there are frequent gaffes in this respect. Bely's genius as an artist lies in the way he matches cosmic disintegration and cosmic swirling with verbal disintegration, with the whirlwind of his style. The vortical swell of words and assonances renders the growing tension of life and the cosmos, which leads to catastrophe. Bely melts and pulverizes the crystals of words, the fixed forms of words, which had seemed eternal, and by so doing conveys the fusion and disintegration of the crystals of the entire objective, material world. The cosmic whirlwinds seem to have broken free, tearing apart and shattering our entire world—fixed, firm, and crystallized as it usually is. "The fabric of the universe there seemed to be the fabric of the Furies." These words of Bely excellently describe the atmosphere in which the action of *Petersburg* occurs. And here is how the city itself seems to him:

> Petersburg, Petersburg! Besieged by fog, you have persecuted me as well with your idle cerebral game; you are a cruel-hearted tormentor; you are a restless phantom; for years you have assaulted me; I have run on your horrible avenues and taken a flying leap to the Iron Bridge that begins at the edge of the earth and leads into the boundless distance. Beyond the Neva, in the semi-dark, green distance, the specters of islands and houses have risen up, seducing me with the vain hope that those bounded parts are reality and not the warring boundlessness which drives the white smoke of the clouds onto Petersburg's streets.

Bely may be termed a literary cubist. Formally he can be compared to Picasso in painting. The cubist method is an analytical one; it does not perceive things synthetically. In painting cubism seeks out the geometrical framework of things; it tears off the deceitful covering of flesh and tries to penetrate into the inner structure of the cosmos. In the cubist painting of Picasso the beauty of the incarnate world perishes as everything is broken down and stratified. Cubism in the proper sense does not exist in literature, yet there does exist in it something that parallels cubist painting. Bely's work represents this cubism in prose, and it is every bit as powerful as Picasso's. In Bely as well, the solid coverings of the world's flesh are torn off; whole, organic forms do not exist for him. Bely applies to literature the cubist method of stratifying all organic existence. Of course, there is no possibility of cubist painting having influenced Bely since he probably is barely familiar with it. Rather, Bely's cubism is his own, organic perception of the world, so characteristic of our transitional epoch. In a certain sense Bely is the only genuine and significant futurist in Russian literature. The old, crystalline beauty of the material world dies in Bely and in its place is born a new world in which beauty does not yet exist. In Bely's artistic method, as with the futurists, everything is displaced from its old position, which had seemed eternally fixed. He writes not agitational futurist manifestos, but symbolist ones; but his very existence, his very work destroys all the old forms and creates new ones. Bely's originality lies in the fact that he combines his cubism and futurism with a genuine, spontaneous symbolism, while the futurists usually consider themselves the enemies of symbolism. Thus in the cubo-futurist *Petersburg* the ubiquitous red domino is a superb, internally motivated symbol of the advancing, but essentially unreal revolution. It is Hoffmann who, in European literature, is the precursor of Bely's artistic method, for in Hoffmann's[6] brilliant fantasies as well, all boundaries and planes blend, everything splits and turns into something else. In Russian literature Bely is the direct successor of Gogol and Dostoevsky. Like Gogol, he sees more ugliness and horror in human existence than beauty and an authentically solid basis for life. Already Gogol had perceived the old, organically whole world in an analytical, dismembered way; man's image for him was layered, and he saw the same freaks and monsters at the heart of life which later, in a somewhat different manner, Picasso discovered in painting. Gogol broke with Pushkin's perenially beautiful and harmonious ethos and world view. And so does Bely.

But it is impossible not to reproach Bely for his occasionally excessive imitation of Dostoevsky, particularly his over-dependence on *The Possessed*. Several scenes, for example the one in the tavern and the one with the detective, are direct copies of Dostoevsky's manner. And precisely in these places Bely goes off into another style, which is certainly not his, thus breaking the rhythm of his novel-symphony. He is internally tied to Dostoevsky, and cannot be blamed for this. But he ought to have been freer in using his own artistic devices, truer to his own style. Bely and Dostoevsky belong to different epochs, and there is a great difference between the two. Bely is more cosmic in his feel for life; Dostoevsky is more psychological and anthropological. Dostoevsky discerned the enormous chasms at the very core of man's being, but for him the image of man was separate from the abyss of cosmic life. Dostoevsky perceived man as an organic whole and always saw God's image in him. Bely belongs to a new era, where the perception of man as a whole has been shaken and man is passing through a process of fission. Bely plunges man into cosmic infinity, he hands him over to be torn to pieces by cosmic whirlwinds. The boundary which separates man from electric lights is lost, and the astral world is revealed. The firm foundations of the physical world used to protect man's autonomy, his own rigid boundaries, his crystal-clear outline from the other side. The contemplation of the astral world, that intermediary realm between matter and spirit, effaces such borders, it decrystallizes both man and his surroundings. Bely is an artist of the astral order into which our world, losing its fixity and solidity, imperceptibly passes. His whirlwinds are all astral whirlwinds, and not whirlwinds of the physical world or the world of man's spirit. *Petersburg* is an astral novel in which everything moves beyond the physical boundaries of the corporeal world and the spiritual limits of human life, in which everything tumbles into the abyss. The senator, after all, sees two spaces, and not one.

Bely reveals in his art the special metaphysics of the Russian bureaucracy. Bureaucratism is an ephemeral reality, a cerebral game, in which everything is composed of straight lines, cubes, and squares. Bureaucratism rules Russia from the center in geometrical fashion. The illusoriness of the bureaucracy engenders an illusory revolution. It is no accident that Nikolai Apollonovich turns out to be a follower of Cohen, i.e., one whose philosophical leanings do not permit him to feel the reality of existence; it is no accident that he is intimately connected to the bureaucracy. Nothing from the heart of Russia, from the depths of popular life reaches ephemeral Petersburg, which passes into the astral plane. The centralism of a revolutionary committee is as ephemeral a reality as the centralism of a bureaucratic institution. The process of putrefaction has progressed from bureaucratism to revolutionism. The agents-provocateurs who, like a thick fog, have enveloped the revolution, reveal its illusory and evanescent character—everything has become mixed up in the satanic whirlwind.

Bely is certainly no enemy of the revolutionary idea. His attitude is completely unlike Dostoevsky's in *The Possessed*. The evil of revolution for Bely is generated by the evil of old Russia. Essentially he wants to expose artistically the illusory character of the Petersburg period of Russian history, of our bureaucratic and intellectual Westernism, just as in *The Silver Dove* he unmasked the darkness and ignorance resulting from the Eastern element in our popular life. The nature of Bely's artistic talent does not, as Gogol's did not, allow him to reveal or reproduce the positive, the bright, and the beautiful. In one of his poems Bely summons his Russia, which he loves with such a strange love, to disperse into space. And from his novels about Russia, we get the same impression of Russia scattering into thin air, turning into astral dust. He loves Russia with annihilating love and believes in her rebirth only through destruction. Such a love is indigenous to the Russian character.

All the illusoriness—bureaucratic, revolutionary, and Kantian-gnosiological—comes together in Nikolai Apollonovich. But in him the author discloses yet another horror. From Vladimir Solovyov[7] Bely has inherited the fear of the Mongol threat. And he senses this Mongol element within Russia itself, and within the Russian people. Nikolai Apollonovich, like his father, the head of a department, is a Mongol, a Turanian. The Mongolian principle rules Russia. The Mongolian East comes to light in, of all places, the Russian West. Bely discerns the Turanian-Mongolian principle in Kantianism as well. He depicts the end of Petersburg, its final atomization. The Bronze Horseman has crushed man in Petersburg. It is this image of the Bronze Horseman which dominates the atmosphere of *Petersburg* and everywhere dispatches its astral double.

Bely lacks a Russian ideology, and we should not try to look for one in him. More than a Russian ideological consciousness, he possesses a Russian nature, a Russian spirit. He is Russian to the core, and in him stirs Russian chaos. His isolation from Russia is external and illusory, as in Gogol's case. Bely both loves and disclaims Russia. Indeed, even Chaadaev[8] loved Russia. Quite recently Bely published a poem which contains the following stanza:

My country, my native land!
I am yours! I am yours!
Take me, sobbing and unknowing,
And cover me with your damp grass.

The poem ends with a confession of faith—that beyond the Russian "night," "He" exists. The "He" who exists beyond the terrible darkness and chaos of Russia is Christ. Bely knows from personal experience how frightening, horrible, and dangerous the Russian chaos is. But he is unable to elicit in himself a Russian will and a Russian consciousness; he still seeks these categories in the West. And we have every right to doubt that he will find them there. I think he will ultimately return to Russia, and seek the light within its depths.

There are some serious artistic shortcomings in *Petersburg;* there is much in it which is aesthetically unacceptable. The style is inconsistent; the ending is arbitrary and internally unmotivated; parts of the book are too dependent on Dostoevsky. But Bely's brilliant creative nature is simply not able to produce a perfect artistic work. There is no catharsis in his work; instead there is always something excessively tormenting about it because he himself is submerged in the nightmare. Bely's novel lacks not only an ideological and intellectual resolution, but an artistic, cathartic one as well. He does not liberate the reader, but rather leaves him in the grips of an oppressive nightmare. He oversteps the limits of perfect, beautiful art. His art is his very being, his chaos, his vortical movement, his cosmic intuition. And this is what is new and unusual about him. One needs to accept it without seeking any consolation. He cannot be approached through the old critical methods. He is an artist of our transitional, cosmic epoch. And he brings literature back anew to the great themes of the classical Russian tradition. His work is tied to Russia's fate, to Russia's soul. He is the first to have written a truly astral novel, which is so unlike the insipid and unartistic occult novels composed in the old-fashioned way. Bely is not a theurgist, but theurgical art may well lie in the direction of the astral division and atomization which characterizes works like his.

Notes

1. *The Bronze Horseman* (*Mednyi vsadnik,* 1833) is Pushkin's narrative poem of 481 lines about a petty bureaucrat who goes mad after learning that his beloved has drowned in the Petersburg flood of 1824, and who imagines that the statue of Peter the Great (known as the Bronze Horseman) is chasing after him.

2. See note 5 in Berdyaev's article on *The Silver Dove.*

3. Scriabin, Alexander Nikolaevich (1872-1915). Russian composer who expressed in music many of the same themes and values that are found in the writings of Russia's leading symbolists. After 1910 he became interested in mystical philosophy, and at least three works, his Third Symphony, his "Poem of Ecstasy," and "Prometheus" are inspired by theosophical ideas which similarly inspired Bely. For an informative discussion of the cultural context of Scriabin's music in Russia, see Ralph Matlaw "Scriabin and Russian Symbolism," in *Comparative Literature* (Winter, 1971), Vol. 31, No. 1, pp. 1-23.

4. Cohen, Hermann (1842-1918). German-Jewish philosopher and founder of the Marburg school of neo-Kantian philosophy. He emphasized ethics and epistomology as opposed to metaphysics. Boris Pasternak came into contact with Cohen and his philosophy during his brief stay in Marburg in 1912.

5. Churlionis, Mikaloius Konstantinas (1875-1911). Lithuanian composer and artist whose paintings (like Bely's writing and Scriabin's music) embody some of the central themes and values of symbolism. He moved to Petersburg in 1909.

6. Hoffmann, Ernst Theodor Amadeus (1776-1822). German writer, critic, and composer. His tales of the supernatural and fantastic were extremely popular in early nineteenth-century Russian literature and they have had a great influence or resonance in Russian literature ever since. Two studies of Hoffmann's legacy to Russian literature are: Norman W. Ingham, *E. T. A. Hoffmann's Reception in Russia* (Wurzburg, 1974) and Charles E. Passage, *The Russian Hoffmannists* (The Hague, 1963).

7. See Gurev, note 5. In May of 1900 Solovyov published his *Three Conversations About War, Progress and the End of the Universal History, With the Inclusion of a Short History of the Antichrist (Tri razgovora o voine, progresse i kontse vsemirnoi istorii, so vkliucheniem kratkoi istorii ob Antixriste).* In this book, which obviously influenced Bely greatly in *Petersburg,* Solovyov talks about a new invasion of Mongols on European soil which will signal the destruction of civilization, the appearance of the Antichrist, and the coming of God's kingdom on earth.

8. Chaadaev, Pyotr Yakovlevich (1794-1862). Mystical philosopher and libertarian of the early nineteenth century. His *Philosophical Letters* (1829-31), with their pro-Western, pro-Catholic views, caused a sensation when they were serialized in 1836. He is mentioned in Pushkin's poetry, particularly in the three poems which Pushkin wrote to him—in 1818, 1821, and 1824.

11

The Inspiration of Horror:
On Andrei Bely's *Petersburg*

Vyacheslav Ivanovich Ivanov (1866-1949)*

Born in Moscow in 1866, Vyacheslav Ivanov lost his father at the age of five and was raised by his mother, a priest's granddaughter whose insistence on providing her son with a solid religious education had an enormous and life-long impact upon him. Ivanov was trained as a classical scholar, was a professor of Greek at the University of Baku between 1921 and 1924, and translated many of the Greek classics during his lifetime. His particular interest was in the Dionysian religion of the Greeks, and when he went on to become a major literary theoretician, critic, and poet of the symbolist period, his fascination with Greek religion and myth showed itself in virtually all his writing. As Zhirmunsky's essay in this collection argues, Ivanov's brand of symbolism (along with Blok's and Bely's) emphasized poetry as a mystical activity and considered the poet to be a priest or prophet. In Ivanov's poetry and prose one finds, not surprisingly given his training, a quite scholarly language and diction; his vocabulary is filled with archaisms and ecclesiastical Russian, and his style tends toward the ornate.

Ivanov is known largely for the work he produced while still in Russia, although he was extremely productive after he emigrated in 1924 to Italy, where he died. Among his major works published in Russia are the collections of verse Pilot Stars (Kormchie zvezdy, *1902)* Transparency (Prozrachnost', *1904),* Cor Ardens *(1907-1911); two books of criticism and theory,* Along the Stars (Po zvezdam, *1909) and* Furrows and Boundaries (Borozdy i mezhi, *1916); the extremely interesting* Correspondence From Two Corners (Perepiska iz dvukh uglov, *1921) with Mikhail Gershenzon; and his lovely* Winter Sonnets (Zimnye sonety, *1919-1920). Two years after emigrating to Italy, Ivanov converted to Roman Catholicism; this fascination with things Roman appears in his major poetry during emigration:* Roman Sonnets (Rimskie sonety, *1924-1925) and* Roman Diary (Rimskii dnevnik, *1944). Westerners are most familiar with Ivanov*

---

*The most complete survey of Ivanov's literary theory and criticism is James West's *Russian Symbolism: A Study of Vyacheslav Ivanov and the Russian Symbolist Aesthetic* (London, 1970).

as the author of an intriguing book on Dostoevsky (1932), published in English under the title Freedom and the Tragic Life. *Ivanov's interest both in Dostoevsky and classical Greek culture is apparent in the review of Bely's* Petersburg *which follows. The two writers were close friends, and it is Ivanov who was responsible for the title of Bely's masterpiece.*

The Inspiration of Horror*

Sometimes I seem to see all of the shortcomings, all of the blunders and deformities of Andrei Bely's work of genius: a certain clumsiness or deficiency here; a forcedness or lack of taste there; in certain places voids and lapses of artistic polish, which are covered up with motley, yet only decorative patches; a frequently excessive indulgence in Dostoevskian devices coupled with an inability to master his style and penetrate the essence of things in his exquisite manner (for Bely, Dostoevsky will apparently always remain a closed book). Yet despite all of this, I would not want his semi-chaotic novel to be changed one iota.

I am aware of the book's non-confomity to the laws of pure art, and I am unable to determine its aesthetic value exactly. For essentially this colorful confusion, in which the ugly and the beautiful coalesce and mutually reflect and inform each other, must be viewed outside of aesthetic categories. One thing I know is that before me lies an unusual and, in its own way, unique work.

I also see how the consciousness which engenders this confusion—a consciousness filled with the horror of its loneliness and connected to the roots of popular life by extremely fine, hardly perceptible threads—is commensurate with the object being depicted: the mystery of Russia's fate and the heart and soul of the Russian land. Yet nonetheless, every time I touch the book's pages, written at the cost of such suffering, a sensation is produced in me akin to a painfully vivid and incomprehensible, yet prophetic dream which may portend good or evil and where everything to the last detail seems highly significant and allows for a contradictory interpretation. You almost avoid examining the author's own suggestive hints, for perhaps he only imagines that he knows something about the meaning of his prophetic dream. What one perceives more vividly is the involuntariness with which Bely conveys this strange revelation, the pure inspiration which makes light of his diligent perserverance both in rationally constructing this capricious epic and in providing adequate justification for this irrational, thousand-hued mirage, which bursts volcanically from his soul in a protracted, ghostly conflagration.

While taking stock of the disagreements and objections which my reason notes and my memory retains in the midst of the fervor with which the poet infects me, I must lodge a firm protest against his artificial disregard for the genuine strengths of the Russian land when depicting Petersburg seized by the storm of 1905 (artificial in an objective sense, for subjectively this disregard is quite in order). I will not insist on developing this thought in terms of treating the events under discussion historically: I

* "Vdokhnovenie uzhasa—O romane Andreya Belogo 'Peterburg'"—published in "Utro Rossii," 1916 (28 May), No. 148, pp. 5-6.

shall grant the author the right to limit himself to the sphere of "hallucination" and completely ignore the sphere of action. But is Petersburg really just hallucination?

Dostoevsky was the first to speak of Petersburg's illusoriness, but he simultaneously reveals to us the direct opposite in his Petersburg novels and tales. And it is he who, perhaps, helped most to connect Petersburg to the Russian land, to reunite the enigmatic "creation of Peter" with the Russian soul. Wherever Dostoevsky may happen to be, there, too, we find the "Russian spirit," there it "smells of Rus'." Bely affirms a belief in Holy Russia, "the Russia of Christ," but he does not reveal this Russia—out of impotence, I should think.

His *Ashes*[1] is a cry of despair, which reaches the point of blasphemous grumbling, against his mother Russia but is not regarded as a sin on the part of her loving son. His *Silver Dove* is in my view metaphysical libel against the latent creativity of those who seek the City of God within our people, a calumny against the dark and mysterious God-seeking of the popular spirit. I know the poet believes that white Phoebe is present in Russia, but the hoped-for sun, according to his horoscopes in *The Silver Dove,* will nonetheless rise in the West. In *Petersburg* the Russian languor of the soul is sketched through the apocalyptic babble of simple souls—obscurely and feebly.

Petersburg, a little circle with a dot inside on the map of the Empire, has only a conditional existence: it is an entity of reason and at the same time it is the meeting point of the forces which produce the variegated and universal Russian delusion. But does not Russia itself (which, the poet assures us, genuinely exists) appear to be a dark Nirvana from this same little circle? Nirvana, according to the hero of the novel, is nothingness. The father of the young Kantian, a dignitary who decides the fates of Russians, compensates for his son by instinctively feeling Russia to be a "given fact," which is being surmounted and reduced to reality, to a kind of meaning, by the "normative" activity of the ruling center, by the "formative" work of the omnipotent, albeit dimensionless dot in the geographic circle. Bely denounces both characters (he is very strong in his negative definitions), but is unable to disprove them in a lifelike way in his work.

Bely knows the Name before Whom all goblins melt like wax in the presence of a flame. But it seems as if he is not satisfied with this Name: he looks around superstitiously for its bearer. Even in his earliest verse *(Gold in Azure),*[2] Bely seeks to identify this Name with deceptive shadows flitting by. Occasionally in *Petersburg,* someone "sad and tall, with stiffening fingers" passes by the terrorist-mystic in solitary detachment. Isn't this most dubious and evasive figure, so corpse-like in appearance, a delusion of horror and deadly anguish?

I shall never forget those evenings in Petersburg when Bely read the manuscript of his still unfinished work, on which he toiled zealously and for which, I remember, he had envisioned an ending less conciliatory and benign than the one that flowed from his pen. The author was undecided about what to call his piece and for my part I assured him that *Petersburg* was the only title worthy of the book, whose leading character is the Bronze Horseman himself. To this very day I still believe that Bely's work easily bears the heavy weight of its monumental title—so great and resilient is its spiritual energy, so convincing is its prophetic significance. And although the entire work is only a dream and an illusion, although all the static forms of its literary exposition seem to be fused into a single surge of musicality and visionariness (the style of the novel is Gogol's reduced to pure dynamism), there is still something firm and stable in the undulating mirage. And I think that these firm and stable features will glimmer with an airy iridescence in the eyes of future generations. This poem will forever hold a place not only in our literary heritage but also in our national consciousness, strange as it may seem to assert this about the delirium of a dreamer, the nightmare of a young poet who is vitally drawn into the maelstrom of ruinous events, and who feels the blow of the bronze hooves of the spectral Horseman on his own psyche.

Indeed, official Petersburg no longer exists; rather there is a certain "Petrograd," as yet totally undefined and therefore problematical, conditional, and meaningless to everybody. One might now say with certainty that the Petersburg period of Russian history has come to a close. Before the end a conflagration occurred which hurled an enormous column of smoke and flames into the air, leaving behind charred ruins and gradual decay. Such, at least, is the "astral" view of the events which Bely describes. For only in a minor, marginal way does Bely's novel touch upon the visible and tangible flesh of historical truth: the poet wants to depict supersensual reality. But "astral" reality must be refracted through the subjective prism of the clairvoyant eye. The novel naturally assumes a subjective quality, but this does not detract from the depiction of what is objectively significant— it merely obscures it, transforming the spiritual chronicle of events into a symbolic cryptograph of a personal, internal experience. Is it surprising, then, that the more carefully I examine this cryptograph the more clearly I comprehend through it the secret course of world events which are now taking place before our eyes?

In those days when the poet read me the manuscript of *Petersburg,* I was delighted by the vividness and novelty of what I had heard, I was shaken by the force of its inner meaning and by the depth of the insights crowding its pages, insights which defy precise analysis. I read the novel in its serialized form and have just reread it in the recently published book edition. Yet I am still unable to approach it in a totally sober, analytical way; rather my synthetic understanding of it has deepened. A kind of semi-conscious feeling commands me, as before, to follow the poem's dizzying pace without looking back, without stopping, for I am sure that the novel will fully resonate in my soul no sooner than the sound of the last word has faded, and that the only thing required here is a synthetic grasp of the whole.

"Like a charioteer, dragged from his course by steeds that spurned the rein, thoughts past control usurp me. Horror lifts, even now, the prelude to her savage hymn, within my heart exultant." These words of Aeschylus' Orestes express for me in one chord all of the separate quiverings which I experience together with the narrator as I skim these pages—now incarnadine, like a crimson glow, now phosphorescently iridescent in the depths of their turbulent, fathomless murk.

Bely's novel is permeated with a genuine inspiration of Horror. Horror overflows in it like the wide and turbid Neva, "teeming with bacilli"; it crouches like the islands on the "far side"; it sits on the waters like the gray granite Peter and Paul fortress; it rears up like the outline of the Bronze Horseman; it winks like the light from the schooner of the Flying Dutchman; it stands frozen like the palace Atlases; it is reflected in the tarnished green mirrors of Ableukhov's rooms and "clatters" in their lunar expanse like the little hooves of the heraldic unicorn; it "smacks its lips" in the secluded nooks of the dirty stone staircase that leads to the garret of the ghost-racked terrorist-mystic; it cries and whines like the toxic streams of rainwater in the gutters and decaying sewers; it flares up in the damp autumn night like the flapping folds of the buffoonish blood-red domino; it grows deathly pale like the sky before the fall of the black and lilac shadows of the night, into which the searchlights will gaze, swiveling and probing the gloom; it "oo's" hollowly from the dark expanses "like the October song of 1905"; it flows along the rectilinear avenues like the crawling, faceless human mass that involuntarily creates from the atoms of its servile whispering and grumbling monstrous, incantatory words of insanity and provocation; it rushes along like the dignitary's black carriage, seized by the same panic which it inspires all around. Horror hides in all of these forms and signs before it finally assumes the guise of a ticking timebomb within the four cramped walls of a human "I," before it becomes a "bomb," swallowed by Nikolai Apollonovich.

In a moment of despondency and bitterness, of intellectual pre-occupation with the nihilistic premises of his gnosiology and methodology, of unfulfilled "froglike" lust, and of aversion toward his own and his father's foul lineage, Nikolai Apollonovich, the Kantian, aristocratic student-intellectual, bound himself with a pledge to a certain party, which now gives him custody of a time bomb; possessed by the absent-mindedness and timorous confusion characteristic of both him and his father when it comes to dealing with real-life situations, he himself sets it at a fatal hour. Agents-provocateurs, who have ensnared the party like a spider web, demand that the holder of the bomb use it to commit parricide. Having finally made the wise decision to throw the "sardine tin" into the river, Nikolai Apollonovich realizes, breaking out into a cold sweat, that the bomb has been stolen from him. And the one who has stolen it, unawares, from his son's room is none other than the small, aged dignitary with the big green ears, Apollon Apollonovich, who has long experienced the agony of a vague but mortal fear of his other "I"—his Kolenka—and who was driven by this fear into his son's room, so crammed with books and variegated, exotic bric-à-brac.

Nikolai Apollonovich, who grimaces painfully throughout the duration of the novel, whether in his sleeveless beaver coat, in his multicolored Oriental dressing gown, or in his buffoonish blood-red domino, is in a state of almost uninterrupted delirium. The young terrorist-mystic, who is visited in his hallucinations at times by Mongolian sorcerers, at times by the Bronze Horseman, the intimate friend of the Flying Dutchman, well understands the peculiar condition of his friend "who has swallowed the ticking bomb," and he gives him some interesting theosophical lectures about how man's initial sensations after death correspond to Nikolai Apollonovich's extremely vivid and accurate impressions of the effect of the metal Fury when it has ticked to its appointed hour; this is supposedly what even the ancients had in mind when they recounted the tale of Dionysus being torn to pieces. The reader begins to feel that the swallowed bomb is a general and comprehensive formula for the conditions governing personal awareness which apply to us all on this earth. "Know thyself!"

This subjective consciousness is symbolized in the novel by the form of space enclosed between four perpendicularly intersecting planes. This space seems unbounded only to the old Apollon Apollonovich, who fears open expanses—both in Russia and in the world, and who does not yet hear either the ticking nearby or the clattering of hooves in far-away rooms. This Homunculus sees the retort which houses him and whose intactness guarantees his very life as a cube—whether it is the black cube of his carriage, in which he hurries along perpendicularly crossing avenues to the "government institution" so that he can magically send out similar perpendiculars from his majestic rectangular chambers through the immense expanses of Russia, or whether it is the four walls of his white bedroom, or the cubical closeness of an even more intimate refuge—the last citadel of lonely self-discovery, where Apollon Apollonovich, after the harmless explosion of the bomb, lets out protracted screams. There he seals himself off from the world, which persecutes him in the form of his frenzied son, who in mad terror pursues him—this, his other, passionately despised and tenaciously beloved "I"—only, it later seems, in order to grab him in his embrace.

The same secret meaning attaches to the garret's four dark-yellow partitions, on whose slimy lathing horrid Mongolian faces appear before the emotionally unstable terrorist-mystic, as well as to the walls of the grimy little restaurant, with their nautical scenes of the flotilla of the Flying Dutchman, where both the terrorist-mystic and Nikolai Apollonovich languish in the paws of the obese voluptuary and agent-provocateur, Lippanchenko, in mortal fear of being ultimately unmasked like the mouse that squeaks in the trap at the very moment that Nikolai Apollonovich is trapped by being given the fatal bundle with the sardine-tin and its "awful contents." Four walls decorated with Japanese landscapes constitute the inner world of the low-browed, dark-haired lady known as "Angel Peri." Within the four walls of his study, illuminated by an icon-lamp, Angel Peri's husband, the blond lieutenant with the face that seems carved from cyprus wood, suffers, prays, and rages with jealousy and nobleness. Within the four walls of the foul bedroom at the suburban villa, the naked Lippanchenko, sweeping cockroaches from the ceiling with a scrub brush, sits on his bed and in the moonlight catches sight of the mad eyes of his assassin, the terrorist-mystic with the small, black, upward-curving moustache (exactly like the Bronze Horseman's), and the new scissors in his hand.

The four walls of the solitary consciousness—here is the lair of all the furies of horror!

Within intersecting perpendiculars all of Petersburg rushes in a stupor. And its collective "I" is as cut off from the Russian land and soul as is the transcendental consciousness of both the Kantian Nikolai Apollonovich and Apollon Apollonovich, the administrator and legislator and scourge of God over Russia who, according to Bely, is just as much a Kantian as his son, although unversed in Kantianism. When the bomb planted by Old Cronos (in whom the poet discerns Mongolian traits), begins to tick in transcendental Petersburg, the sociopolitical events which constitute the novel's backdrop are set into motion.

The bomb goes off, causing only partial damage to the Ableukhov house and the dignitary's retirement. Indeed, looking at it from the outside, no one would say that anything very significant had happened. The terrorist dies; the provocateur dies; the Kantian shows an interest first in ancient Egyptian mysticism, then in contemporary Orthodox mysticism.

And the Bronze Horseman gallops on as always; and everywhere there again appear the Mongolian shadows which can so successfully assume the guise of Kant and Cronos, the dignitary from a distinguished, formerly Tartar line, and the provocateur Lippanchenko. Nocturnal shadows glide and wander about the smouldering remains of the fire to consolidate at times into hostile hordes, and at some future time to rise up *en masse* against Christian Russia, according to the poet's prophecy, by a new Kalka, on a new Kulikovo Field.[3]

The "yellow peril" haunts the poet's imagination. But what is this peril, whose herald in Russia was Vladimir Solovyov?[4] Is it merely the latter's "pan-Mongolism?" Bely does not accept all of Solovyov's prophesying about "pan-Mongolism," but he addes to it new and original features.

The coming pan-Mongolism grows out of ancient roots: the sorcerous

Turanian of the immemorial past is reborn in it. It lives primarily in our blood and defiles it. At the same time it is a poison which circulates in the veins of European culture; it even lives in the substance of our brains. Thus not only Russia, but Western Europe as well is infected by it.

A pernicious spirit, the ancient intimate of home and clan, Aeschylus' "Alastor,"[5] nourished by the blood of interminable crimes, has from times of old been growing fat by Russian hearths and gathering strength for its ultimate victory. What is the essence of this demon? Here he is, "the venerable Turanian ancestor," wearing miniature golden dragons, dropping by the study of Nikolai Ableukhov, the descendent of the ancient Ab-Lai:

> Nikolai Apollonovich rushed toward his guest (one Turanian to another, the underling to his superior), a pile of notebooks in his arms:
>
> "First paragraph: Kant (proof that Kant was also a Turanian).
>
> "Second paragraph: Value understood as nothing and no one.
>
> "Third paragraph: Social relations based on values.
>
> "Fourth paragraph: The destruction of the Aryan world by means of a system of values.
>
> "Conclusion: The ancient Mongolian affair."
>
> But the Turanian answered:
>
> "The task has not been understood. Instead of Kant, you should have the Avenue. Instead of values, numeration: by houses, floors, rooms, forever and ever. Instead of a new order, the even rectilinear circulation of the citizens of the avenue. Not the destruction of Europe, but its immutability. This is the Mongolian affair."

Here is a concurrence of antitheses and a system of perfect identity. Here all of the nerve fibers of horror have been gathered into one center. The terror of the son and the reaction of the father are one and the same: both amount to absolute, mystical Nihilism. Value (it is likewise numeration), understood as nothing and no one, means the destruction of the personality, the destruction of man, the destruction of Christ. The explosion of the bomb means the revelation of the noumenal Nothingness behind the phenomenon of the number, reunification with a single Nothingness.

> Nikolai Apollonovich was a Kantian, moreover a follower of Cohen.[6] In this sense he was a nirvanic person. By Nirvana he understood Nothingness.
>
> Nikolai Apollonovich particularly worshipped Buddha, believing that Buddhism had surpassed all religions in two respects: psychologically it had taught love for every living being; and theoretically this logic had been lovingly developed by the Tibetan lamas. Nikolai Apollonovich remembered that he had once read the logic of Dharmakirti with commentaries by Dharmottara.[7]

And the low-browed Angel Peri, who looks Japanese and is surrounded by views of Fuji-Yama, tries at this time to master a book by "Henri Besançon" (as she confusedly renames Annie Besant).[8]

The yellow peril exists for Bely primarily in the blood and in the spirit.

It is inherent in us; it is a bomb ticking away in our bellies. The Turanian rises up among us and from us; Gog and Magog will stir when "Alastor," the spirit of the anti-Christ, has grown sleek inside us. And at a new Kalka, on a new Kulikovo Field, Russia is fated to stand up for the whole Christian world, for Christ himself.

> There will be a new Kalka!
> Kulikovo Field, I await you!
> And on that day the last Sun will shine forth over my native land. O Sun, if you do not rise, then, O Sun, the shores of Europe will sink beneath the heavy Mongol heel, and foam will curl over those shores. Earthborn creatures again will sink to the bottom of the oceans, into primordial and long-forgotten chaos.
> Arise, O Sun!

Thus does Bely utter crucial and important prophecies, "from Horror," as the Greeks would have said. In his *Phaedrus* Plato distinguishes different forms of divine possession of the spirit. One proceeds from Apollo—this is the sphere of prophetic clairvoyance. The second proceeds from Dionysus—this is the realm of mysticism and spiritual purification. The third proceeds from the Muses, who move poets and artists. The fourth proceeds from Eros, who commands the obedience of those in love with the divine beauty of the eternal essences. Andrei Bely seems to me to be possessed by Horror.

Here the other divinities, including the heavenly Muses and Eros himself, recede in confusion, and only from a distance hold out protective hands over the Gorgons[9] themselves, who turn all that lives into nothingness or into stone.

Contemporary culture had to exhaust itself completely in order to reach this threshold with "Horror" inscribed on its flagstones, a threshold from which the curtain is imperiously torn by the Russian poet of Metaphysical Horror, who thus exposes the deepest recesses of our most refined consciousness.

Notes

1. *Ashes (Pepel)*—Bely's second collection of verse (1909). Like many symbolist writers Bely was extremely disillusioned by the failure of the 1905 Revolution, and this book of poetry best expresses his mood of pessimism and pain.

2. *Gold in Azure (Zoloto v lazure)*—Bely's first collection of verse (1904). The mood is highly optimistic and the imagery bright. The major influence is of Vladimir Solovyov (See note 5 in Gurev).

3. The river Kalka; Kulikovo Field. Cites of a major turning point in Russian history. The Tartar hordes, which had subjugated Rus to their power for over 150 years, suffered a decisive blow in 1380 on Kulikovo Field, after which their hold slowly disintegrated. This heroic moment in Russia's past is treated lyrically by Alexander Blok in his 1908 poem "On Kulikovo Field" ("Na pole kulikovom").

4. See note 7 in Berdyaev's article on *Petersburg*.

5. Alastor in Greek mythology is an epithet for Zeus the avenger and is also applied to any avenging deity or demon. Ivanov has in mind the *Agamemnon,* where, according to Clytemnestra, it is a supernatual agent (i.e., Alastor) who takes revenge on Atreus' descendents for his crime.

6. See note 4 in Berdyaev's article on Bely's *Petersburg.*

7. Dharmakirti was an Indian Buddhist philosopher of the seventh century. Dharmottara was a legendary Buddhist monk.

8. Annie Besant (1847-1933). An English writer, social reformer, and one of the leaders of the Theosophist movement, under whose influence Bely also fell.

9. Gorgon is a monster figure in Greek mythology.

12

Symbolism's Successors

Viktor Maximovich Zhirmunsky (1891-1971)

Philologist, critic, professor, and theoretician of literature, Viktor Zhirmunsky belonged to a select and distinguished group of Soviet literary scholars which included such luminaries as Boris Eikhenbaum, Yury Tynyanov, Viktor Shklovsky, Boris Tomashevsky, and Viktor Vinogradov. Zhirmunsky's first article, published in 1914 and entitled "German Romanticism and Contemporary Mysticism" ("Nemetskii romantizm i sovremennaya mistika"), revealed what was to be a life-long interest in German literature, language, and culture. He wrote a classic study on the question of literary influence and cross-influence, Goethe in Russian Literature (Gyote v russkoi literature, *1937), and all during his life he published articles and monographs on the German language. But Zhirmunsky's first love was Russian literature, particularly poetry, as the following and quite early article demonstrates. Among his major, nontheoretical works in the area of Russian poetry are* The Poetry of Alexander Blok (Poèziya Aleksandra Bloka, *1921),* Valery Bryusov and the Heritage of Pushkin (Valerii Bryusov i nasledie Pushkina, *1922), and* Byron and Pushkin (Bairon i Pushkin, *1924). Zhirmunsky had a special interest in Blok and, not long before his death, published a full-length study of Blok's drama* The Rose and the Cross (Drama Bloka—"Roza i krest," *1964).*

Shortly after the Revolution, and still quite early in his career, Zhirmunsky became attracted to the Russian school of criticism known as formalism, which paid great attention to problems of literary form and poetic speech. For a while he was part of the Petrograd group of formalists known as OPAYAZ (an acronym which in Russian stands for "Society for the Study of Poetic Language"). Although he was quite close to their thinking on many issues, he just as often quarrelled with them and, ultimately, failed to be fully accepted by the group as one of its true members. Zhirmunsky's works which engage in literary theory and show the most significant formalist leanings are Rhyme—Its History and Theory (Rifma, ego istoriya i teoriya, *1923),* An Introduction to Metrics (Vvedenie v metriku, *1925) and* Problems on the Theory of Literature (Voprosy teorii literatury, *1928).*

Symbolism's Successors*

I. *The Symbolist Poets and the Poets of "Hyperboreus"*[1]

There have been three generations of symbolist poets in the history of Russian poetry over the past twenty-five years, three waves of symbolism which have affected the consciousness of those of us who live for art and philosophy: symbolism as 1) a perception of life, 2) a world view, and 3) an aesthetic culture. We can designate these generations by the poets who are most closely associated with them: the first by Balmont and Bryusov; the second by Vyacheslav Ivanov, Andrei Bely and Alexander Blok; the third by Kuzmin. Behind each of these leaders stands a whole series of lesser poets and writers who have been inspired by their new creative vision. Several prominent forerunners of this literary movement stand somewhat removed—major writers who remain outside of my scheme: Fyodor Sologub and Zinaida Gippius.[2]

For the poets of the first generation (Balmont, Bryusov, and their pupils) symbolism was predominantly a liberation from the constricting and ascetic moralism of Russia's liberal intelligentsia. There suddenly emerged from the intellectual monastery an exit to the free, wide world: "The world is beautiful! Man is free!"**

We must submit to life and live it to the full—spontaneously, intensely, passionately, and outside the categories of good and evil, happiness and unhappiness. Life's meaning and justification exist by virtue of our experiences.

> Let us be like the sun! It is young,
> And so beauty orders us to be.

Let us burn with life, accepting and blessing it in its joy and in its grief, in its heights and in its depths. And this applies not only to external life: the new school introduces into poetry the profound and rich content of the individual human soul. Everything in man's life is interesting and valuable, all that is passionate and intense deserves attention. The rich and introspective personality of the poet becomes poetry's major theme. The poetry of this epoch bears the character of an individualistic lyricism; the earliest symbolists were complete individualists in their feel for poetry and life. Their activity parallels and reflects the influence of Nietzsche, as well as other writers who only then became known to us—Ibsen, d'Annunzio,[3] Przybyszewski.[4]

---

* "Preodolevshie simvolizm"—published in *Russkaya mysl'*, 1916, No. 11 pp. 25-56.

** So writes Vyacheslav Ivanov about the mood of this first epoch of symbolism in his *Furrows and Boundaries.*

The appearance of the second generation of symbolists (V. Ivanov, Bely, and Blok) dates to the beginning of this century—to around 1900. The term "symbolist" applies to these poets in a narrower and more authentic sense. The richness and fullness of life, the beauty and brilliance of earthly existence for which their predecessors strove, are revealed to this second generation as a divine fullness and beauty, as an eternal and sacred mystery. The world is awesome and marvellous; one feels the spirit of the infinite in all that is finite; the infinite exists in the world and in man's soul; natural life is a symbol of Godhead, and human life is defined by its connection to the divine. The second generation of symbolists are mystics. The presence of the infinite in their experience alters the very nature of this experience. Each of life's sensations is deepened. Instead of simply and joyfully accepting life in oneself and the world, life now unfolds as a profound and complex religious tragedy where every experience and act is but a step on the road to the salvation or damnation of man's soul. In this sense poetry is a religious ceremony; poets are prophets, perhaps pitiful and weak, but ones who nevertheless see God's radiance in this world.

The teacher of this group is Vladimir Solovyov,[5] both in his role as religious thinker and lyric poet; their past comrades-in-arms were the early German romantics.

As is always the case in the history of poetry, a new sensibility constituted the foundation of the new aesthetics. A more intense personality, a refinement of individual experience, an increased emotionality, and, most importantly, an introduction of mystical feelings into poetry demanded new words and new poetic techniques. Poetry becomes more musical in this period; via melodious combinations of words it tries to suggest moods which are verbally inexpressible. Instead of representing logical and clearly delineated concepts, words must now function as hints, half-tones and half-shades in order to suggest moods which are logically vague but musically significant. Just as earthly life disclosed its divine meaning for the poet's mystical contemplation, so poetic images became symbols, the living flesh of more penetrating revelations. They alluded to the ultimate depth of the human soul which could not be relayed distinctly and rationally, but which could be felt only in allegory and song.

Kuzmin represents the third generation of symbolists. He is tied to symbolism by the deep, mystical character of his experiences; but he does not translate these experiences into unvanquishable, vague, and palpitating chaos. Art begins for him the moment chaos is overcome: life's divine sense is already found; it is the absolute center of the world around which all objects are placed in correct and beautiful order. One needn't approach life with exaggerated, individualistic demands, for that is when the interrelation of all things begins to come apart. Kuzmin's poetic world is not distorted by this excessively subjective, demanding, and passionate approach; an even, soft, joyous light falls upon all objects of this world, large and small.

The spirit of trifles, delightful and airy,
Of love-filled nights (at times coddling, at times stifling),
Of an unthinking life spent in lighthearted mirth.
I am faithful to your flowers, o gay earth,
Although far from your obedient miracles.

In this childlike wisdom, which has overcome chaos and now freely and joyously accepts the whole world without distorting it by excessively individualistic demands, we can already see symbolism's demise. All the precise and delicate forms of the external world come to life under Kuzmin's free and blessed gaze. He loves the finite world and the sweet boundaries between objects and experiences which, even as they arise out of the Dionysian depths of symbolism, always bear the trace of "Apollonian" clarity. His sophisticated simplicity in the selection and combination of words is either conscious art or a spontaneous gift, but in any case he is a pupil of Pushkin's. In general a rebirth of the Pushkinian tradition has played a large role in the formation of the young generation's artistic tastes...

In his article "On Beautiful Clarity" (*Apollo,* January 1910), Kuzmin advanced a whole series of demands which unquestionably had a powerful effect on the aesthetic tastes of the young poets brought up under his influence. "There are artists who bring chaos, perplexing horror, and spiritual disintegration to people, and there are others who give the world harmony. There is no particular need to say how much greater and more sanguine is the latter's talent. Without entering into a discussion of the notion that aesthetic, ethical, and religious duty obliges a person (and especially an artist) to seek and find peace within himself and the world, we consider it indisputable that the works of even the most intransigent, vague, and inchoate writer must submit to the laws of clear harmony and strict form." And so, after a religious and ethical demand on the poet's soul, we now have an aesthetic one. "Whether your soul be unifed or splintered...I entreat you, be logical—and excuse this cry from my heart—logical in the design, construction, and syntax of your work.... Be a skillful architect in the small details as well as in the whole. Let your tale tell its story, let your dramas be dramatic, preserve lyricism for your poetry, love the word like Flaubert, be thrifty in your means and meager in your words, be precise and genuine and you will find the secret of a wonderful thing—*beautiful clarity,* or what I would call *clarism.*"

The success and influence which Kuzmin's programmatic article had point to a certain change in the spiritual mood and artistic taste of recent years.* The generation of poets which follows Kuzmin can,

---

* Related to this change is also the remarkable poetry of Innokenty Annensky who occupies a special and somewhat detached place among the late symbolists. Like Kuzmin, he had a great influence on the poets of "Hyperboreus." See Annensky's collection of verse, *The Cypress Chest,* 1910[6]

to a larger or smaller degree, be seen as overcoming symbolism. A certain duality characterizes these young poets vis-à-vis the tradition which had informed their epoch: the stylistic achievements of symbolism are preserved, cultivated, and modified for the transmission of the new psychic state; then the psychic state which generated these achievements is discarded as tiresome, cumbersome, and unnecessary. It seems that poets were tired of immersing themselves in the soul's ultimate depths, of constantly ascending to the Golgotha of mysticism. They again wanted to be simple, more spontaneous and human in their experiences; they wanted to reject the excessively individualistic demands on life which had broken and torn asunder life's living links and the everyday bonds between people. There was a desire to be "like everyone," as these poets tired of the excessive lyricism, emotional agitation, and uncontrolled chaos of the preceding epoch. There was a desire to speak about the clear and simple objects of external life and about ordinary, uncomplicated human affairs without feeling the sacred need to prophesy ultimate divine truths. Before the poet now lay the external world—varied, distracting, and bright, and almost forgotten in the years of individualistic lyrical self-absorption.

Even more significant for the poets who have overcome symbolism is the gradual impoverishment of emotionality and lyricism in their work.

Experiences are concrete, distinct, and separate. Lost is that special coloring which the mystical presence of the infinite in the finite gives to each experience; instead of a religious and mystical tragedy a simple, intimate tale of life is told. We generally do not encounter solitary and complex personalities lyrically withdrawn within themselves: the new poetry provides an outlet to exterior life, it loves the precise outlines of external objects, and it is more pictorial than mystical. The persona of the poet may lose itself totally in the contemplation of things, but it does not violate the boundaries of artistic form by directly and painfully disclosing its empirical reality. For all this, as we have said, the literary achievements of symbolism have retained their significance. These are first and foremost a conscious liberation of language from the norms of rational logicality and an attitude toward language as a work of art. The symbolists advanced the study of meter and rhyme, of verbal instrumentation (i.e., the acoustical property of words), and of the structure and rhythm of images, as they artistically affect the listener's perception. Yet here, too, symbolism's traditions and aesthetics are not only preserved but also modified in conformity with the young generation's new sensibility. Attention to the artistic texture of words now emphasizes not so much the significance of the poem's melodiousness or musical effects as it does the pictorial, graphic precision of its images. The poetry of allusions and moods is replaced by an art of exactly measured and precisely weighed words; the conscious and demanding artist uses them like bricks. With the disappearance of lyrical

melodiousness and mellifluous harmony as the direct expression of
emotional agitation, with the penetration into the distinct and discrete
qualities of emotional life, the rational element of words and phrases once
again becomes highly significant. But now this element is considered from
an artistic point of view, as a component of the aesthetic effect, and it
assumes artistic shape not as inadequately expressive, prosaic discourse,
but rather as a pointed, highly polished and expressive epigram. This last
feature, as do the others mentioned above, allows us to compare the new
poetry not with the musical lyrics of the romantics, but with the precise and
deliberate art of French classicism and the French eighteenth century—
emotionally spare, always in rational possession of itself, but graphic and
rich in the variety and refinement of visual impressions, lines, colors, and
forms.

   In the winter of 1912-1913 several young poets deliberately split off
from symbolism as a literary school; not very successfully they gave the new
trend the vague and inexpressive name "acmeism." Soon after this the
"acmeists" founded a small journal of poetry and a publishing house called
"Hyperboreus." Gorodetsky's[7] and Gumilyov's acmeist manifestos, published in *Apollo* (No. 1, 1913), informed the world of the philosophical and
artistic reasons for the young group's split with symbolism. The manifes-
toes speak largely of expelling mysticism from art as its required theme and
basic goal. "Russian symbolism," writes Gumilyov, "directed its major
energies to the area of the unknown. By turns it flirted with mysticism,
theosophy, and occultism." Furthermore, "the unknowable, by virtue of
the word's very meaning, cannot be known.... All attempts in this
direction are tainted.... The childishly profound, painfully sweet sensation
of one's own ignorance is what the unknown gives us." In rejecting
mysticism, i.e., the direct experience of the divine, the acmeists have by no
means denied God: they have accepted religion as an object of personal
faith and religious feeling as "material" for artistic depiction. "To be sure,"
continues Gumilyov, "knowledge of God, the beautiful lady of Theology,
will remain enthroned, but we acmeists do not want to reduce her to the
level of literature nor elevate literature to her diamond-like coldness." With
the expulsion of mysticism as poetry's exclusive concern and indispensable
goal, the diverse and resplendent earthly realm again commands primary
attention. Gorodetsky talks about this: "The struggle between acmeism
and symbolism... is first and foremost a struggle for *this* world, for our
planet Earth—with its sounds, colors, forms, and dimensions of time and
space... After all the "rejections," acmeism accepts the world with all its
beauty and ugliness." With equal clarity the two poets distinguish
symbolism's aesthetics from the poetics of acmeism. For the symbolists the
word was a hint, an allegory; there existed secret correspondences between
words and between things, and all boundaries dissolved in the general
atmosphere of musicality and lyricism. Gumilyov sees the influence of

German mysticism in this. "The Romanic spirit is too fond of the element of light, which distinguishes individual objects and precisely delineates line. Symbolism's connection of all images and objects and the changeability of their features could arise only in the foggy mists of a German forest.... Our new movement.... resolutely prefers the Romanic spirit to the German one." Gorodetsky also argues for the deliberate separateness of words, the graphic quality of lines in place of the musical coalescence of moods, and the artistic vagueness of allusions. Art is stability, he says. Symbolism on principle ignores these laws of art. It has tried to utilize the fluidity of the word.... and has intensified this fluidity by all means possible; but in so doing it has destroyed art's supreme prerogative—to be serene no matter what the situation or methodology." If the symbolists referred to Baudelaire's theory of "correspondences" and to Verlaine's words, "Music above everything... No colors, only tones!" then Gumilyov cites the words of his beloved Théophile Gautier:[8]

> Creation is all the more beautiful,
> If its material
> Is impassive—
> Poetry is marble or metal!

And so instead of the complex, chaotic, and solitary personality we have the multiplicity of the external world. Instead of emotional, musical lyricism we have precision and graphicness in the joining of words. And most importantly, instead of mystical penetration into the secret of life, we have simple and precise psychological empiricism. This is the program which unites the "Hyperboreans."

Already in the spring of 1912 Anna Akhmatova's collection of poems *Evening,* which represents the new literary movement's first serious achievement, appeared. In the same year the theoretician of acmeism, Nikolai Gumilyov, revealed certain traits which artistically separated him from the teachings of symbolism. We can see a similar fissure in the first volume of Osip Mandelstam. The name Akhmatova became instantly famous and beloved for all young Russians. And many experts and aficionados of poetry see Mandelstam and Gumilyov as genuinely significant poets. The time has come for an attentive look at the works and achievements of Russia's new poetic generation and an examination of the peculiarities of the new artistic movement which they represent.*

---

* The following books have been used for this investigation: Akhmatova—*Rosary* (3rd edition, 1916), *Evening,* 1912; Mandelstam—*Stone* (1916); Gumilev—*The Quiver,* (1916), *Pearls* (1910), *Foreign Sky* (1912); Georgy Ivanov—*Heather* (1916),[8] *The Chamber* (1914); G. Adamovich—*Clouds* (1916).[9]

II. Anna Akhmatova

Akhmatova's poetry is not exhausted by the handful of features which we will take note of here. Akhmatova is not only the most outstanding representative of the new generation of poets: there are eternal and individual qualities of her verse which are not confined exclusively to the peculiarities of contemporary poetry—certain aspects of Akhmatova's work liken it to the poetry of the symbolists. The nature of her talent has been most clearly revealed in her recent verse. But what interests us here is not the eternal or deeply personal aspect of Akhmatova's lyrics or their point of contact with symbolism. Rather, we are concerned with those features which make her poetry particularly modern and different from the artistic strivings and emotional outlook of the last quarter century. These uniquely non-symbolist features compel us to see Akhmatova as the most typical representative of the new poetry.

Symbolist poetry essentially derives from the spirit of music; indeed, harmony and melody determine a poem's very effectiveness. Words do not convince us as concepts or by the logicality of their content; rather they create a mood which corresponds to their musical value. It seems that before words there existed in the poet's imagination tunes or melodies out of which words were born. In contrast to this, Akhmatova's poems are not melodic or sonorous; when they are read they don't "sing," and it would be difficult to set them to music. Of course, this is not to say that they do not contain a musical element, but this element does not predominate, it does not predetermine the poem's very verbal structure, and it has a different character than its counterpart in the poetry of Blok or early Balmont. In them the sonorousness and melodiousness of the verse occasionally recall the romance; in her there is something akin to the transparent and pictorial harmonies of Debussy, to the unresolved and frequent changes of rhythm which in contemporary music replace the customary melodiousness which has ceased being effective. Therefore alliteration and internal rhymes are rare in Akhmatova; even traditional rhymes at the end of a line are not mandatory or terribly lavish—in fact, they are as inconspicuous as possible. Akhmatova loves to use imperfect rhymes: "uchtivost'-lenivo," "luchi-priuchit'," "vstretit'-svete," "gub-beregu," "plamya-pamyat'." In this way an element of dissonance is introduced into a harmonious chord; and now combinations of words, not overly sonorous but still new and unexpected, become possible in creating rhymes. Akhmatova also loves enjambement, i.e., the incoordination of the sense unit (the sentence) and the metrical unit (the line), and transitions which begin in one line and continue into another. This latter device also deemphasizes the excessive precision of the poem's metrical and musical structure, and the rhyming becomes less noticeable:

True tenderness you will confuse
Not with anything, for it is quiet.

Nor does the wealth and originality of the rhythmic quality which defines the nature of Akhmatova's musical gift increase the poetry's melodiousness. She loves interrupted, retarded, syncopated rhymes and she combines various alternations of binary and ternary feet in the same stanza or line. Conforming to the psychological content of the poetic lines rather than being governed by their free and mellifluous harmony, she moves poetic diction close to conversational speech. Her poetry introduces the impression not of a song, but of a refined and witty discussion, an intimate conversation.

As simple courtesy orders
He came to me, and smiled;
Half-tenderly, half-sluggishly
He touched my hands with a kiss...

Or here is another example of intimate conversational speech converted into poetic form:

True tenderness you will confuse
Not with anything, for it is quiet.
In vain do you carefully wrap
My shoulders and bosom in furs,
And in vain do you speak
Of first love with words of humility—
How well do I know these obstinate,
Ravenous looks of yours!

As always, at the base of this poem lies Akhmatova's exact and perceptive observation of the barely noticeable external signs of an emotional state and her precise, epigrammatically severe, almost formulaic transmission of the thought which expresses her mood vis-à-vis the addressee. The poem opens with a general observation taken extremely personally but expressed aphoristically; in its totality it might be called an epigram in the old sense of the word. But an epigram cannot be melodious; it approximates logically precise and deliberately simple conversational speech.

Akhmatova's vocabulary displays her conscious striving toward conversational speech and everyday words, usually far removed from the closed circle of lyrical poetry. Her construction of sentences gravitates toward the syntactic freedom of the living, unwritten word. She speaks so simply; her words seem like crystallized snatches of lively conversation in verse. But this conversational style never verges on prosaicness, it always remains artistically effective: it reveals Akhmatova's enormous artistic skill, her desire for the chaste simplicity of the word, her fear of unjustified poetical exaggerations, excessive metaphors, and worn-out tropes, and the clarity and deliberate precision of her diction.

The epigrammatic quality of her poetic forms constitutes one of Akhmatova's most important trademarks. This explains her kinship with the French poets of the eighteenth century and with the poetics of French classicism in general, as well as her poetry's profound dissimilarity to the musical and emotional lyrics of the romantics and symbolists. The preciseness of observation and refinement of her vision, the ability to generalize and express generalizations in a succint verbal formula, the polish of her style—all of these are features which sharply counter the musical lyrics of the old and new romantics, and they are the necessary conditions of an epigrammatic style. But for all this there is a significant difference between Akhmatova and the French. For while the French adapt the general and aphoristically formulated observation to every occasion, despite the conditions which gave rise to it, Akhmatova, even in her most generalized sentiments, conveys her personal voice and private mood. Here are characteristic examples of epigrammatic lines:

> The requests one always has of a beloved!
> The once-loved receives no requests.

This is a general observation, an epigrammatic formula, but its artistic impact is tied to a personal experience. Dependent upon the tragic development of the entire poem, the formula is colored by certain intimate and personal overtones. The same holds true for other, similar examples:

> And he doesn't know that from happiness and glory
> Hearts grow hopelessly decrepit.

Or:

> For a woman to be a poet is absurd.

Even more frequently there lies at the base of Akhmatova's epigrammatic formulas a precise and delicate perception of something in the external world or even just a keenly and subtly relayed sensation—or the expression of the psychological fact which stands behind this sensation. These lines from Akhmatova's poetry stick in one's mind and constitute the genuine achievements which belong to her alone:

> How unlike embraces
> Is the touch of these hands.

Or:

> He again has touched my knees
> With an almost steady hand.

Or still further:

> My brittle voice rings out and out,
> A ringing voice having known no happiness.

The use of such epigrammatic lines to end a poem is especially characteristic of Akhmatova. Often this ending constitutes an ironic, concluding twist to a lyric mood which pervades the poem, such as occurs in the late romantics and Heine:[11]

> Sighing, I shouted: "All that was,
> Was a joke. If you go, I shall die."
> His smile was calm and quite awful,
> As he said: "Don't stand in the draught."

At times instead of such a contrast we have an epigram which rounds off and summarizes the mood of the poem:

> And the passers-by think confusedly:
> True, only yesterday she was widowed.

Or:

> And like an undying beam of light
> Grief lay upon my life, and my voice was dull.

The muting of emotionality on the psychological plane corresponds to the absence of melodiousness in the formal structure of Akhmatova's verse. More precisely Akhmatova conveys the emotional fluctuations of psychic life along with various changes of mood not spontaneously or lyrically, but rather through their initial reflection in external phenomena. And here again we have a basic feature of her poetic profile. She doesn't speak about herself directly; instead she relates the external environment of a psychic event, the affairs of exterior life and the objects of the outer world. And only in her original selection of these objects and in her changing perception of them is the real mood, the special emotional content of each word felt. This makes Akhmatova's poetry emotionally austere and abstemious. She says nothing more than do things themselves. She doesn't thrust herself onto the reader. She doesn't explain in her own name.

> We met for the last time
> On the embankment, where we always met.
> The Neva's waters were high,
> And people feared a flood in town.
> He spoke of summer and said that
> For a woman to be a poet is absurd.
> How I recalled the Monarch's towering house
> And the Peter and Paul fortress—
> And that the air did not belong to us,
> But was like a gift from God—so magical.
> And at that time there came my way
> The last of all my senseless songs.

The words sound deliberately restrained, removed, and dispassionate. She recalls only the trivialities of the situation, the unnecessary details of the conversation which remain so distinctly fixed in her memory at the moment of such extreme emotional agitation. Only the word "last" (repeated twice, at the beginning and end of the poem) speaks directly of her psychic state, as does the disturbed, emphatic raising of her voice in the lines:

> How I recalled the Monarch's towering house
> And the Peter and Paul fortress.

And still, in her story about external events she relates a great emotional tale—providing not only the bare facts of its content, but also its psychic overtones and her own private feelings. Here is another example of psychic state relayed via subtly noted external perceptions:

> *Confession*
>
> The voice which forgave me my sins is silent.
> A lilac dusk extinguishes the candles,
> And the priest's dark stole
> Covered my head and shoulders.
> Isn't it the same voice that said: "Arise, maiden"?
> My heart beats faster and faster...
> And through the cloth there is
> The touch of a hand absentmindedly blessing me.

Despite the profound and explicit lyricism of this poem, it is built exclusively on keenly perceived sensations: auditory (the sounds of a voice), visual (the extinguishing candles, the dark stole of a priest), tactile (the touch of the priest's stole and the passing of the hands through the cloth). Even the "beats of the heart" are apprehended not as a direct reflection of emotional agitation, but rather as a mere bodily sensation.

Each psychic state, each mood in Akhmatova's poetry is signified by a corresponding phenomenon in the external world. Recalling childhood means:

> My books and pencil box were tied in small straps,
> I was returning home from school...

And this:

> To be again a seaside girl
> And wear slippers on my feet,
> And tie my braids in a bun,
> And sing in an agitated voice.

Languishing, her unanswered love sounds thusly:

> The pupils of my blinded eyes
> Have grown dim, are already dead.

Or thusly:

> How futile, pitiful and torrid it is
> To stroke my cold hands.

Here is an expression of emotional disarray:

> I cannot raise my tired eyelids,
> When he pronounces my name.

And one even clearer and more external:

> I put on my right hand a glove
> That really belonged to my left.

Love is the image of the beloved. And the male image, the impression of masculine beauty is depicted to the limits of visual clarity. Here she is on eyes:

> There was only laughter in his placid eyes,
> Under the gold of his eyelashes.

Or:

> And the eyes of cryptic, ancient
> Faces stared down upon me.

Or thus:

> My imagination submits to me
> In my description of gray eyes.

Here are "his" lips:

> And if you knew how pleasant to me now
> Are your dry and rosey lips.

And his hands:

> But on lifting his dry hand,
> He lightly touched the flowers...

And here are still other hands:

> How unlike an embrace
> Is the touch of these hands.

These examples will suffice. But besides them we note in every one of Akhmatova's poems, and each time differently, although still distinctly and clearly, the sound of his voice, his movements and gestures, his dress, his manners, and a whole slew of other insignificant aspects of his external appearance.

Of course, these details are not accumulated indiscriminately, for the sake of photographic precision, as in works of literary realism. Sometimes it is only a detail, only one slight touch of the artist's brush, but it is always an acute and specific observation and not a lyrical allusion, and it reveals the emotional sense of what has been experienced. Nowhere is this more clear than in the following lines:

> I'm in possession of a smile
> Such that the lips seem hardly to move.
> I'm holding on to it for you
> For it is given to me by love.
> No matter that you're insolent and mean,
> No matter that there are others you love.
> Before me is a gold lectern
> And with me my gray-eyed beloved.

In this poem the precisely and carefully perceived detail—"the lips (which) seem hardly to move"—suddenly develops into an entire narrative which discloses the profound emotional content enclosed in this detail.

Details in Akhmatova's poetry cannot be called symbols. By symbol we always mean the embodiment of eternal, mystical content in earthly and finite form. Here we are not dealing with mystical experiences taking the shape of images and words, but with simple, concrete occurrences which are severely wrought and sharply outlined. One cannot say the same about the lyrical and emotional infusion of feeling into external objects which causes these objects to live a life similar to the soul; such an infusion of feeling is most common in poems about nature (for example, Fet).[12] In Akhmatova the events of emotional life are totally distinct from the facts of the external world. The soul does not overflow its boundaries or inundate outer reality; inner experience and exterior fact develop parallel to, and independently of, one another, and indeed occasionally in opposite directions. Thus, in the above-cited poem "The Last Time We Met," the calm flow of external life sharply contrasts the mood of separation, just quoted in the words "the last time."

In just this way Akhmatova's unique experiences are rendered comprehensible. These experiences are always definite and distinct, clearly outlined, discrete, and separate from one another. In symbolism poetry is born from an almost ecstatic emotional intensity, from psychic depths which are still indistinct; all the different sides of the soul are fused together and the spirit's integral and creative unity speaks more profoundly. In Akhmatova wholeness and indivisibleness are replaced by a discreteness which is accompanied by straightforward, precise, and strict self-observation. Moreover, the emotional content of her poetry does not pour itself out directly and musically in song; rather each separate experience is tied to a specific fact of external reality. It is precisely these external facts, so distinct and graphic, which allow us to see the divisions in what is usually a fused and formless mass of psychic events. This is especially clear in relation to the religious feeling which plays such a large role in symbolist poetry. Here this feeling is a mystical mood, a direct sensation of the infinite and the divine, a fusion of the human soul with Godhead; it is a feeling which is restless and deeply agitated, fluctuating between ascents and descents. In Akmatova's poetry religiosity is no less genuine, yet its nature is not one of mystical insight, but of firm and simple faith which becomes the basis of life. And this firm, calm, positive faith enters life itself, acquiring living, historical, everyday forms, and it manifests itself in the conditions of daily existence and in the customary rituals, acts, and objects of religious devotion.

> There is a worn carpet under the icon:
> The cool room is dark,
> And thick and dark green ivy
> Curls around the large window.
> The roses are sweetly aromatic;
> Hardly burning, the icon lamp chirrs.
> The room's furniture is brightly painted
> By the loving hand of a craftsman.

The factual grounds for the soul's every movement are always provided with such precision and always reflect such concretization of psychic experience. And these factual grounds introduce a completely new narrative element into the poem. Many of Akhmatova's lyrics can be called short stories or novellas; usually each poem is an excerpted novella which describes the action at its tensest moment and allows us to sense the flow of all preceding actions. This observation applies not only to such a genuinely narrative poem like the one which relates the death of a beloved boy ("The high vaults of the church... "), but to lyrics which are very common in Akhmatova, such as the above-cited "We met for the last time," or "The requests one has for a beloved," or "The Guest." As narratives about something which has already occurred, these verse-novellas begin by relating a fact in the past tense: "My love left me at the new moon."

The very feelings which Akhmatova treats are not those which attract us to symbolist poetry. There we are dealing with the most profound confessions of the spirit and not the soul, with the disclosure of certain metaphysical premises and strivings of the lyric persona, with mystical flashes, and with the struggle for God—all permeated by a divine atmosphere. Such is the case in Blok, for example, whose young radiant love for the Beautiful Lady and late tragic verse, written "at the edge," are stages of the struggle between God and the devil, with the poet's soul constituting the field of battle. Such is also Zinaida Gippius's yearning for what has never been and longing for a miracle ("O, let there be what has never been and never will be!," "But the heart wants and requests a miracle!"). This reflects a desire for such happiness and light, the likes of which human life has never experienced and the existence of which renders meaningless all that is ordinary, simple, and earthly. Akhmatova speaks of a simple earthly happiness and of simple, intimate, and personal grief. Love, separation, unfulfilled romance, infidelity, the radiant and happy faith in one's beloved, the feeling of grief, abandonment, loneliness, despair, that which is close to everyone and which everyone experiences and understands, although not so deeply and personally. To what is simple and everyday she gives an intimate and personal character; therefore the tender and human love for her deeply human poetry is so understandable. I will cite as an example a poem which seems especially accessible and convincing in its human content and in the simple and delicate sadness which pervades it. We feel in it that singular mood which belongs to Akhmatova's art and which makes its universal content inimitably personal.

> You have come to console me, my dear,
> And tender, and gentle one...
> I can hardly lift my head from the pillow,
> And the windows are covered with grating.
> You thought you would find me dead,
> And you have brought a rather flimsy garland.
> How you wound my heart with your smile,
> My affectionate, sarcastic and sad one.
> What are death's torments to me now!
> If you should choose to stay with me,

> I will obtain God's forgiveness
> Both for you and those you love.

Clearly, Akhmatova's muse is not the muse of symbolism. She understood the unique style of the symbolist epoch and made it fit the expression of new experiences which were discrete, simple, concrete, and earthly. If the symbolists' muse saw in the image of woman a reflection of the Eternal Feminine, Akhmatova's poetry speaks about what is enduringly female. The mystical profundity, intuition, and revelation disappear.

> Not a shepherdess, nor a queen,
> Nor even a nun am I—
> In this grey and ordinary dress,
> In these worn-out heels.

The singularity of her emotional life requires us to see Akhmatova as a successor to symbolism and her poetic gift as the most significant among the younger generation.

III. Mandelstam

Next to Akhmatova, Mandelstam is the most interesting representative of acmeism. In terms of verbal mastery Mandelstam is hardly inferior to Akhmatova. But his poetic interests are too specified, and he demands too much erudition and high culture from his reader for his poetry to enjoy wide popularity. For our purposes his second volume already distinguishes him as an original, serious, and genuine poet.

Mandelstam's poetry reveals the entire course of his development from symbolism to the sensibilities and poetics of acmeism. His early poetry is marked by an authentic, albeit extremely restrained lyricism. The world of his poetic experience consists of a specific range of feelings which likens him to several early representatives of symbolism, especially French symbolism. In his poetry Mandelstam perceives the world not as a living, tangible, and solid reality, but as a play of shades, as an illusory veil cast upon real life. Life is not real; it is a mirage, a dream created by someone's artistic imagination. Nor is the life of the poet himself real; rather it is illusory, like an apparition or dream.

> I am as indigent as nature,
> And as simple as the heavens,
> And my freedom is illusory—
> Like the voice of midnight birds.
> I see the lifeless mirror
> And the sky is deader than canvas;
> Your strange and sickly world
> I accept: it is emptiness!

Sometimes the poet interprets the feeling of this world's illusoriness in the spirit of philosophical idealism: the whole world is the vision of my consciousness, my dream; I alone exist in this world. Here Mandelstam's words recall the solipcism of Fyodor Sologub:

> I am a gardener and also a flower,
> In the world's prison I am not alone.
> My breath and my warmth
> Already lay on the window of eternity.

But, as we have said, the poet can also doubt his existence and the authenticity of his life:

> Am I indeed real,
> And will death actually come?

The fake and illusory world in which we live loses the correctness of proportion and shape, along with its genuineness and reality. The world seems doll-like; it is the kingdom of funny and absurd games:

> In the forests the Christmas trees
> Burn like golden tinsel;
> Toy wolves with terrifying eyes
> Glare from the bushes.

When the boundaries of time and space are no longer firm, but seem rather unsteady, changing, and subjective, there occur spatial dislocation and distortion among phenomena, which is also characteristic of an idealistic perception of life.* Mandelstam preserves this peculiarity in his mature verse; in his earlier poems we read:

> So what if above a fashionable store
> There hangs an ever-twinkling star
> Which might suddenly descend
> Into my heart like a long pin.

Thus Mandelstam's early verse allows us to penetrate his emotional world and to compare his feel for life with that of several symbolist poets. The illusory and mysterious world—playful, inauthentic, and frightening—exists together with its irreality. All ties are severed from living and

---

* See Gogol's "Nevsky Prospect," the description of night on Nevsky. In contemporary poetry this occurs in Blok's ballad of the "Unknown Woman": "And the drooping ostrich plumes sway in my mind / And blue, fathomless eyes flower on a distant shore." Bely's remarkable novel *Petersburg* presents a whole series of examples of the distortion of the spatial perception of things.

stable reality, from life's flesh; there are no roots in life, no pegs to grasp onto in the solidity and gravity of earthly existence. Rather there is something uniquely disturbing, something fragile, transparent, and tender: this is how the poet's soul opens up before us. As we have said, this feel for life contains a corresponding lyricism, deliberately veiled and unclear, yet with a definite emotional cast.

Mandelstam's participation in the new poetic movement has not changed his poetry to the extent that it significantly approximates real life, but it has allowed his artistic development to move in an unexpectedly fruitful direction. Neither Mandelstam's soul nor his personal, very human moods appear in his mature verse; in general the direct and lyrical element assumes second place, as it does in the other acmeists. But Mandelstam not only ignores the lyricism of love and nature, which is the usual theme of emotional and personal poetry; he generally never talks about himself, his soul or his direct perception of either external or internal life. Using Schlegel's[13] terminology, we can call his verse not the poetry of life, but the poetry of poetry (die Poesie der Poesie), i.e., poetry which has as its object not life which is directly perceived by the poet himself, but a foreign, artistic perception of life. Peculiar to Mandelstam is an intuition into other poets and literary cultures, and he perceives these cultures uniquely, with a penetrating and creative imagination. He renders strange tunes comprehensible, he retells others' dreams, he creatively synthesizes and reproduces an alien perception of life which has already taken artistic shape. To quote his own words:

> I have received a blessed inheritance,
> The vague dreams of foreign poets ...

The poet stands immutably before this objective world like an extraneous observer looking out of his window at the absorbing spectacle. The origin and relative value of the artistic and poetic cultures he reproduces are of no matter to him. How successfully, and with what sympathetic understanding and faint mockery he conveys the special flavor of the cinematographic impression, the sentimental exaggeratedness and absurdity of the program:

> A movie house. Three stools.
> A flush of sentimentality.
> A rich aristocratic lady
> In the nets of a wicked rival.
> The flight of love is unstoppable:
> She is guilty of absolutely nothing!
> She loved an ensign in the fleet,
> Selflessly and like a brother.
> But he's wandering in some wilderness—
> The natural son of a greying count.

Thus begins the cheap love affair
Of the beautiful countess...

Next to this expressive and finished print place his description of a
different milieu and artistic style—the commercial life of old London
reflected in the novels of Dickens:

Ask Charles Dickens
About the London of those times:
Dombey's office in the old City
And the yellow water of the Thames.
Rains and tears. A blond
And gentle lad—Dombey's son;
And he alone can understand
When the office clerks make their puns.
Broken chairs fill the office;
And such an abundance of shillings and pennies;
The figures of the fiscal year
Are like bees swarming from a hive.

Here, as in Akhmatova, two or three concrete details, graphically and
precisely formulated in words, reproduce the external setting and psychological sense of the event. How much more precisely can one convey the
impression of Ossian's[14] majestically melancholic poetry than Mandelstam
does in the following words:

I have not heard the tales of Ossian
Nor partaken of ancient wine;
Then why do I dream of a glade,
And the bloody moon of Scotland?
And I hear in the sinister silence
The exchange of raven and harp;
And the wind-swept scarves of the retinue
Keep flashing in the light of the moon.

Or here, how concisely and effectively Mandelstam conveys his artistic
impression of the Petersburg period of Russian history in which you
simultaneously sense its psychological import:

And on the Neva are embassies of half the world,
The Admiralty, the sun and silence!
And the robust purple of the State
Seems so poor, like a crude hair shirt.

Like Akhmatova, Mandelstam transmits his impressions epigrammatically. He does not hint suggestively at some vague mood in the picture
he reproduces; rather he relays this picture through an original and precise
verbal formulation. He also likes to make his poems more pointed by

ending them with an epigram; the lines in which the conclusion is given are almost always read separately, like a formula. The poet concludes the poem about a religious heresy:

> Every time we love
> We fall into it again.
> Anonymously we die,
> As does love together with our name.

Another example is the conclusion of his poem dedicated to Akhmatova:

> Thus Rachel once stood—
> An indignant Phèdre.

Like Akhmatova, Mandelstam also reveals similarities to French classicist poetics in his love for the epigrammatic verbal formula. But Akhmatova's formulations always bear a private character, conveying a sense of personal involvement or emotional excitement. Mandelstam is actually closer to the French. He is most naturally attracted to Latin culture, to which his best poems are devoted. He understands "pseudo-classical" drama better than any of his contemporaries (the poem to Akhmatova, the poem about Ozerov, and particularly the remarkable "Phèdre"); he finds words to describe Racine which show profound aesthetic intuition:

> The theater of Racine! A mighty screen
> Divides us from another world;
> A curtain whose folds are deep
> Lies between it and us.
> Classical shawls fall from shoulders,
> A voice dissolved by suffering fortifies itself,
> And the playwright's heated words
> Through indignation reach their angry pitch.

In his large compositions he is drawn to the pseudo-classical ode, to its archaic vocabulary and its somewhat intellectual stiffness and splendor. As in the French classicists, his verbal formulations do not proceed from personal emotional agitation or troubled observations, which is true of Akhmatova. Rather, he constructs purely abstract verbal schemes which correspond to the rationality of what is being depicted.

It is interesting to examine how Mandelstam selects those details which convey the sense of a given culture. He can least of all be called an impressionist who spontaneously, arbitrarily, and dissociatedly reproduces visual patches which constitute merely the first, and as yet unrealized sensation of external objects. Consciously chosen by his aesthetic tastes, details can seem at first arbitrary and inconspicuous; their significance in the poet's creative imagination is excessively exaggerated; a small detail grows to fantastic proportions, as in an intentionally distorted grotesque. At the same time the proper correlation between large and small objects disappears; near and far in a projection on a plane are found to be of equal proportion. But in this intentional distortion and fantastic exaggeration a previously insignificant detail becomes highly expressive and characteristic of the object being depicted.

Thus in the poem "The Abbot" Mandelstam describes the life of a French priest who preserves "the remains of the power of Rome" within non-believing secular society. Two details, each receiving equal attention, express this life:

> Preserving silence and decorum,
> He needs to eat and drink with us (1)
> And hide in his joyous appearance
> The honor of his radiant tonsure. (2)

If the poet's artistic consciousness greatly overstates the tragic significance of the first circumstance, then the final detail which is placed alongside of it seems deliberately grotesque, especially the exaggeratedly solemn words "radiant" and "honor." But in the further development of the narrative the life of the abbot is presented in the same grotesque style, alotting an enormous, almost mystical significance to all of the peculiarities of his behavior and worldy habits, all of which yields an effect of somewhat ironic grandeur:

> Falling asleep, he reads
> Cicero on his bed:
> So birds in their own brand of Latin
> Prayed to God in days gone by.

The same effect of grotesquely caricatured and fantastically exaggerated detail is produced at the end of "Dombey and Son," where the suicide of the bankrupt financier is described:

> The laws are on the opponents' side:
> There is no way to help him!
> And weeping, the daughter clings
> To the trousers' checkered print.

Placed at such a tragic point, the checkered trousers represent a deliberate distortion of the poem's artistic balance in favor of a fantastically exaggerated detail. But, exaggeratedly distorted, this detail becomes extremely graphic and characteristic, conveying in its very exaggeratedness the aesthetic uniqueness of the "old City."

So it is in other poems that the distortion of perspective and the fantastic exaggeration of isolated details and their significance in the work's overall structure convey with particular acuity and force the uniqueness of the culture Mandelstam reproduces. How well Mandelstam speaks of Tsarskoe Selo (I shall cite only excerpts from the poem):

> Free, thoughtless and passionate,
> The cavalry soldiers smile there,
> Atop their firm saddles....
>
> Barracks, parks and palaces,
> And on the trees—wads of cotton,
> And to the shout of "Splendid, chaps!"
> Burst out peals of "Hail",...
>
> One-storied houses,
> Where narrow-minded generals
> Amuse their old age
> By reading Dumas and "The Grainfield"...
> Private mansions and not just houses!
>
> And the carriage, inspiring secret dread,
> Returns home—
> Where else but to the kingdom of etiquette,
> With the relics of a gray-haired fräulein.

Of course, the smiling cavalry soldiers, the shouts of "hail," the narrow-minded generals reading Dumas and "The Grainfield"[15] in their homes, and the gray-haired fräulein in her carriage do not fully exhaust the artistic effect of Tsarskoe Selo; indeed, they reconstruct this effect in an extremely fractured, fantastically unexpected way. Moreover, further analyzing those details which form the overall effect, one can say that they imply a one-sided and original perception. But in this fantastic exaggeration and distortion, Mandelstam's imagination preserves what had been the work's point of departure—the precise observation of details and the graphic severity of their reproduction. In this same way all of the uniqueness of the literary culture which Mandelstam depicts appears with characteristic exaggeratedness and acuity.

In his metaphors and similes Mandelstam always compares precise and graphic images—maximally dissimilar, fantastically unexpected, anchored in objective reality, inherently discrete—and, as always, he does this all in the same severely wrought, epigrammatic form. He describes a tramp after an evening brawl:

> And his eye, bruised in the depths of night,
> Shines like a rainbow.

He formulates his impression of Bach's music via contrast:

> And like Isaiah you rejoice,
> You hyperrational Bach!

The map of Europe evokes the following simile:

> Like an inland crab or a starfish,
> The last continent was cast out by the water.

From the idealistic perception of life characteristic of his early poetry Mandelstam retains this shift of perspective which makes small objects as significant as large ones, as well as his grotesque and fantastic exaggeration of details. Therefore he cannot be considered a realist. In his grotesquely exaggerated and graphically precise style he is the same kind of realist-magician as Hoffmann[16] is in his tales. If Hoffmann enlarges a single characteristic piece of trivia, a single exaggerated peculiarity to fantastic and frightening proportions, thereby concealing the larger features of life and people and reproducing them in the manner of distorted grotesque, then Mandelstam, by virtue of his poetic technique, is as much a magician of words as the German poet is a magician vis-à-vis his images and narrative structure. But what links Mandelstam to the acmeists is the absence of a personal, emotional, and mystical element reflected in a spontaneous, melodious manner, a highly conscious use of words, and a love for graphic details and epigrammatic formulations.

IV. Gumilyov

Gumilyov's literary career began long before the peculiar sensibilities and independent poetics of acmeism came into being. *Romantic Flowers, The Path of the Conquistadores,* and *The Pearl* (1906-1910) were written when symbolism was at its height. But already in his early verse we can see those features which made Gumilyov the leader and theoretician of the new movement. His active, frank, and unabashed masculinity, his intense emotional energy and temperament distinguish him from the other poets of "Hyperboreus." He himself admits his isolation among the younger generation on this score:

> I'm on good terms with life,
> But between us there's a barrier,
> Everything that mocks it, proud one,
>   Is my only joy.
> Victory, glory, deed—these poor
>   Words are forgotten nowadays.
> But they ring in my soul like thunder,
>   Like God's voice in the desert.

And further:

> I rage like a metallic idol
> Among toys made of china.

But like a true acmeist, Gumilyov does not express this psychic intensity, vigor, and masculinity in sonorous lyrics which directly reflect his emotionality. Content-wise, his poems are emotionally and musically sparse; he rarely speaks about intimate and personal experiences, and like the majority of the poets connected to "Hyperboreus," he avoids poems about nature and love which are too confessional and painfully self-reflective. He creates an objective world of intense and vivid visual images to express his moods; he introduces a narrative element into his poems and provides them with a quasi-epic quality—a "ballad-like" form. The search for forms and images which would correspond in power and vividness to his temperament leads Gumilyov to depict exotic countries where his dream finds its visual and objective incarnation in colorful and motley visions. Gumilyov's muse is the "muse of distant wanderings."

> Today I again have heard
> How a heavy anchor was raised,
> And saw how a five-decked ship
> Sailed out to the far-off sea,
> And this is why the sun breathes,
> And the earth speaks and sings...

This is from his recent poetry in *The Quiver,* but he sang quite similarly at the beginning of his career, in *Pearls* (see "The Captains").

The themes which Gumilyov narrates in his ballads relate his impressions while traveling to Italy, the Levant, Abyssinia, and Central Africa. More frequently, however, he speaks about unknown lands, where the earth is still primeval, where plants, beasts and birds, and people, who resemble these beasts and birds, grow out of its bowels in all their richness, in all the originality of their lines and colors, which are absent from the cold and "intellectual" nature of the north. In this sense, as the author of exotic ballads, Gumilyov has rightly called himself a pupil of Bryusov's, although the timbre of Bryusov's dream is more individualistic, producing an epic narrative much more precise and conscious of its lyrical roots—which in Bryusov is invariably connected to the feeling of love. Like Bryusov, the early Gumilyov loves extremely bright images, lush words, and exaggeratedly sonorous rhymes. He is not only a good poet, but also a masterful rhymist...

In his latest collections Gumilyov has matured into a great and pronounced master of the word. He still loves the rhetorical splendor of lush words, but he has become more sparse and selective in his choice of them, combining his previous desire for intensity and brightness with graphic precision.

Like all of the poets of "Hyperboreus," he has experienced the turn toward a more deliberate and rational use of words, toward the sharpened aphorism and the epigrammatically strict verbal formula. The best of his "exotic" poems in *The Quiver* can be paragons of verbal precision and austerity...

But Gumilyov's muse has really found its true self in his "war poems." The arrows in *The Quiver* are the sharpest; here the poet's spontaneous and intense masculinity expresses itself most fittingly and appropriately. War as a serious, severe, and sacred matter, where the entire strength of the individual soul and the whole value of human will unfold in the face of death—such is the mood of these poems. A deeply religious feeling accompanies the poet upon fulfilling the military deed:

> And truly the business of war
> Is a wonderful and sacred thing,
> Angels, bright and winged,
> Are seen behind the warriors' shoulders.

After glory and heroic action, death seems simple and uncomplicated:

> There are so many worthy lives,
> But death alone is worthwhile,
> Only under fire, in tranquil trenches,
> Do you believe in God's banner, in his heavens...
>
> The heavenly firmament will open up
> Before the soul, and snow-white steeds
> Will speed that soul
> To the blinding heights.

Gumilyov dedicated poems to the pathos of battle and victory, when in the face of death "the sun of the spirit" rises. Here the individual life force fuses in its ultimate intensity with the supra-individualistic and reaches infinite, mystical heights:

> I shout and my voice is wild,
> It is sword against sword,
> The bearer of a great thought,
> I cannot, just cannot die.
> Like thundering anvils
> Or the waters of angry seas,
> The golden heart of Russia
> Beats rhythmically in my chest.

Both Gumilyov's war poems and Akhmatova's, which reflect war in the soul of "those who remain," in the soul of the woman, are the best and most important things which the world war has created in Russian poetry. If the fear of experiencing such simple, bright, and direct feelings and such cheerful words evokes doubts about their artistic worth in the minds of some excessively refined critics, Gumilyov has the right to answer these judges:

> Victory, glory, deed—these poor
> Words are forgotten nowadays,
> But they ring in my soul, like thunder,
> Like God's voice in the desert.

V. Toward An Evaluation of the Poets of "Hyperboreus"

We have examined the work of the three most important poets of "Hyperboreus" and have found something new and artistically significant in them. It was not mere enmity which alienated the younger generation from the symbolists, and what united it was not a fortuitous closeness, but rather an internal kinship, a harmony of mood and direction, an inner divergence from the "teachers," which was symptomatic of the new literary epoch. The most obvious features of this new sensibility are a rejection of a mystically perceived and intuited life and an escape from a lyrical absorption in one's self to the diverse external world abundant in sensual impressions. We might cautiously call the new poets' ideal *neo-realism*, understanding artistic realism as the exact transmission of discrete and precise impressions primarily of exterior, but also of spiritual life, both of which are perceived from an external, more removed and precise point of view and with minimal distortion by subjective emotional and aesthetic experiences. One proviso: the young poets are obviously not beholden to the naturalistic simplicity of prosaic speech (which seemed inescapable to the earlier realists), because they inherited from symbolism a new attitude toward language, as well as toward artistic creation.

In order to pass judgment on the new literary movement its significance must be measured on a scale of values established by the personal outlook of the judge himself. From this point of view one can suggest that the determining factor in such an evaluation is really whether the critic accepts or rejects mystical knowledge as an experience of the individual human soul. But if an assessment which proceeds from this position is likely to be acceptable only to people of similar faith, then we can utilize another critical methodology in evaluating the new poetry, one which assesses its achievements and the general course of its development from within, from its own perspective. To begin with, if we see the acmeist poets as practitioners of a new realism who once again bring all the riches and diversity of the external world into literature, then we need to inquire about the extent to which their work constitutes objective, realistic poetry.

Has that subjectivity, that insularity, and that spasmodic distortion of
one's visual capacities, which distinguishes the individualistic poetry of
symbolism, really disappeared from the new generation's poetic perception
of reality? Of course not. The seductiveness of individualism has too deeply
penetrated into the very perception of life of the generation who was raised
on symbolism. There is Akhmatova's world, very personal and very
feminine; there is Mandelstam's world, somewhat abstract, extremely
cultured, and with a characteristically grotesque distortion of the mutual
relationship and proportion of objects; and there is Gumilyov's world,
intense, exotically colorful, passionate, and masculine. But there is no real
escape from their lonely souls into worldly life, no real humility or
submission of the individual persona to life's objective truth. In particular,
several offshoots of the emotional disintegration which accompanies
individualistic poetry, several aspects of decadent aestheticism and amoralism have survived undefeated in the new poetry's structure. Let me cite an
excerpt from a poem by Akhmatova depicting an artists' cabaret, in which
she employs a formula of a decadent cast, not at all foreign to the acmeists:

> All here are revellers and whores,
> And how unhappy we are together!
> On the walls flowers and birds
> Seem to languish among the clouds....
>
> The windows are completely covered:
> What's out there—hoar frost or storm?...
>
> O, how my heart fills with anguish!
> Am I not awaiting the fatal hour?
> And she who is dancing now
> Is certain to go to hell.

The beginning of a new and broadly realistic current is impossible
without escaping from an individualistically distorted and solitary perception of life into the fresh air of real and spontaneously perceived
existence, without rejecting personal alienation and submitting to life's
objective truth. Of course, such poetry will no longer be primarily lyrical.
In any case, a certain duplicity already manifest itself among the acmeists,
insofar as they have undertaken the creation of a pictorial poetry directed
to the outside world whose form is that of lyric verse, which is essentially
private and musical in nature.

On the other hand, the acmeists' extreme awareness of the word as
such, as well as the graphic quality, precision, and balance of their style
constitute an achievement when compared to the musical vagueness which
characterizes the poetry of hints and moods. And the acmeists are superior
because emotional content seems totally embodied in the word, and this
yields the enticing artistic polish of their poetic formulas. But the formal

perfection and artistic balance of acmeist poetry are achieved by a series of basic concessions and by a voluntary restriction of the tasks of art which constitute not the victory of form over chaos, but rather the deliberate banishment of chaos. Everything is incarnated because what cannot be incarnated is removed; everything is expressed fully because what cannot be expressed is rejected. It was precisely the desire to express the inexpressible, to say the unsayable which brought on the artistic revolution of symbolism, the poetry of allusion and allegory. Now the narrowing of the emotional world again allows poetry to be graphic, precise, and sober-minded. In Akhmatova this narrowing manifests itself in her refusal to become absorbed in the single, all-encompassing, and chaotic interior of her soul, in her love for clear, discrete and, of necessity, peripheral experiences. In Mandelstam the narrowing appears in the total exclusion of the poet's personality from his poetry, in its dissolution through contemplating literary cultures not his own. In Gumilyov the narrowing appears in his exclusive love for the exotic ballad as an objective, non-individual expression of emotional experience, and in the younger members of "Hyperboreus" it is manifested in the contraction of horizons, in emotional impoverishment, and in the miniature, diminutive character of all experience.

Be this as it may, the significance and value of a poem are not measured by artistic polish alone. All art, and poetry more than any other, lives not only by its artistic effectiveness, but by a whole series of extra-artistic experiences which the aesthetic experience calls forth. Of course everything in art must be artistically effective; there can be no lapses of inexpressiveness in the swift flow of artistic perceptions. But what effects us aesthetically, what is expressed in a work of art and what we experience under the influence of artistic persuasion can in itself be examined and understood *not only from an artistic point of view,* and, in fact, is not perceived and comprehended solely from this point of view. When a feeling of love, of devout prayer, of emotional depression, or loneliness is related in the artistically effective form of a poem, the artistic perception creates in the listener's consciousness aesthetic images which, once they are formed, leave the sphere of art and enter into the world of our customary likes and dislikes, where they are evaluated in terms of their meaning, as values of another, extra-aesthetic order—philosophical, moral, religious, or indivi-dual-experiential. Even in painting, the most objective of the arts, intellectual associations and values play a large role. The mistake of the impressionists and their followers, and one which is extremely typical and widespread, was precisely the desire to expel intellectual associations from painting once and for all and respond instead to the entire area of painting as the combination of lines, forms, and colors without any thought about the essence of the object being depicted. Indeed, the expressiveness of a portrait or the significnace and exalted pathos of a religious painting also constitute the tasks of art, and to treat the artistic function of a portrait or of an image of the Madonna as an ornament or a beautiful wall hanging means to narrow the tasks of painting as art. It is from this point of view that we should approach the artistic difference between symbolism and acmeism. The symbolists, who had stood at the furthest boundaries of art, really could not fully convey in poetry the inexpressible content of the soul; only by allusion and allegory could they lead us to a presentiment of the soul's secrets. But even with their works' deliberate imperfectness which, claim the theoreticians of acmeism, destroys art's majestic harmony, the symbolists are incomparably richer and more interesting than the poets of "Hyperboreus." And if Blok mastered the art of the expressive word less perfectly than the acmeists, then he was certainly more important than them as a poet, offering a presentiment of emotional realms of enormous intensity and immeasurable scope.

Will acmeism be the poetry of the future? Certainly over the last years we have observed a turning toward a new realism both within symbolism itself and from without it. But we would hope that this new realism will not forget the achievements of the preceding epoch, that it base itself on a firm and unshakable religious feeling, on the positive religion which has entered history and everyday life, illumining all things in their harmonious interrelatedness. . . . Yet even if our much-awaited literary future does not belong to the acmeist poets, their work has nonetheless echoed a need of the times: the search for new artistic forms and noteworthy accomplishments.

Notes

1. "Hyperboreus" appeared in 1912-1913 in only ten issues. Edited and published by Mikhail Lozinsky, the journal was largely an organ of the acmeists, although symbolists such as Blok and V. Ivanov also contributed to it.

2. Gippius, Zinaida Nikolaevna (1867-1945). A major symbolist poet, critic, short story writer, and playwright who emigrated to Paris with her husband Dmitry Merezhkovsky (see note 6 in Nevedomsky). A recent and interesting work about her is V. Zlobin: *Zinaida Gippius, A Troubled Spirit* (1970), translated, edited, and introduced by Simon Karlinsky (Berkeley, 1980).

3. Gabriele d'Annunzio (1863-1938) was an Italian writer of a decadent cast whose novels and dramas were especially popular among the symbolists and their supporters.

4. See note 1 in Ivanov-Razumnik.

5. See note 5 in Gurev.

6. Critic, translator, and poet of extreme depth and refinement, Innokenty Annensky (1856-1909) exercised a considerable influence on the acmeist poets. Annensky taught Greek literature at Pushkin's former school, the Lyceum at Tsarskoe Selo and, like the acmeists, represented what Zhirmunsky terms "the rebirth of the Pushkin tradition."

7. See note 2 in Gurev's article.

8. Théophile Gautier (1811-1872) was a French novelist and critic who was one of the earliest supporters of "art for art's sake." Gautier's view that the artist must strive to attain perfection of form was especially close to the acmeists. Baudelaire dedicated his *Fleurs de Mal* to Gautier.

9. Ivanov, Georgy Vladimirovich (1894-1958). One of the best poets of the Russian emigration who began his career as a pupil of Gumilyov, and a minor acmeist.

10. Adamovich, Georgy Viktorovich (1884-1972). Poet with acmeist sympathies and an influential literary critic in France, where he emigrated in 1922.

11. Heinrich Heine (1797-1856) was an extremely popular German lyric poet whose poems were frequently used for the lieder of such composers as Schubert, Schumann, Mendelssohn, Brahms, and Hugo Wolf.

12. See note 3 in Gurev.

13. Schlegel, August Wilhelm von (1767-1845). German critic, poet, and major translator of Shakespeare into German. He is one of the most influential figures in the history of literary criticism and theory.

14. Ossian. Irish warrior-poet of the third century who became extremely popular when new works were "discovered" and really invented by the Scottish poet James Macpherson. These so-called Ossianic poems were particularly popular among the romantics, such as Goethe.

15. "The Grainfield" ("Niva") was a very popular "illustrated family journal," published monthly between 1870 and 1918.

16. See note 6 in Berdyaev's article on *Petersburg*.